D1507490

Anything
for a
T-Shirt

Sports and Entertainment
Steven Riess, *Series Editor*

Other titles in Sports and Entertainment

The American Marathon
    Pamela Cooper

Black Baseball Entrepreneurs, 1860–1901: Operating by Any Means Necessary
    Michael E. Lomax

Catching Dreams: My Life in the Negro Baseball Leagues
    Frazier Robinson

Diamond Mines: Baseball and Labor
    Paul D. Staudohar

The Fastest Kid on the Block: The Marty Glickman Story
    Marty Glickman with Stan Isaacs

Glory Bound: Black Athletes in a White America
    David K. Wiggins

Great Women in the Sport of Kings: America's Top Women Jockeys Tell Their Stories
    Scooter Davidson, Toby and Valerie Anthony, eds.

Playing Nice and Losing: The Struggle for Control of Women's Intercollegiate Athletics, 1960–2000
    Ying Wushanley

Running with Pheidippides: Stylianos Kyriakides, the Miracle Marathoner
    Nick Tsiotos and Andrew J. Dabilis

Sports and the American Jew
    Steven A. Riess, ed.

Anything for a T-Shirt

Fred Lebow and the

New York City Marathon,

the World's Greatest Footrace

Ron Rubin

With a Foreword by William A. Burke

SYRACUSE UNIVERSITY PRESS

Copyright © 2004 by Syracuse University Press
Syracuse, New York 13244–5290

All Rights Reserved

First Edition 2004
04 05 06 07 08 09   6 5 4 3 2 1

Permission to use material from the following publications is
gratefully acknowledged: Robert Brody, *Whatever It Takes:
Athletes Against Cancer* (Waco, Tex.: WRS Publishing, 1993);
Dick Traum and Mike Celizic, *A Victory for Humanity* (Waco,
Tex.: WRS Publishing, 1993); Sri Chinmoy Marathon Team,
Fred Lebow: A Celebration of His Life (Jamaica, N.Y., 1994);
Road Race Management Newsletter; Road Runners Club of
America, *FootNotes;* and *Runner's World Magazine.*

The paper used in this publication meets the minimum requirements of
American National Standard for Information Sciences—Permanence of
Paper for Printed Library Materials, ANSI Z39.48–1984.∞™

Library of Congress Cataloging-in-Publication Data
Rubin, Ron, 1942–
  Anything for a t-shirt : Fred Lebow and the New York City Marathon, the
world's greatest footrace / Ron Rubin ; with a foreword by William A. Burke.—
1st ed.
      p. cm. — (Sports and entertainment)
  Includes bibliographical references and index.
  ISBN 0-8156-0806-3 (pbk. : alk. paper)
  1. New York City Marathon. 2. Lebow, Fred. I. Title. II. Series.
GV1065.22.N49R83 2004
796.42'52'097471—dc22   2004016645

Manufactured in the United States of America

For Meir,
who crossed the finish much too soon

Ron Rubin, a professor of political science at the Borough of Manhattan Community College (BMCC), City University of New York, holds bachelor's and doctorate degrees from New York University and a master's degree from Brown University. In addition to his professorship at BMCC, he has taught as a visiting senior lecturer at Haifa University.

The author has worked as a legislative assistant in the United States House of Representatives and is the author of books on American foreign propaganda, Soviet anti-Semitism, and Rudolph Giuliani. He is also an avid "back of the pack" runner who has schlepped himself to the finish line of the New York City Marathon six times.

Contents

Illustrations

Foreword

William A. Burke
President, City of Los Angeles Marathon

HE WAS SLIGHT OF BUILD and very soft-spoken, but his presence was almost overpowering. In his world he was bigger than life, but he was one of those rare individuals whose fame did not diminish his ability to be a regular guy who always had time for anyone with a legitimate question about running.

I met him more than twenty years ago when I was attempting to become the race director of a marathon in the Bermuda Triangle of marathons, the City of Los Angeles. If you were attempting to organize a marathon in those days, it was mandatory that you make a trip to New York and get those nuggets of wisdom from the dynamic duo of Fred Lebow and Allan Steinfeld. The night my partner, Marie Patrick, and I were to meet them was also the night of the New York Road Runners Club board meeting, and it ran late. Our meeting didn't begin until 11:30 P.M., and it went until 1:30 A.M. It was truly like being back in college, trying to absorb a deluge of what to do and not to do. At 1:30 we were summarily dismissed with the following admonition: "Get these things done, and I will come and check on your event."

Two months before our first race Fred Lebow appeared at our office unannounced, telling us that he had heard through the grapevine that we were doing all the things he had suggested and he wanted to see the results firsthand. It was his first trip, and he kept coming back for the next seventeen years, as long as his health allowed. He was an unrelenting critic and a world-class cheerleader. He was not too proud to steal a good idea and certainly not hesitant to tell you when one was stupid. He did not suffer fools easily.

When his health was failing and it was obvious the end was near, I told him we should start another marathon with the two of us as co-race directors. He pretended to love the idea and threw out dozens of ideas on how we would make it unique, such as letting only American elite athletes participate in order to drive up television ratings. I will never forget the morning I called to tell him my newest idea of having a Brinks truck with a million dollars as the pace car. If you break the world's record, you get to keep the truck and the money. He really laughed.

When he stopped laughing he said he missed me and would like to see me, so I casually said I'd come to New York. There was a pause in the conversation, and in a voice that was even softer than normal, he said, "Come soon." I left Los Angeles that night and saw him the next morning. We laughed and talked for hours. It was the last time I ever saw him alive. When he died it was the end of an era in our sport. The king had died.

And now, with the help of this valuable book by Professor Ron Rubin—himself one of the hundreds of thousands of "back of the pack" runners for whom Fred Lebow's vision had made distance running a possibility—those touched by the creator of marathon running who were not as privileged as I to have met him in person can meet him in print.

Long live the king!

Preface

FRED LEBOW WAS A DREAMER, the kind of dreamer who pursued his dream and made it a reality. And today, more than thirty years later, the world is still reaping the rewards of his vision and hard work.

In between escaping the Holocaust and succumbing to cancer, Fred Lebow the survivor became Fred Lebow the visionary, the entrepreneur, the gritty promoter, the unschooled marketer, the shrewd recruiter, the director—whatever he needed to be to create what is the world's best-known and best-loved marathon festival, the New York City Marathon.

Redefining the marathon wasn't his original goal. To begin with, his dream had been simply to reshape the world of distance running in order to share something wonderful with others . . . and that he did, in a big way. The New York City Marathon and the marathons around the world that emulate Lebow's "street party" were simply the best way for the racing impresario to get everyone out there running.

And as one of the schleppers—the ordinary, middle- and back-of-the-pack grassroots runners convinced by Fred Lebow that they could go the distance—I was a firsthand recipient of the gift he created. I am one of those who ran the race and made it to the finish line in Central Park—and the experience was so rewarding I went on to do it five more times.

Shortly after the passing of Fred Lebow, the running icon whose creation had given me such pleasure, I began doing research into his life. What I found was a story that embodied almost all of life's—and history's—most important themes: surviving adversity, rising above challenges, overcoming humanity's worst nightmares and reaching for our individual dreams, working hard to achieve our goals or volunteering to help others accomplish theirs, the people and the places, the politics, the hype and the shtick, competition and controversy. . . . Just about every imaginable emotion and experience was there.

Fred Lebow's life was a story just waiting—and deserving—to be told.

Acknowledgments

MY THANKS TO THE MANY PEOPLE I interviewed who helped me figure out how Fred Lebow convinced the ordinary folks of this world that running a 26.2-mile marathon was a happy fete worth striving for. Kristine Schueler, photo editor of the New York Road Runners Club, was instrumental in helping me choose pictures for this work. My colleagues, Professors Jules Cohn, Bert Kabak, Ting Lei, and Harvey Rosenfeld, provided faith and probing comments. My devoted editor, Peri Devaney of PERIodicals (peri_odicals@yahoo.com), was truly indispensable. My love and gratitude to my aunt Roslyn Grubart, who, when I was a young boy, introduced me to the life of the mind and taught me how to dream.

I have been blessed with five wonderful daughters and three wonderful sons-in-law—Mishalea and her husband, Jeff; Shulie and her husband, Dan; Rena and her husband, Jeff; Talia; and Sarah. They supported and encouraged me throughout and were sensitive enough not to ask too often how my writing was coming along!

Most of all, my thanks to my beloved wife, Miriam, whose warmth and sweetness transformed what might have been a marathon literary burden into a cakewalk.

Anything
for a
T-Shirt

Chutzpah's Destiny

LYING AT DEATH'S DOOR at Manhattan's Mount Sinai Hospital in early 1990, Fred Lebow was not about to allow himself to be defeated. Earlier that day, doctors had given him the bad news—a tumor the size of a tennis ball swelled in his brain. In all likelihood, he had no more than six months to live.

His visitors having gone home, Lebow tossed in bed, tears in his eyes. As the spindly race director took account of his life, he was overcome by one private sadness. He had never run in his own creation, the five-borough New York City Marathon. This race, which consumed him more than anything else in his life, had developed into the Big Apple's happiest, most unifying, most inspiring day of the year—and the grandest of all the "people's races" that followed his blueprint and transformed the traditional 26.2-mile marathon from a grueling, sweaty athletic competition into a fun spectacle, a piece of urban street theater.

Befitting the show he'd designed in 1976 as a one-time event honoring the nation's bicentennial, Lebow had been busy each year since, leading the pack as his marathon's number-one star performer . . . but always from his pace car, never on foot. Although he had run in sixty-eight marathons around the world, he had never completed the course of the festival he had launched.

Now, coming to terms with his life, the fifty-seven-year-old race director promised himself that if he survived this disease, he would finally go the distance in his own marathon. True to his commitment, he struck out down the hospital passageways, figuring out how many hallway lengths to the mile, even when he had only the faintest strength to do so. Although the hospital hallways were not the ideal locale for marathon training, these forays enabled him to stay in motion. By so doing, he refused to be defeated by his disease. Motion was the sign that he remained in control over his life.

Ever the running missionary, he did not allow other patients to sit on the sidelines. Between chemotherapy sessions, the beat-up race director mustered his fellow patients, in their hospital gowns and bathrobes, to follow him up and down the hallways. Such heroics were not foreign to Lebow. His resourcefulness came naturally: he had survived the Holocaust and honed his "can-do" style in improvising during his years as a garment-center knockoff designer.

Lebow's hospital walks were much more than an example of exercise: they became a lesson in fighting despair. His cancer not only served as a catalyst for recapturing his running stride, but also forced him to "recapture" himself. Previously a pragmatic, bottom-line promoter obsessed with producing the most fun-filled marathon party possible, concentrating all his thought on the shtick with which he could hype his marathon party, Lebow realized during his hospitalizations that staging a marathon festival was not the only thing that mattered. His family and a reconnection with the religion of his youth emerged as new priorities, and a softer side appeared. He was more willing to listen to others and to delegate tasks. He took on a new identity—cancer patient and then, gratefully, cancer patient in remission.

Back home, rather than curse his misfortune, Lebow raised himself one step at a time to the point where he could master the 26.2-mile marathon distance. He trained in Central Park, cradle of his vision of a people's race. Sometimes Allan Steinfeld, his Bronx-born alter ego and technical director, accompanied him. For longer sessions, he joined classes given by his Road Runners Club. As a result of the chemo and radiation treatments he underwent during that period, there were stretches where he lost his hair and beard, but regardless of how concerned he was about his looks, it was not his style to give up; he simply ran in the park hidden under a hood so as not to be recognized.

Lebow mobilized his resources against the darker aspects of his disease with the same determination that drove him to showcase his marathon theater. Told by doctors to expect to live between three and six months, he would survive for more than four and a half years. If during that time he could defy the odds and run his five-borough creation for the first time—a self-bestowed sixtieth birthday present—he could inspire millions of spectators. Such a feat could stir hope in cancer patients and their families everywhere, and in the most physical way possible. If he could cross the finish line, his achievement would be an incentive for patients to stay in shape despite pain and weakness. To others stricken with cancer, and to their relatives and friends, Lebow could send the message that running was the best medicine to kill the disease.

So run he did. Almost three years later, in the 1992 New York City Marathon, Lebow fulfilled his "deathbed" promise to himself and entered his own show. With an escort of close friends running alongside to guard him, he faced his challenge. As he ran, fragments of memories from marathons past surely flickered through his mind—memories of his wild run-in with police during his first five-borough show, of his successful negotiations with surly teenage "turf protectors" in Brooklyn, of placating Fourth Avenue worshipers when marathon spectators blocked their entrance during services, of the response of Bedford Avenue Hasidim to his Yiddish plea for water for the runners, . . . these memories and so many more.

Would the aging race director have the stamina to finish? Could he push through the weakness and pain? And would he win the race within?

The Starting Line

A Showman and His Show Are Born

1

From Arad to Central Park

"I LOVE THE PARADE ATMOSPHERE," Lebow reminisced, thinking of himself as the boy with Hasidic-style earlocks who was so excited when the Romanian king's entourage jauntily cascaded down the main street of his birthplace, Arad, in the late 1930s. "I love the flags, music, bands, banners. . . . You know—the hoopla!"

Fred Lebow recaptured his childhood excitement each year by challenging runners to face themselves in his joyous urban theater, his own parade of "royalty"—the New York City Marathon. The trajectory of Lebow's life would take him from the Holocaust through Brooklyn's knitting factories and the doubting old guard of America's distance runners before he cleverly created his athletic version of the "show" he so loved as a boy.

The unlikely beginning of a man destined to permanently change the sport of marathoning and distance running—the man originally known as Ephraim Fishl Lebowitz—occurred on June 6, 1932, in the city of Arad, in the province of Transylvania, in western Romania, not far from the Hungarian border. Arad's population included some ten thousand Jews. Despite its relatively small Jewish population, the *Jewish Encyclopedia* notes that the city boasted a wide network of Jewish benevolent institutions, a factor that perhaps contributed to Lebow's inclusive marathon vision.

In the Orthodox Jewish Lebowitz family, Fishl was the sixth of seven children, with four older brothers, one older sister, and a younger sister, Sarah, who would later emphatically insist, "We are '*Lebowitz*.' . . . '*Lebow*,' *it* sounds good in French."

Fishl and his family occupied a stone house with a courtyard in back, and the grass behind the home served as the grazing area for young Fishl's pet goat, Lily. Fishl spoke mainly Yiddish at home, and Hungarian and Romanian on the outside. Prayer and the study of Jewish classical sources in an exclusively Jewish elementary school called a cheder dominated his childhood.

His father, Tzvi, was a produce merchant who bought and shipped freight-car loads of fresh fruit and vegetables to Bucharest. Lebow's partiality to all varieties of produce during his years in New York stemmed from the exposure he was given to these foods through his father's business.

In their own way, Tzvi's business practices would serve as a model for the future race director. Just as Tzvi's business was based on the honor system as far as his customers' finances went, for the adult Lebow, a handshake rather than a contract would cap negotiations. Similarly, the boy Fishl noticed very little bookkeeping in his father's business, and years later, the man Lebow was much less concerned with his marathon's financial details than with the staging of his show, giving it the flair and glitz that would capture the world's attention.

In the aftermath of World War I, several ethnic groups set up enclaves in the eastern European area surrounding Arad. Fishl enjoyed accompanying his father on his rounds to these diverse communities.

It was in his childhood home that Lebow learned the value of appearances, a lesson that would serve as the touchstone of his marathon festival. His parents went to great lengths to ensure that the children dressed in clean, fancy clothes. Even when hiding from the Nazis, they were dressed immaculately.

The Lebowitz family hardly saw Fishl as destined for greatness. As he later admitted to girlfriend Heather Dominic, "ugly duckling" was the term applied to him by his siblings. As Sarah, the sibling with whom he was closest, explained, "Fred as a kid was not colorful. All my [other] brothers were gorgeous. All of them had the best personalities. Fred faded into everything."

Sarah spoke sentimentally of the family's "wonderful life in Romania. We were always singing and laughing." Yet it was during this wartime experience that Fishl honed the skills to live by his wits and to improvise. Survival depended on cleverness in sizing up a situation, and being strong in the face of danger. There was nothing casual about his approach to life. "These early years taught me to be on my toes," he said in 1982. "As a twelve-year-old, I was always on the lookout. I still am—even today."

In 1942, although the Nazi crematoria were already operating at full pitch, ten-year-old Fishl and his family, like so many Jews at the time, refused to believe the rumors they were hearing. The Germans they knew could not commit such horrors. Luckily, before the Nazis got to Arad, the Romanian government had convinced them that the Jews were more valuable as a labor force to build up the country's defenses against Russia than as ashes. Instead of being exterminated in the concentration camps, Mr. Lebowitz and his older sons were imprisoned in local work camps.

Mrs. Lebowitz was able to get provisions to them, and with a bit of chutzpah—a trait Fishl would learn from her—she even managed to sneak them some of her homemade white bread, a treat that was illegal because of the high cost of bleached flour. All she did was add a little brown sugar to her recipe to disguise it.

Slowly but surely, the horrors of the Holocaust became more and more apparent to the Jews of Arad and to the young Fishl, as it did to all Jewish communities throughout eastern Europe. Soldiers boasted about the atrocities they committed and openly displayed their hatred for the Jews.

As the Nazi threat drew closer, the family saw they had to escape. Fishl, his mother, and some older brothers—dressed as farmers— walked miles in the dark to neighboring villages where they received a cold reception. Explosions and gunfire racked the air. Young Fishl's knees were trembling, a reaction that would stay with him his whole life—when frightened, his knees would automatically shake.

After Russian soldiers took the city from the Germans, the Jews of Arad learned that they had escaped planned Nazi gassings by only one day. Liberators these Russians were, but as confiscators of private property, they set off panic among the Lebowitz family and the other Jews of Arad. Not only in matters of business, but also in all things social, the Jews resented the depersonalization and forced uniformity of Communist values. Fishl's family concluded that they had no future under Communist occupation, but since Jews were prohibited from leaving as a family, the Lebowitzs were forced to split up. They bade each other farewell, clinging to the dream of reuniting one day in a new State of Israel.

In 1947, fifteen-year-old Lebow, together with his brother Michael, who was two years his senior, managed to get permission to leave with a group of several hundred Jewish refugees for Czechoslovakia, and thus began a period of several years of wandering. In later life, Lebow would term this the "vagabond" era of his life and claim that this moving around set the stage for his inability to plant roots.

At the Hungarian border, Lebow had to think fast when guards came aboard the train searching for kids who were too young or too short to belong in the transport. Fishl and Michael fell into that category, but they avoided being thrown off by hiding behind the taller kids. At the Czech border, the two hid in the baggage compartment, and, in order to escape detection, they bribed the baggage watchman. The young refugees reached Marienbad, enrolled at a free Hebrew school, and carried out odd jobs.

Not much is known about this stage of Lebow's life—his autobiography simply notes that after a couple years he started roaming again, to Belgium, Holland, England—but it is known that he enjoyed the travel opportunities provided by his unfettered lifestyle. He and his brother became experts at train hopping, concealing themselves in baggage cars and spreading judicious bribes along the way. Contrasts surfaced between the two teenage Lebowitz boys, with Michael taking to his studies and Fishl, always adept at beating the system, getting involved with smuggling.

At first the teenage courier dealt in sugar, but later turned to the more lucrative diamond trade. His routine consisted of smuggling the diamonds by boat from Ostend, Belgium, to Dover, England, each trip earning him about two hundred dollars. He packaged the diamonds in double prophylactics, concealing the shipment in his body. Forgetting his wares' strategic location on one mission, Fishl used the shuttle boat's bathroom, and the diamonds disappeared down the toilet bowl.

The young smuggler never returned to Belgium. His next stop was Ireland, where he was lodged in a castle in County Westmeath while attending Hebrew school. Here, too, he had trouble with his studies, so, having been granted a passport as a stateless Irish citizen, Fishl headed west to America. He decided against joining his parents and most of his siblings in Israel, to which they had escaped from Romania, because the United States was too tempting a prospect to turn down.

In 1949, Fishl's first stop in America was Brooklyn's Yeshiva Torah Vodaath, led by Rabbi Shrage Feivel Mendlowitz, a pious Hassid with an untrimmed beard, uncompromising in his commitment to Orthodoxy, and also an immigrant from Europe. But Fishl had become estranged from his family's Orthodoxy during his years on the run in Europe, and, seeing himself less Orthodox, he craved adventure in the enticing secular world.

Seizing the opportunity to leave Brooklyn, the young man named Fishl enrolled at a newly opened yeshiva in Kansas City. Yet even in this more open mid-American setting, Lebow sensed that academics were not for him. Never officially graduating from high school—in either the United States or Europe—Fishl quit school and joined his brother Morris in Cleveland, Ohio.

Since he had immigrated to the United States on a student visa, Fishl Lebowitz was not legally permitted to work, so it was time for a new identity. He dropped the name Lebowitz, and at the Social Security Administration's office, a man with a card bearing the official name of Fred Lebow replaced the man who had been Arad's Fishl Lebowitz.

The new Fred Lebow took a job as a salesman for a wholesale television distributor. He became a member of the Cleveland Council on Foreign Relations; this affiliation, out of character for someone of such limited formal education, foreshadowed the international focus he would later incorporate into the New York City Marathon. After hours, he produced shows, a talent he would refine in his marathon spectacle.

Lebow became part owner of an improvisational-comedy theater, the Left-Handed Compliment, based in the suburb of Cleveland Heights. In focusing on this particular type of theater, Lebow once again showed his improvisational talents. Improvising was a theme throughout his life, from surviving the Holocaust to knockoff-dress production in the New York garment center to devising shtick for his marathon party.

Shtick: This Yiddish word, meaning roughly a show-business routine, gimmick, or gag, perfectly describes the characteristic traits and the entertainment routines and gimmicks that became so vital in Lebow's efforts to secure the recognition and attention needed to make his marathon vision a reality. However, *shtick* has a depth of meaning no English word can seem to capture, like *chutzpah,* another oft-used Yiddish word describing another trait Lebow would reveal over and over again.

Eventually, Lebow quit his job, concentrating on the nightclub that took as its model Chicago's Second City. The hustler skills he later showed in recruiting athletes for his marathon were now exhibited during trips to New York to scout performers. His showman expertise was definitely behind the scenes rather than onstage, as demonstrated when one of his actors took ill and he had to substitute in the cast. Though the theater was improvisational, there were still some lines he had to remember. When he forgot everything, he recognized clearly that improvising as a showman was not the same as improvising as a doughty performer.

The Cleveland club's shows ended when no reviews were being written because of a local newspaper strike. Lebow opened his next scene in New York. It was 1962, and Lebow found employment in the garment industry. Jews had been the key ethnic group in the industry's development decades earlier, but by the time Lebow arrived, Jewish predominance was fading. His first contact with the garment industry was in the nitty-gritty technical end rather than the entrepreneurial side. He specialized in double knits, the clothing rage of the early 1960s, and eventually his improvisational talents won out, bringing him to knockoff productions.

Lebow worked as a knitter at Berg & Berg Knitting Company on Brooklyn's Knickerbocker Avenue, a site not far from his eventual marathon route. Starting at the company's women's sweater factory in 1966, Lebow's first job was to make sure that no mechanical problems would stop the expensive machines from churning out fabric. It was a union shop, and company owner Martin Schloshberg was not allowed to permit a knitter to operate more than four machines at one time. "[But Lebow] didn't stand on ceremony," recalled Schloshberg. If one of the factory workers called in sick, Lebow took the initiative to operate six to eight machines. His main function, according to Schloshberg, was to troubleshoot for damages in the machinery: "If a broken needle was in the machine, we would have to throw away the fabric."

After working in the position of knitter for almost one year, Lebow rose to the next level of expertise at the factory, that of mechanic. In that role, Lebow was responsible for repairing the machinery, not simply attending to needles.

Always adept at seizing the moment, Lebow eventually opened a Brooklyn factory producing knockoff fabrics. "Knocking off" meant manufacturing cheaper imitations of expensive women's garments by skimping—possibly a shorter jacket, fewer buttonholes, no lining, false pockets. In order to produce first-class garments and not skimp on style, Lebow sometimes had the work done in Hong Kong or Taiwan.

For Lebow, "knocking off" was yet another outgrowth of the survival skills of improvising and manipulating he had developed in the years of living on the edge in Europe following World War II. Both fashion designing and marathon hyping were enterprises that would highlight his abilities to spot trends, move fast, and give the customer what he or she wanted. The fashion runway was as strategic a site for improvising as his racecourse would become. And his shtick—whether in the form of fashion accessories or marathon glitz—was directed at attracting an audience. Appearances, again, were everything.

Beyond the world of fashion, knocking off conveyed an equalizing quality similar to what would be his theme of a people's marathon. The elitist connotation of a designer dress smacked of an exclusiveness he liked to tear down, as he did later in attacking the elitist notion of marathoning.

In addition to the knockoff-production factory, which he owned with a partner, Lebow worked as a consultant to other manufacturers. To improve his skills, he took three courses at New York's Fashion Institute of Technology in 1965: basic textiles, knitting, and the knitting industry.

Professionally, during his garment-center career, Lebow never revealed the flair that would mark his style as director of the New York City Marathon. "He was not an outgoing guy," Schloshberg commented. "He was very calm, not excitable, matter-of-fact. Everybody liked Fred. He did more than he had to."

Praise came from throughout the industry. Jerry Goldman of Scottex Corporation, a company Lebow was involved with as Schloshberg's contact for yarn work, remarked, "The garment center is not filled with decent people, but [Lebow] was a very decent man. I remember him fondly. He dealt with us professionally."

"Fred took one day at a time," proffered Maurice Dickson, another of Lebow's early supervisors. His preoccupation or absentmindedness—traits that colleagues noted in his years of race-promoting prominence—was also obvious to garment-center associates. Dickson cited one incident when Lebow, in the process of cutting material on the tailor's table, absentmindedly cut the tie he was wearing: "Sometimes I wondered why he never cut his hand off."

Money clearly mattered little to Lebow. Although once he started his own business he proudly reported in his autobiography an income in the "middle five figures," he earned little as an employee and hardly seemed driven to earn more. "Fred couldn't care less [about what he earned]. . . . He was a man of simple needs," said Schloshberg, who first hired him at a salary of $225 a week. And, according to Dickson, who was comptroller of the company, by the early 1970s he earned about $300 weekly.

"Why do I need money?" declared Lebow to Schloshberg, who indicated that Lebow's $69-a-month walkup apartment at 226 East Fifty-third Street contributed to his nonchalance toward money. It was, in fact, Lebow's need to climb the eighty-eight steps up and down to his sixth-floor apartment daily, joked Benon Sevan, his roommate, that provided his first exposure to running. Sevan, a friend from Cleveland who later became an assistant secretary at the United Nations, said, "We used to plan how many times we went downstairs and upstairs. And if we wanted people to come and stay, we made sure they came late, so that they would be so scared of climbing down that they would stay overnight."

Lebow distanced himself from *most* things material, not only money. "Whatever I want, I get," he told Dickson. Despite his work in the world of fashion, Lebow had no interest in his personal wardrobe. "I'd go up to his apartment, open a drawer, and find only loose black socks lying around," said Dickson.

The green Volkswagen convertible Lebow owned testified that his life during that period was not *completely* ascetic. He drove the car to work in Brooklyn, and used it for making headway on dates. Lebow enjoyed the company of women, especially during the garment-center stage of his life. "He had a lot of chutzpah in picking up women," reported Dickson. "But he was a bachelor at heart. Women liked his personality. They found him different. He was interesting, exciting, smart, and had a good sense of humor." He specifically remembered one red-head who lived in the fire-escape apartment opposite Lebow and "who was always running after him." (Later, toward the end of the 1970s, being preoccupied with promoting his running vision, Lebow would sell the Volkswagen to Dickson.)

It was during his garment-center years that Lebow took up running, and he tried conveying the sport's infectiousness to business associates. Although they were amused by his enthusiasm, little did they expect him to emerge as a running-world icon. "Fred, the knitter from Brooklyn?" commented a skeptical Schloshberg, "Not in a million years would I have thought he would have achieved such fame." "He was one of the last guys I would have thought would become a celebrity," echoed Jules Marder, one of Lebow's clients.

Long before he emerged as a master promoter, the only sport Lebow played was tennis. In the late 1960s most of his tennis games were against one of his Manhattan walkup roommates, Brian Crawford. But repeatedly losing to Crawford drove Lebow to look for strategies to improve his game, and the coach of the Midtown Tennis Club advised him to build up his strength by joining a health club. After quickly becoming bored with lifting weights at the health club, he was told to try jogging and was directed to the 1.5777-mile oval track around the Central Park reservoir.

The reservoir loop, which was to emerge as the heart of both the New York running scene and Lebow's personal marathon tune-ups, was planned in the late 1850s, even before Central Park. At first a path for gentlemen and ladies carrying parasols, it had become a road for service vehicles. With the fitness movement already under way, runners had started using the track by the time of Lebow's initial foray.

Lebow convinced Crawford to accompany him for his first go around the reservoir. They each brought a date to cheer them on. Making the race competitive, Lebow and Crawford bet a few dollars on the outcome. Crawford, who was heavier, gave up after a mile, but Lebow kept going and finished. He ran the distance without stopping. Lebow afterward never lost another tennis match . . . because he never played another tennis match! Enamored of running, he became a regular in going the distance around the reservoir.

Though new to running, Lebow was not new to the values of self-discipline and self-control necessary for success along the course. Before taking up running, Lebow tried to eliminate distractions from hindering his goals. Fancy clothes and fancy apartments were not among his priorities. He also fought so that food needs would not determine his schedule. In his early garment-center days, the future race director felt a compulsion to eat at least three meals a day, as well as three or four snacks in between. Distressed at allowing himself to blow up to 175 pounds, Lebow embarked on a program of occasional fasting.

At first, he refrained from eating for periods of twenty-four hours. Then the regimen was extended another twenty-four hours, where only water or soft drinks were had. This routine ensured his independence from food. His appetite became subservient to his schedule, rather than the other way around. Likewise, he reduced his need for excessive sleep. Gradually, he cut down the time he spent in bed to one hour a night.

The New York City running world that Lebow entered in the 1960s was far removed from the dramatic people's marathon he later built. The marathon boom of the 1920s had declined to the point that, by the 1950s, there were only two marathons regularly held in the United States—in Boston and Yonkers. The great names in running were French or British. Long-distance running, wrote Joe Cody in the April and May 1983 issue of *New York Running News,* was seen by the American public "as something of a sideshow."

Races longer than two and a half miles were considered extraordinary and limited to the gifted few. The Amateur Athletic Union (AAU), the governing body for all American athletics until 1958, hardly considered distance running a priority. In England, by comparison, the sport (under the direction of the Road Runners Club) was taken much more seriously.

To uplift the cause of distance running, H. Browning Ross, an Olympic marathoner from Woodbury, New Jersey, had called a meeting in New York City of prominent Americans competing in the sport. This meeting, held at the Paramount Hotel on February 22, 1958 (the weekend of the national track and field championships), created a Road Runners Club in America. Soon afterward, some local runners formed the Road Runners Club of America (RRCA), New York Association.

Comprising forty-two members, the group elected Ted Corbitt, an Olympic marathoner and its most noted runner, as president.

Organizationally, this club, which directed New York City distance running, barely survived its formative years. The AAU refused to recognize it until 1964, and, as Corbitt later remarked, the lack of a firm agenda brought it "that close to being dissolved." Still, this small group of New York distance runners refused to be deterred by political problems. A year following its formation, the New York Road Runners Club (NYRRC) (officially, the group was then known as RRCA, New York Association) put on its own marathon in the Bronx, called the Cherry Tree because it was held on George Washington's birthday. In 1970, Lebow competed in this marathon, the first of the sixty-nine he eventually ran.

The initial running of the Cherry Tree Marathon was found afterward to be one mile short, having been based on an inaccurate measurement by a car odometer. Following the 1960 Cherry Tree Marathon, therefore, Corbitt worked to devise an accurate method and pioneered a technique of course measurement, using a surveyor's wheel, that became widely accepted.

A fellow Central Park jogger told Lebow in 1969 about an upcoming five-mile race sponsored by the Road Runners. The course consisted of eleven laps around Yankee Stadium in the Bronx. The jogger also advised Lebow to buy a pair of real running shoes, Adidas, for the meet. Lebow followed the advice, but remembered that pair as the only pair of running shoes he ever bought. Afterward, manufacturers supplied all his running shoes.

In this first competition with the New York Road Runners Club, Lebow was one of only a few dozen runners. The race was broken down into two categories, fast and slow, and a cautious Lebow signed up with the slow runners. Everyone passed the neophyte Lebow except one elderly man, whom he estimated to be sixty-five years of age. His not coming in last in that maiden race shifted the course of running history. The New York City Marathon would have never materialized in the wake of a last-place finish by this fledgling competitor. Such a dispiriting result in his first race, noted the race director years later, would have ended his running career early on.

Later that year Lebow paid three dollars to join the club. He competed in all its meets, mainly cross-country races at Van Cortlandt Park in the Bronx, but he was unhappy with how coldly he was received by the other members. The club's lack of outreach to nonelite runners grated on him.

To be sure, the predominantly blue-collar membership of the club felt a strong sense of camaraderie. Lowering their cholesterol level, taking part in an urban festival, and obtaining a T-shirt were not factors motivating their running. "I don't know if we did it for our health," said Kurt Steiner, the distance-running pioneer. "We did it for the competition. We did it because we loved the sport."

At those Bronx starting lines, no one, despite their improvised running outfits, was a stranger. "Everybody knew each other," said Harry Murphy, a founder of the New York Road Runners. "In fact, you knew everybody so well, you usually knew where you'd finish."

But the heavily accented Lebow, with his Jewish Romanian lineage, felt alienated from that crowd. Lebow lamented that the club consisted of "a small clique of men" who seemed reluctant to share their world with outsiders, which included him. Eager to break out of his slow running pace, Lebow wanted more tips from these experienced runners. He found them uncommunicative, and their vocabulary—*splits, paces, surging, drafting*—represented a foreign language Lebow did not understand.

Lebow was not the only critic of the club's lack of outreach. Vince Chiapetta, later codirector with Lebow of the first New York City Marathon, observed, "We had to move out of the small club thing. We wanted to see running as fitness. We had to reach out to the larger public, but we didn't want to lose our clubbiness."

Always pushing himself, Lebow directed his training to the 1970 Cherry Tree Marathon. Considered the mother of the New York City Marathon, the race started at Yankee Stadium across the MacCombs Dam Park, site of other Road Runners Club races. The course consisted of four times up and down Sedgwick Avenue. A tree on Ogden Avenue, facetiously called the Cherry Tree by the runners, served as the turn-around point.

The course itself, void of any scenic significance, was chosen for its lack of both traffic and spectators. Gordon McKenzie, a ten thousand-meter Olympian in 1956 and second-place finisher in the 1961 Cherry Tree, described the running outfits: "We wore what we had in the house. Long Johns and cotton sweats." Footwear was even more rudimentary. For his 1961 race, McKenzie created his own version of running shoes by asking a shoemaker to insert a layer of soft white rubber in his tennis sneakers.

It never dawned on these Cherry Tree marathoners to close streets, hire bands, hang balloons, or put up banners hyping the race. T-shirts and finisher medals were not necessary to set a mood of excitement. Instead, the main concession from New York City officialdom, said Vince Chiapetta, was that "the police in the Forty-fourth Precinct didn't give us tickets if we parked our cars by the starting line."

Launched with twenty starters, the Cherry Tree Marathon had grown to two hundred by 1970, the year Lebow competed. Most runners participated in this Bronx marathon as preparation for the venerable Boston Marathon held later in the spring. For his marathon debut, Lebow wore "some crazy-looking long Johns and a turtleneck," recalled Chiapetta. "His beard gave him a look of savoir faire." But this neophyte marathoner sensed something was missing at the Bronx competition: "There was no water, no press, no spectators, it was cold."

Some refreshments, however, were available. "Each loop, I passed a man who handed me a cup," said Lebow. "It was bourbon. I thought this was the way you run a marathon. Every few miles you took some bourbon. On the last loop, I was handed water and I was so disappointed."

Meanwhile, Lebow's good friend Brian Crawford was driving a car alongside him, heckling, "Drop out, Fred, drop out." Lebow's girlfriend was also in the car, shouting similar advice with a smile on her face. Between the whiskey and the needling, Lebow found it hard to go the distance.

Though Lebow finished his first marathon in four hours and nine minutes, he did not glory in the achievement. His disappointment in the race's drab surroundings overcame his joy. "This is a stupid place to have a race," he bluntly told Chiapetta. The tenement bu the course, the automobile traffic, kids throwing stones a all reinforced Lebow's distaste for the Bronx route.

Rather than relegate this marathon to a remote ou

Lebow urged Chiapetta, then president of the New York Road Runners Club, to switch it to Central Park, in the heart of the city. This new location not only would avoid the obstacles in the Bronx, but also had the benefit of a wide road meandering through its trees. Lebow's vision was buttressed by the decision of New York City mayor John Lindsay earlier that year to close the park to auto traffic on weekends in order to accommodate sports enthusiasts.

Strengthening his case, Lebow revealed to Chiapetta that there were some "millionaire" joggers who ran with him in the park. These wealthy runners would help defray the cost of a relocated marathon, promised Lebow. Questioned as to the identities of these potential benefactors, Lebow refused to disclose their names. "There were no marathon runners in Central Park," confessed Chiapetta. "I know them all." And to confirm his hunch, he secretly canvassed the seasoned runners in Central Park as to whether they recognized Lebow. "No one ever heard of that guy."

Convinced of the value of a Central Park marathon, Lebow was handicapped by his lack of social ties with top long-distance runners. But he was savvy enough to realize New York City's primacy as the home of many of the pioneers of American road running: Ted Corbitt, considered the founder of American ultramarathoning; Aldo Scandurra, president of the Metropolitan AAU; Joe Kleinerman, coach of the Millrose Athletic Association; and Kurt Steiner, the former French Foreign Legionnaire and racewalker.

To his chagrin, Lebow's vision of promoting distance running was not shared by many of the movement's longtime players. "There's an element that feels I've robbed them of something," Lebow said in a *New York Times* article published on October 20, 1981. "Before I came," the quote continues, "there was a group that ran in Van Cortlandt Park. They did things there and no one knew about them. The only thing I did was move the program to Central Park. A lot of runners resented that move." He felt they were content to keep marathoning in obscurity, a sport devoid of hoopla and glitz.

Organizationally, the Road Runners Club struck him as merely a "paper organization" limited by its not even having an office, so he decided to take the initiative and call the Metropolitan AAU with his proposal for a Central Park marathon. Unimpressed, the group asked Lebow to send a letter in triplicate.

Displaying his chutzpah, Lebow decided to make a pitch to the membership of the small Road Runners Club of New York. Buttressing his case, Lebow promised the help of wealthy friends in sponsoring the race. By his own later admission, Lebow "exaggerated a little" in citing these nonexistent friends.

The elders of distance running assembled around Lebow's kitchen table found big problems with the Central Park proposition. The Parks Department would never allow it, they asserted. The police would refuse to cooperate. Runners would not compete because of the park's unsafe reputation. After the running club members voted down Lebow's proposal, Chiapetta suggested that they themselves produce the race.

Two years earlier, Chiapetta had tried to organize a race in Central Park, but the Parks Department had turned down the request. As fate had it, the Parks Department official who rejected Chiapetta's application resigned around the same time that Lebow arranged an appointment for Chiapetta and him to make their case.

"I represent a committee of millionaire joggers," declared Lebow to the Parks Department administrators at the June 1970 meeting. Chiapetta was impressed with Lebow's immaculate attire in a polyester knit suit. Chiapetta did most of the explaining. He stressed the growth of the running movement and the prominence of the organization he represented. Surprisingly, permission from the Parks Department was forthcoming. "I don't think they quite knew what we were talking about," said Lebow, "but they gave us permission for the marathon."

Launched as the New York City Marathon, the race basically circled Central Park four times, from Fifty-ninth to Seventy-second Streets, and added two more miles in order to meet the distance requirement. The original plan called for Chiapetta, then a New York University graduate student in biology, to hold the title of race director, but Chiapetta added Lebow as codirector. Lebow's allure was his promise to pay for food and prizes. The entry fee was one dollar. Chiapetta typed the entry blank. Course-measurement pioneer Ted Corbitt made sure the distance was accurate.

Lebow tried to get all the publicity he could, but as the summer dragged on, the marathon counted only a handful of entries. Desperate, a week before the marathon in September, Lebow made a trip to the newsroom of the *New York Times,* but no one at the newspaper had heard of this New York City Marathon or of Lebow. But when the race codirector cleverly boasted that Ted Corbitt would be running, things changed. Corbitt, an Olympian, generated marquee value because he held many records in epic twenty-four-hour and fifty- and one hundred-mile runs, and was the second man in history to complete one hundred marathons.

The Corbitt association worked—the next day the paper ran a story about the race, and Lebow learned an important lesson he would apply down the road in promoting his marathon party: the hype of the big name. From then on he knew that names were critical in showcasing his events.

Meanwhile, Chiapetta also took to garnering publicity. The day before the race, he went to the *New York Daily News* and enticed a photographer with the promise of plenty of beer on hand.

Naturally, Lebow's fictitious "wealthy friends" never appeared, leaving it to Chiapetta and him to sponsor the race. They bought a few cases of soda at a Greenwich Village supermarket because they were three cents per can cheaper there than uptown. Unfortunately, the soda never hydrated the thirsty runners during the race because Lebow somehow forgot to bring a can opener to Central Park.

Chiapetta worked in his Greenwich Village apartment until 4 A.M., typing up the program. By that hour, Lebow, also involved in preparations, had already fallen asleep on the floor of Chiapetta's living room.

This first New York City Marathon drew a mere 127 starters, including two women who never finished. However, appearances by both New York City mayor Abe Beame and Manhattan Borough president Percy Sutton helped ensure that the race was not held in complete obscurity. Fittingly, the starting gun was shot by Ed Levy, a Bronx public school principal and manager of the Pioneer Club, whose inclusive membership policy was part of the foundation Lebow built on with his populist vision of marathoning—Pioneer was a racially integrated club admitting any athlete seeking to join. Despite his own budding prowess as a race director, Lebow was still known by his garment-center affiliation, and the *New York Times* on September 14, 1970, identified him as "an executive with Taylor Knits."

In the unseasonable eighty-degree temperature, Lebow, Chiapetta, and Corbitt were among the runners, Lebow's time being four hours and nine minutes. Lebow, running in a pair of Tretorn tennis shoes, desperately craved something to drink in the heat. He stopped a push-cart vendor in the hope of getting some refreshment. The vendor shook his head negatively when learning that Lebow carried no money in his running shorts. Fortunately, a woman standing nearby took pity on the exhausted Lebow, treating him to a soda. Looking back, Lebow confessed it was unlikely that either the woman or the vendor had any idea that a marathon was under way.

Actually, most of the "spectators" at the 1970 Central Park marathon were merchants on hand to sell their wares rather than to cheer on the runners. "It is a matter of unassailable history," wrote Bob Ottum in *Sports Illustrated*, "that most of the spectators were the gentlemen standing beneath the gaily striped umbrellas of their pushcarts, yelling, 'What's the big rush? Stop and buy a pretzel already.' "

By Lebow's reckoning, the Central Park New York City Marathon was successful if only because it avoided the drawbacks of its predecessor, the Cherry Tree Marathon. Frisbees were thrown amid the panting runners, and not too many people were paying attention, but at least in the park there were no cars, traffic, or rock-throwing teenagers to harass the marathoners.

At the awards ceremony, Lebow once again showed his knack at improvising. Since not enough money was available to buy trophies, old baseball and bowling trophies were recycled as running awards. But the number of trophies was still not enough. So Lebow handed them out onstage and secretly retrieved them from local runners to redistribute them to unsuspecting out-of-towners. The top winners were awarded wristwatches costing ten dollars each.

As though he had conspired to follow Lebow's "makeshift" strategy, thirty-year-old marathon winner Gary Muhrcke, with a 2:31:38 finishing time, had not even been sure he would show up at Central Park. As a New York City fireman, he had spent a busy "night before the race"—not carousing at carbo-loading parties, but fighting fires instead. "We had a lot of fires and a couple of close calls," he recounted, "and I was up all night. It was a majority decision just to go to the marathon the next morning. I wanted to go to bed, but we had three small kids and my wife wanted to get out of the house." So, to avoid a domestic squabble, the jaded fireman brought his family to Central Park to watch him run.

The year 1970 was a busy one for Lebow in regard to Lebow's own marathoning. He competed in thirteen marathons, including Oslo, Stockholm, and Paris. In Syracuse, New York, he set his lifetime best of 3:19.

It was with a dash of chutzpah that he finished his first Boston Marathon in the spring of 1971. "They had no water and no food on the course," he related. "I was trying to break four hours. I was so hungry. About three miles from the finish, I saw a little kid with a Hershey bar. I said, 'Can I . . . ' and then I just took it. I heard a voice, 'Daddy, he stole my Hershey!' *That* will teach him. . . . I finished in 3:59:58 because of that Hershey bar."

Veteran runners such as Nina Kuscsik knew what to expect in the hilly environment of Central Park. "We didn't have these water stops, food stops," she said, referring to what the future marathons would include. "I used to know I'd run out of energy. I used to take Tootsie Rolls with me, some sugar cubes. I'd find that if I took them every 20 minutes with water, they kept me in good stead."

Lebow's success with his first Central Park marathon spurred him to stage the event again. He again sponsored the 1971 race himself, but this time the field doubled to 246 starters and 164 finishers.

The 1971 marathon paid off for another of Lebow's visions, that of promoting women's marathoning. Seeking to enhance his field, he asked Beth Bonner's coach, Dave Romansky, if she would compete in his race. Bonner, a nineteen-year-old from New Jersey, had run a then stunning time of 3:01 in a marathon earlier that year. Romansky, who was an Olympic team racewalker also committed to improving women's distance running, noted, "Women got absolutely no respect. We didn't know how to coach them. We had no idea what women could do in a marathon."

In winning Lebow's marathon that year, Bonner became the first woman in the world to run a marathon officially in under three hours (2:55:22). In those early days of amateurism, Bonner's record didn't elicit a money prize. For her victory, Lebow presented her with a sweat suit and paid her train fare.

After meeting Bonner at Grand Central Station before the marathon, Lebow had taken her to "a little French place" for dinner. "He looked at me rather strangely," Bonner remembered. When the time arrived to order dessert, he asked her for her choice. Still hungry from her trip, she told her surprised escort, "I want another main dish."

Originally, Bonner was supposed to stay overnight at Lebow's girl-friend's apartment. Somehow, that arrangement did not work out, so he invited her up to his apartment, instead, in order to save hotel costs. Despite the womanizing reputation he developed in later years, Bonner did not detect any advances, so she agreed. What struck her about the apartment were his knockoff-dress creations hanging from ceiling hooks. "He let me pick out a blue dress with white trim to wear for dinner," she said.

The oddly scripted arrangement in Lebow's apartment carried over to the race itself. On the Central Park course, Bonner sensed nature's call. She divulged that when she was told by a male runner keeping pace with her that portable toilet amenities were not provided, "I sped up and made a turn into the woods and went to the bathroom."

The serendipitous quality of the race was exemplified by how the men's winner, Norm Higgins, a thirty-four-year-old Fuller Brush sales-man from Connecticut, happened to run in it: "I came down here today," he said, "because I thought they were running a 5000-meter race, but when I got here I found out it was a marathon. So, I decided to run anyway."

By 1972, the sixth-floor walkup apartment Lebow shared with Brian Crawford became the club's unofficial office, and Lebow in-stalled a club telephone. In those days, there was neither the money nor interest to provide more lavish quarters. Nina Kuscsik, one of the pio-neers of women's distance running, recalls how she once went to his apartment "to get some T-shirts to take with me to Puerto Rico, where I was going to be the first woman to run in a race. Those orange T-shirts that he always had . . . Fred threw them out of his apartment window! He kept everything for the club there."

In 1972, following two years of paying for the race with his own money, Lebow decided to put the marathon into high gear. His running club's membership had already risen to 250. There was no more reason, he felt, for subsidizing the race as a money-losing proposition.

The strategy called for promoting his marathon with an attractive two-color entry blank. This catchy design, he believed, would even impress competitors at that year's Boston Marathon. He also sought to build the marathon up with a magazine-style program carrying ads. The total outlay for this publishing enterprise came to three hundred dollars. Lebow thought approval from the club elders, whom he invited to eat and drink at his kitchen table, would be immediately forthcoming. But although the runners gathered in his apartment agreed it was a terrific idea, one guest asked what would happen if the venture lost money. In response, Lebow promised to cover any losses.

Despite Lebow's assurances that ads would cover the cost and that he would make up the difference, doubts persisted. Further explanations from Lebow became pointless after one club veteran posed the ultimate question: Suppose we supply the money and tomorrow you die? Ignoring the club's failure to back his proposal, he produced the program on his own.

The program's cover featured Gary Muhrcke, the New York City fireman who had won Lebow's 1970 Central Park marathon. The twelve inside pages included photos of the 1971 marathon, the race Lebow himself had run, although he never finished. One of the pictures showed him running side by side with Erich Segal, author of *Love Story*.

The club's race schedule, some twenty year-round events, and the names, ages, and personal-best running times of every entrant were also listed. Lebow sold all the ads to his contacts in the garment center, where he was still employed.

In a bolder move, Lebow tried to enlist General Motors, which had just opened its magnificent Fifth Avenue skyscraper, as a sponsor. Lebow interpreted the automaker's refusal to company pragmatism— masses of marathoners would make cars obsolete!

He sent out a letter to the club's more than two hundred members asking for donations. Forty-three members sent in money, and as a result, Lebow ended up kicking in very little of his own funds for this innovative running publication.

The marathon was held on Sunday, October 1. Earlier that summer American marathoning had received a big boost when Frank Shorter won the gold medal at the Summer Olympics in Munich. The victor was not only an American, but also a clean-cut Yale student with whom the burgeoning singles population of Manhattan's West Side identified. The running boom that Lebow had earlier prophesied might now be imminent, he thought.

"Everyone saw Frank's victory in the Olympics on TV and that got the ball rolling," said Bill Rodgers, a three-time Boston Marathon champion and future winner of four consecutive New York City Marathons between 1976 and 1979. "That's when America discovered the marathon."

By the end of 1972, Lebow was clearly onto a developing phenomenon. The image of the hard-training athlete was taking hold. More leisure time, emphasis on fitness, communing with nature along training trails . . . these were elements drawing jaded baby boomers. In 1972, at least 124 marathons were staged in the United States, though none along the lines of the show Lebow eventually produced.

The lure of distance running brought a few hundred additional members into the New York running club in 1973. Many of these new recruits first worked in races as volunteers, then took up the sport themselves. Lebow, always on the lookout for volunteers, liberally distributed T-shirts promoting his utopian vision of running as the key to happiness. Socially, these new members were more educated and had higher incomes than the primarily blue-collar mainstays of New York distance running in the late 1950s and the 1960s. They supported Lebow's more inclusive focus toward running.

Elected club president in 1972, Lebow's vision, ambitious for its day, called for transforming the notion of distance running in New York City. He dreamed of a club boasting one thousand members, a year-round schedule of races, an office, an awards banquet. Absent from his original vision was the shtick he would use to hype his marathon—money to attract the best runners and schemes to find million-dollar sponsors—but that year he moved to a new promotional level in marathoning by signing up his first corporate sponsor, Olympic Airways.

Lebow had help from Kathrine Switzer in advancing his sponsorship agenda. In addition to her running prowess, Switzer shared with Lebow the quality of chutzpah. She entered the men's-only Boston

Marathon as "K. Switzer." A few miles into the race, the marathon director recognized her as a woman and physically tried to push her off the course, but Switzer's boyfriend, who was also competing in the marathon, came to her rescue and knocked the director away. Photos of her struggle added support to Lebow's quest for the legitimacy of women's distance running.

Switzer introduced Lebow to Nancy Tuckerman, a former personal secretary to Jacqueline Kennedy Onassis, who directed public relations for Olympic Airways, then owned by Aristotle Onassis. In May 1973, Lebow, confident in his product, took Tuckerman to the Yonkers Marathon, which she found captivating and which convinced her to arrange for Olympic to sponsor Lebow's 1973 marathon with five thousand dollars. In addition, the airline agreed to fly the race's winner to the Pan Hellenic Marathon in Athens.

During the first year of his running club presidency, membership grew to eight hundred. New runners such as George Spitz, reluctant at first to run competitively, accepted Lebow's assurance that the six-mile distance was doable and signed up for Lebow's races. "I guarantee," said Lebow, "you won't finish first or finish last, but you'll finish." Away from the racecourse, Spitz, a New York State civil servant, volunteered to do publicity for Lebow's races, and Lebow showed his gratitude over the years by contributing to his political campaigns as a Democratic Party candidate, usually in the thirty- to forty-dollar range.

The 1973 marathon drew 406 starters, including 12 women. The number of finishers stood at 287. Waxing historical in promoting the race, Lebow arranged for the finish to be at Columbus Circle, right outside Central Park's southwest corner. He located the finish line there based on the belief that the first marathon in New York City, run in 1896, had also ended at that spot. But Lebow had been sold a piece of mistaken history. Actually, the finish line in that landmark race stood at Columbus Oval in the Bronx, not at Manhattan's Columbus Circle. For his first five-borough marathon in 1976, Lebow transferred the finish line back to Central Park's Tavern on the Green.

The early seventies were, for Lebow, a period for propagating the running lifestyle in its broadest sense. With its few hundred starters, the marathon did not yet consume much time. It wasn't until later years that, boasting an international field of thousands of competitors, the marathon became his main focus.

Seen in contrast to the streets of the backwater Bronx where his club previously competed, the beauty of Central Park, site of most of his Sunday races, helped the race director put his goal on firmer footing. Young athletes, like New Jersey's Tom Fleming, honed their skills in Central Park under the tutelage of the elder statesmen in Lebow's club: Joe Kleinerman, Harry Murphy, and Kurt Steiner. The camaraderie of these Central Park runners strengthened this new running constituency. "We trained with each other," said Dick Metz, a golf instructor. "We talked about our running times, our splits, gave each other training tips, recommended the best sneakers to wear."

Schmoozing took place after races over hot chocolate and coffee at the Church of the Heavenly Rest, across the street from Central Park at Eighty-ninth Street. Between 150 and 200 runners traded stories and compared performances. Lebow was regarded as just one of the middle-of-the-pack runners, with no inkling of the icon he would later become.

"All the races were very social," said Metz, a feature Lebow encouraged because it drew Manhattan's burgeoning singles population. Lebow joked from his bullhorn before races that running helped one's sex life. "Women were attracted to running," Metz continued. "They would see all those guys running. 'Maybe I could meet one,' they thought."

The foundation of what would develop into Lebow's world-renowned marathon party was being laid in these early Central Park races. The marathon became a work in progress, with Lebow specializing in introducing his unconventional shtick. He handed copies of the club newsletter, edited by Ted Corbitt and announcing race activities, to passersby in Central Park.

When necessary, his blueprint called for making over a runner's specialty. For example, Lebow did wonders for British runner Chris Stewart's career, convincing the track and field champion to risk lengthening his running distance to marathons. According to Lebow's autobiography, he lured Stewart to run increasingly longer distances by fixing up dates for him with increasingly more attractive women. The race director supplied garment-center models for the lonely Brit.

For 1974, Olympic Airways increased its sponsorship to eight thousand dollars. But a weather-conscious New York City Parks Department expected the race to be canceled due to a rainstorm that day, and Parks Department personnel stayed home, forcing Lebow to scramble at the last minute to find substitute volunteers. The race went off smoothly, and the New York City bureaucracy learned that the spirit of marathoners would not be dampened by mischievous weather.

Always looking for promotional breaks, Lebow scored a coup that year when winners Norb Sander and Kathrine Switzer were invited for the first time to do television interviews and appeared on the *Today Show*. But on the downside, that year's marathon struck future-winner Bill Rodgers as unexciting, and he claimed there was nothing spectacular about it and nothing to arouse the imagination and interest of the general public. He went further to say that the New York Road Runners Club put on the race with only "a minimal effort" and that things were so disorganized that while he ran, "bicycles and Frisbees were zipping by."

So what made Lebow stand out as a leader in this emerging running movement? According to Olympian Frank Shorter:

> People were willing to allow him to be the leader because they saw that he truly loved to run. They saw that all he wanted was to put on a great race. He wasn't pretentious about his own running. He wasn't greedy about his success. He didn't come across as a person who would throw his power or influence in anyone's face. He had tremendous organizational skills, and was willing to give credit to volunteers. His open agenda appealed to people in New York.

Membership in the NYRRC had grown to nearly two thousand in response to the running boom. Lebow himself was becoming more of a fixture in Central Park. His touting the message of "running for the common runner" led to the opening of a closet-size office at the West Side YMCA in 1975.

Lebow suffered a sharp setback for the 1975 marathon, losing his main corporate sponsor, Olympic Airways, as a result of Aristotle Onassis's death earlier that year. Ironically, while more New Yorkers were embracing Lebow's run-for-fun philosophy, tight money threatened the survival of the three area marathons: Lebow's marathon, the Yonkers Marathon, and the Earth Day Marathon. Lebow decided to continue his marathon even in the absence of a sponsor, and, according to George Spitz, "He was a desperate guy that year [but] his real greatness came out then."

Failing to find another sponsor, Lebow begged all over for money. Donations came in from 160 people, but the marathon still ended up losing money. Yet public awareness of the marathon was growing, enabling Lebow to score two big promotional advances that year. First, the AAU sanctioned the marathon as the National AAU Women's Championship, a major switch from the organization's previous opposition to women competing in a race of that distance at all. Second, Percy Sutton, the savvy Manhattan Borough president with designs on becoming the city's first black mayor, stepped up to champion Lebow's cause. After an introduction by a politically connected Spitz, Lebow invited Sutton to serve as the race's official starter. Rather than leave after he fired the starter's pistol, Sutton remained until the winner crossed the finish. For his reward, Lebow asked Sutton to place the laurel wreath on the head of Kim Merritt, the twenty-year-old University of Wisconsin women's winner. The photo of Sutton bestowing this honor on Merritt made the page-one cover of the *New York Daily News* on September 29, 1975. This publicity breakthrough transformed the Big Apple's impression of the race from a small run-of-the-mill marathon to one of flamboyance. Maybe going the distance, hinted the photo, was a fun thing to do.

But Sutton's contribution went beyond this one picture. Though he never captured city hall, Sutton helped bring Lebow's vision of a people's race closer to reality the following year, as the nation sought entertaining ways to celebrate its bicentennial.

2

Framing a Five-Borough Party

A DASHING FIGURE HIMSELF, borough president Percy Sutton admired the chutzpah of Lebow's showmanship, whose spiel, as Sutton saw it, was intended not simply to generate media hype, but also to help define the New York experience in a spirit of inclusiveness. In that sense, Sutton saw the race director's vision as similar to his own. Among the country's civil rights leaders, Sutton spent most of his time by the mid-1970s moving beyond his Manhattan political base to stress the ethnic diversity of the city. His message, he hoped, would carry enough strength to not only promote ethnic goodwill, but also persuade the electorate of his capacity to serve as New York City's first black mayor.

"Fred was a hustler," commented Sutton. "In Harlem, we call a man with a vision a hustler. He was a hustler in the best sense of the word . . . a man who gets things done."

Sutton sometimes could not understand Lebow's Jewish Romanian accent, but knew that the race director stemmed from a group historically denied entry. Forging opportunities for "people who felt left out" was one of Sutton's main political goals. And, in addition to his idealism, the savvy borough president responded to Lebow because he caught the timeliness of the running movement. "I'm a dreamer," said Sutton. "When I talked with Fred, I saw he also held a dream."

Despite these dreams, the New York City Marathon, wrote one sports historian, was no more than "an inconspicuous event" for the first six years of its running in Central Park. Drawing only about five hundred competitors in 1974 and 1975, sponsors perceived the marathon as holding little commercial value.

True, the gold medal that clean-cut Yalie Frank Shorter captured in the 1972 Munich Olympics made it easier for yuppies to embrace marathoning, and upper-status Americans began to see running's benefits—such as cardiovascular fitness, weight control, and social companionship—instead of its monotonous repetitiveness. But although he was identified publicly with the running boom, Lebow did not always, during this period, find peace and harmony within the ranks of his running club. The old-timers challenged his undemocratic leadership style, which consolidated power in his own hands rather than emphasizing input from members. Some club veterans were also unhappy with Lebow's courting of the more casual recreational runners.

To offset the loss of these dissident old-timers, Lebow cultivated volunteers as manpower for his marathon and the club's other races. As a result of what historian Pamela Cooper termed the "gentrification of marathoning," these volunteers, along with the runners, were stirred by the emerging "theater." T-shirts, training classes, and special ceremonies were among Lebow's techniques in expanding his volunteer base, and these volunteers joined his club, many times becoming runners themselves, further marginalizing Lebow's old-line critics.

Even Vince Chiapetta, who had cofounded the Central Park New York City Marathon with Lebow in 1970, was threatened by the politics of the club, warning Lebow, "Don't try to push me out." He considered challenging Lebow for the club presidency but dropped the idea, sensing how consumed the race director had become by the running movement: "I could've taken back the presidency in 1976, but for me running was only an avocation. I knew Fred would devote the time and energy to it." Chiapetta felt politically safe in the club because of his national prominence in distance running and his presidency of the Road Runners Club of America. To Lebow, Chiapetta represented an instrument with whom to promote his populist running vision: "He needed my power in other places," said Chiapetta, "to do what he had done in New York."

By 1975, there was barely any excitement left to Lebow's Central Park marathon. "Look at all those crazy people," mocked one spectator about this sports eccentricity on a television-news commentary. Horseback riders, dogs, bicyclists, and pedestrians freely crossed the Central Park runners' lane during the race. And during a European visit, Tom Fleming, whose two victories in the Central Park marathon were totally ignored, lamented, "They knew me as the guy who lost Boston."

How to hype the marathon? How to showcase it not merely as an endurance event, but also as fun, as sufficiently entertaining to draw more yuppies and more sponsors? These were Lebow's challenges, and two key players in Lebow's circle, Ted Corbitt and George Spitz, independently came up with schemes to help mainstream the event.

As first editor of the NYRRC's newsletter, Corbitt wanted to broaden access to his sport. Musing on a way to bolster the Central Park event, he came up with the suggestion of having teams from each of the city's five boroughs compete for a New York City Marathon championship. He conceived of this race as a one-time event to celebrate the nation's bicentennial.

A politically minded Spitz sought a more appetizing recipe to make the marathon not only a vehicle to showcase running, but also a means of boosting a New York City that was in a deep economic downturn. *New York Daily News* columnist Jim Dwyer, in describing the depressing backdrop for Spitz's proposal, wrote, "Business was fleeing. The Bronx was burning. City Hall was bankrupt. The popular wisdom was that most people wanted to run away from New York, not around it." But Spitz mistakenly thought Corbitt had proposed a race *covering* the city's five boroughs, so, shortly after the 1975 marathon and knowing Lebow's enthusiasm for shtick, he went to the race director with a five-borough marathon proposal.

Lebow rejected the idea of this citywide race. Staging a marathon through the city streets struck Lebow as so ridiculous he refused to give the proposition a second thought, for as much as Lebow wanted to hype his young marathon, he was, at the core, a pragmatist. Troubles producing the sponsorless 1975 marathon made him wary of taking on additional burdens.

Undeterred, Spitz contacted Sutton with the five-borough marathon proposition. Himself a Democratic Party activist, he had followed Sutton's rise in New York City politics and was impressed with the borough president's support of the marathon in 1975. "The Road Runners," wrote Spitz, "had seen too many politicians come to the starting line, smile for the cameras, fire the gun, and then leave without finding out how the race came out." Sutton endeared himself to Spitz when he "broke with political tradition by remaining for the finish." Sutton told Spitz he would cooperate. "My prime consideration was that the event should highlight the various ethnic groups in New York City." Sutton wanted the city's spirit celebrated in the structuring of the five-borough course.

Unable to stall any longer, Lebow was forced to go to a meeting at the Manhattan home of David and Lynn Blackstone to discuss the proposed five-borough race. Both Blackstones were active runners. Attending this historic meeting, in addition, were Spitz, Sutton, and Lebow's roommate, Brian Crawford. Sutton quickly took charge, laying out the arguments for this novel race. Not the least of the benefits, argued Sutton, would be its contribution to the city's commemoration of the country's bicentennial.

A reluctant Lebow spelled out his worries about a marathon extending beyond its Central Park confines: difficulties obtaining cooperation from city agencies such as the police to close off streets and coordinate crowd control, expected high financial costs, and losses sustained by the running club in paying for the sponsorless 1975 marathon. Staging the type of marathon conceived by the other guests would cost twenty thousand dollars, he said, doubting the costs would be that high, but purposely introducing the intimidating number to end further discussion.

Sutton, no less manipulative than Lebow, was not scared away: "If I can get you the money, and get you the proper police protection and all, would you still object to it?"

Lebow was cornered. Of course he couldn't object to Sutton's offer. Yes, he answered. Diplomatically, he went along with what he told himself would prove to be a nonstarter.

Sutton's first step was selling the merits of such a marathon, especially as a celebration of the bicentennial, to Mayor Abe Beame, who approvingly responded, "You take care of it." With that one nod, worries about cooperation from the city's police, fire, sanitation, highway and traffic, and neighborhood services departments were erased.

Next, to come up with the money Lebow needed, Sutton called on real estate developers Lewis and Jack Rudin of the Rudin Management Company. Not one to forget useful data about his campaign contributors, Sutton remembered that their late father, Samuel, who founded the company, ran marathons with an athletic club in the Bronx between 1917 and 1923. "He helped me when I headed the NAACP," said the borough president of his relationship with Samuel.

Expecting that he would have to bargain with these seasoned businessmen, Sutton asked for a sponsorship of twenty-five thousand dollars—five thousand dollars more than Lebow had said he needed. But the proposal sold itself, with Lewis showing immediate excitement in sponsoring a five-borough marathon whose winner would receive a silver trophy in memory of his father. "If my brother didn't want to chip in," Lewis thought to himself, "I'll do it alone." But as it happened, brother Jack gladly agreed to join in. For the Rudins, as for Sutton, sponsoring the marathon fitted their strategy to boost New York City. A civic-minded race touting the city was hardly an aberration to the check-writing prowess of these superphilanthropists. Their decision to sponsor this first five-borough marathon was based not on a relationship with Lebow, but on confidence in Sutton's judgment and their own vision of the potential such a race held for renewing morale in the Big Apple. They hardly knew Lebow when they pledged their twenty-five thousand dollars to borough president Sutton.

Once Sutton had secured the political help of Mayor Beame and the Rudins' sponsorship, Lebow saw there was no turning back. Still employed full-time in knockoff-dress production, he was, at first, genuinely frightened by the enormous work that would be involved with staging the first-ever five-borough race in New York City's history. But on second thought, the showman in him was excited by the challenge.

After investigating costs, Lebow realized that the money Sutton had been promised would not be enough. More money must be raised, but where to turn? Given New York City's role as the world's financial capital, banks seemed an obvious source, so Lebow wrote Citibank asking for a sponsorship of ten thousand dollars. The officer reading his request did not even bother to draft a separate reply letter. He scribbled a note on Lebow's letter saying the bank was not interested.

At the time, Charles McCabe, a vice president of Manufacturers Hanover Bank, was taking golf lessons at the Madison Avenue studio of Dick Metz. A runner himself, Metz had told Lebow in 1975, while they were both training in Central Park, "If you need money for any of your races, let me know." Remembering Metz's offer, the race director asked for help. According to Metz, who was already supplying "Manny Hanny" with logo golf balls for the bank to distribute at Westchester County country clubs, "Fred said he was short between $8,000 and

$9,000," and McCabe had filled Metz in "about some of the things we were doing—basketball shootouts, T-shirts, things like that—to get your name in the community." At that point, Metz brought Lebow the fund-raiser around.

The banker struck Lebow as knowing little about running and even less about the marathon, but he impressed Lebow as a sharp promoter, the type of person who appreciated the marathon production Lebow had in mind. "Wouldn't it be wonderful," thought McCabe, "to have thousands of people running around New York City in our T-shirts?" He offered five thousand dollars.

Lebow was displeased not only with the paltry figure, but also with the prospect of his precious T-shirts being burdened with the bank's long, formalistic name. For a shorter name, teased Lebow, he would settle for five thousand dollars. "Fred asked for $7,500," said McCabe. "Eventually it became $20,000."

Lebow's experience with Olympic Airways served as an incentive to find another airline to fund his five-borough race. He hoped to sign up Finnair because Finland was home to some of the world's greatest distance runners, including Lasse Viren. If he secured Finnair, fantasized Lebow, the airline might persuade Viren to compete.

Rather than send a sponsorship request through an agent or on letterhead, Lebow and Spitz jogged over to the airline's Fifth Avenue office one summer afternoon to do their spiel. Finnair's executives were not turned off by the sweaty outfits the two were wearing because most of them were also runners, and they promised to help, but only to the tune of five thousand dollars. Deciding not to press for more money, Lebow proposed a barter deal for the airline's sponsorship, suggesting that Finnair fly in some ten to fifteen of Europe's top runners and have its European offices publicize the five-borough marathon in European running clubs.

Agreeing that Lebow's proposal made sense, Finnair saw the marathon's business potential. It organized a package for Finns to spend a week in New York City and run in the race. Lebow, in turn, put the airline's name on the marathon T-shirts, which were paid for by the airline, and he set up a "Finnish" line in Central Park.

George A. Hirsch, publisher of *New Times* and later of *Runner's World* magazine, became a sponsor for five thousand dollars. Himself a marathoner, he signed up to run in Lebow's race. Although he had run the Boston Marathon several times in the 1960s, he saw the five-borough race as the beginning of a new era in distance running. "We were doing it in relative obscurity," said Hirsch of his earlier marathons. "It meant nothing to anyone else. It was our world. There was an incredible sense that our day had come, that we, as runners, had come into the big time. I do think we had the moment—that marathon."

Sutton's office on the Municipal Building's twentieth floor was transformed into the unofficial headquarters for planning the citywide race. His staff, at Lebow's disposal, readily opened the doors to the city's bureaucracy. With their help, it became easier for Lebow to ensure that streets would be closed, traffic regulated, and police on hand. The marathon entry blank was even printed in Sutton's office.

Sutton provided demographics for the marathon and insisted on tracing the city's ethnic landscape in drawing up the route. But how were they to draw the route? The only basics were the precise requirement of 26 miles, 385 yards and the inclusion of all five boroughs. The marathon's route was designed to link the city's social, income, and ethnic mélange: not simply to touch geographically on all sections of the city, but to capture its variegated ethnic flavor as well. But how many runners would sign up for the race? Were the streets wide enough? What would be the response of New Yorkers to blocked bridges, closed streets, and half-naked marathoners? Lebow had no clues, no answers.

In December 1975, Lebow and other ranking club members—Ted Corbitt, Joe Kleinerman, Paul Milvy, Harry Murphy, and Kurt Steiner—began laying out a course. Geographically, they agreed that the marathon would start in Staten Island and finish in Manhattan. Crowd size and crowd hype, key considerations for Lebow in mapping out the strategy for later marathons, were not weighed seriously. He wanted a course that would bring the least amount of traffic disruption.

Lebow's crew, with the experienced Corbitt as the guiding force, measured possible routes using car odometers. They ran though the streets themselves, getting a feel for road conditions. Focusing on traffic control, they eliminated options such as the Triborough Bridge because of the disruption that shutting it down would cause.

The race would begin at Staten Island's Verrazano-Narrows

Bridge, with the army's Fort Wadsworth, adjacent to the bridge, designed as the staging area. On the Brooklyn side of the bridge, the route skirted the old Brooklyn Navy Yard, where traffic was minimal.

For Lebow, it was imperative that the Williamsburg section of Brooklyn be included, the antimodern black-frocked Hasidim presenting an obvious contrast to the scantily dressed runners with their ethos of fitness. "When we built the course, I made sure we went through Williamsburg," said Lebow. "It's the safest neighborhood in the city. The Jewish runners are excited to go through the Chasidic [*sic*] neighborhood. They like to shout *'Shalom!'* to the Chasidim. For the non-Jews it's like going to a new country. They're exhilarated." In preparing for the first five-borough race, Lebow met with the leaders of the community to explain what he had in mind. A boyhood friend from Arad, Rabbi Chaim Stauber, was among the leaders, but despite the connection and the Yiddish dialogue, the Hasidic policy makers were not impressed. Lebow's decision to add Yiddish to the No Parking signs in Williamsburg on Marathon Sunday did nothing to ingratiate them. Their turnaround wouldn't come until years later.

Judy Woodfin, vice president of public affairs for Hertz and Lebow's driver in her company-sponsored lead Jeep in the 1981 and 1982 marathons, noticed the "dissonance" in Williamsburg and reported, "The Hasidim looked on us like we were invaders. They didn't clap and cheer. They were polite. We were *die anderer* (the outsiders). [But] Fred saw the humor in this scene," and the runners were thrilled about the experience, the response of the Hasidim possibly fitting their notions of how such a pious group should react.

Crossing into Queens, at the halfway point, was the Pulaski Bridge, and about two miles later a climb up the Queensboro Bridge—better known as the Fifty-ninth Street Bridge—into Manhattan. The course then headed north in Manhattan on the sidewalk along FDR Drive, hugging the river. Runners were required to go up and down several flights of stairs adjoining the highway overpasses, a feature hardly part of a standard marathon course.

The Bronx, the last of the boroughs to be tapped, was reached via the Willis Avenue Bridge. Snaking through just a few yards of the Bronx, the route returned to Manhattan via the Madison Avenue Bridge to 1st Avenue, crossed at 106th Street to Fifth Avenue, and proceeded to 102nd Street. There, runners mounted the low hills of Central Park for the final three miles, finishing at Tavern on the Green.

Once the route was drawn, Lebow picked a date for the marathon. He chose Sunday, October 24, because it did not compete with any other marathons and it was free from holidays, particularly the fall cycle of the Jewish New Year.

Next, Lebow had to organize the marathon itself, a task he pursued as though a man on a mission. His strategies were designed for maximum impact for both the runners and the New York City public. "Elite runners" had to be recruited, applications drawn up, and the runners' T-shirts produced. Logistical problems such as transporting the runners to the Fort Wadsworth staging area, scoring and timing, setting up the start and finish areas, and schlepping equipment abounded. Though he was learning how to make "news" largely by trial and error, Lebow wanted to be assured of media publicity for this historical event. He also had to put together an awards ceremony where winners, supporters, and politicians could take bows.

Lebow needed volunteers for all stages of the race. While he had developed a cadre of volunteers for his Central Park races, the five-borough run would require technical skills he never called for before: medical personnel had to be on hand, and radio communications were crucial in linking such a long course. In September, he hunted for volunteers at the main ham-radio group in the area: the Tri-State Amateur Repeater Council. Steve Mendelsohn, secretary of the ham operators, considered Lebow's pitch ridiculous: "I turned to the president and told him that Fred was an idiot. You can't run a race through the five boroughs of the city. Nobody will shut down the streets." He was wrong.

The press conference Lebow announced for Central Park in the early summer of 1976 revealed that, as a showman, he still had much to learn. Percy Sutton took time from his busy schedule to lend support, but the two were left schmoozing alone because no reporters showed up. Lebow, always a quick study, learned a basic promotional lesson from the press conference failure—the value of names in promoting his show—so he went after the two runners most venerated by his emerging yuppie constituency: Frank Shorter and Bill Rodgers.

The race director stood truly in awe of Shorter. This Yalie was the first Olympic gold medal winner that Lebow, a "mere" garment-center knockoff designer, had ever met. In the 1976 Montreal Olympics, Shorter had added a silver medal to the 1972 Munich Olympic gold that had made marathoning more intriguing to his countrymen, his prep school and Ivy League credentials making it socially acceptable for Americans to emulate his agenda. Shorter also sensed his impact: "Winning the marathon in Munich made my running, in the eyes of others, legitimate. Suddenly, it was okay to be a runner, to train for two and three hours a day. There was a purpose behind it, something to be gained."

And Shorter was no stranger to New York City, having been raised some fifty miles north in Middletown, New York, and boarding as a youngster at Manhattan's St. John the Divine Choir School. "My initial impression of Fred was, "Here is a guy who is smart and who really wants to put on a race in the five boroughs.' He was talking positively about all that he could do. He didn't talk about all the incredible obstacles, but he was excited about it. With that type of personality, he might just pull it off."

The Olympian sensed Lebow's ability as a showman simply by his smile. "You read people. Fred had a good idea of what would work. He was open to ideas, and gave credit to others for their ideas. He told you an idea that was PR-based, and I could tell in an instant from his smile that he was a showman." But Shorter was more intrigued by how pandemonium would be avoided in a race through the streets of New York City than by the unifying concept of a five-borough marathon. "This is New York. How are they going to be able to shut the streets down to be able to go through?"

After Shorter agreed to run, the race director capitalized on the Olympian's reputation with a press conference held September 16. Lebow paid to fly Shorter to New York. "Fred personally drove out to the airport in a Fiat X19 and drove me into New York," said Shorter. "In any of the entrepreneurial success stories, that's how you start out. You must do everything."

Mayor Beame and four borough presidents were c
photo op. Shorter ran a few sprints against Sutton and

ough heads. Mayor Beame fired the starter's gun. This time, the press was present and photos appeared in the newspapers. Lebow had successfully learned his lesson in marketing.

Though Bill Rodgers finished fourth in the 1974 Central Park marathon, Lebow and he had never met at the race. Suffering from leg cramps, Rodgers had skipped the awards ceremony, all the better for the race director, because the Bostonian's nonappearance probably postponed the public feud between the two that would last for years. Privately, they seemed friendly enough—going out to dinner and sharing fun times—but publicly, Rodgers spelled trouble for Lebow. In his autobiography, the race director divulged that nobody had tried to discredit him more than Rodgers. Unable to explain their paradoxical relationship, Lebow had to accept it as a given because in 1976, Rodgers, a teacher of emotionally disturbed children in Everett, Massachusetts, was the type of celebrity Lebow was looking for. A year earlier, he had finished third in the World Cross Country Championships in Morocco. Later that spring, in winning his first of four Boston Marathons, Rodgers set an American record time of 2:19:55.

In August 1976, while at Cape Cod's seven-mile Falmouth Road Race, Lebow invited Rodgers to compete in his upcoming marathon. Rodgers readily accepted, but soon afterward, someone who appeared to be directing Rodgers's business turned up, demanding money for the Bostonian to run in New York. Lebow doubted that, on his own, Rodgers would have shown such gall.

Despite his own experience with bribing his way to survive in post-Holocaust Europe, Lebow did not expect to need money to draw elite athletes to his marathon. *Amateurism* was clearly the byword in distance running at the time, and no runner had ever asked Lebow for a "smear." The race director had no problem paying such expenses as travel or hotel accommodations for elite athletes, but he was appalled at the excessive amount Rodgers sought—two thousand dollars.

Since Lebow's official budget lacked provisions for paying athletes, he knew that any funds to pay Rodgers would have to come out of his own pocket, but he agreed to pay, speculating that showcasing Rodgers would put his marathon on the map. In Lebow's vision, he needed stars because he was promoting a show, not simply an athletic event. Name performers generated publicity. He never regretted the payment because the investment paid off, and the 1976 marathon launched New York into the big leagues, right on the crest of the running boom.

The big question was *how* to pay Rodgers? Given the code of amateurism in running competitions, his public budget could not include an entry for such a payment. So Lebow relied on Brian Crawford, treasurer of Lebow's running club, who emerged as a dependable courier. Shortly before the marathon's start, bag in hand holding two thousand dollars, Crawford showed up at Rodgers's hotel room.

News of the payment angered Tom Fleming, winner of Lebow's Central Park marathon in both 1973 and 1975. Fleming, who also finished among the top ten in six Boston Marathons, felt snubbed. "I found that certain people were getting money, and I never wanted Fred to take me for granted," said Fleming. "Why wouldn't the champion from the year before get paid?" When confronted by Fleming, Lebow's defense was that as a "local runner," he did not require payment.

Seeking cachet for his race, Lebow wanted to sign up top foreign runners, but his international contacts at the time consisted more of Hong Kong dress manufacturers than global running clubs. After convincing sponsor Finnair to bring over Finland's Pekka Paivarinta, Lebow turned for leads to the one solid international runner he actually knew—England's Chris Stewart—who was indebted to Lebow on two accounts: professionally, Lebow's nudge to change his running focus to distance events instead of shorter races enabled Stewart to carve out an extraordinary reputation in this new running arena, and personally, Lebow continued to set the Englishman up with gorgeous garment-center models as postrace diversions during his American trips.

As a result of Stewart's contacts, Lebow drew athletes from ten countries, including British runners Ian Thompson and Ron Hill. But not all Lebow's foreign entrants reached the starting line unscathed. Jack Foster, the New Zealand masters champion with a 2:11 running time at age forty, unsuspectingly jumped into a cab at Kennedy Airport where two waiting robbers were seated. "Jack was rolled in the drive to the hotel," reported Frank Shorter. "Fred took the incident personally. He was genuinely distraught that this happened to one of his runners."

Arriving in the Big Apple, these foreign competitors not only had to be accommodated, but also had to be entertained. Dick Metz was enlisted by one of his golfing students, marathon sponsor Manny

Hanny's Charles McCabe, to show the athletes around town. Metz drove them to the city's top sites in the bank's "Anycar," a comical vehicle hobbled together from parts of other cars, including a Rolls-Royce that showcased the bank's name.

Metz invited some one hundred guests, including some twenty-five foreign athletes and Lebow and a date, to a party at his two thousand-square-foot apartment at 142 East Eightieth Street. Tapping his bagful of stories, Lebow was the hit of the evening. With McCabe's bank picking up the bill, Metz also hosted an athletes' luncheon at Club 21. A surprised Metz watched as Bill Rodgers, despite standard training rules, smoked cigars at the restaurant.

As the marathon date came closer, Mt. Sinai Medical School scientist and veteran distance runner Paul Milvy recruited Allan Steinfeld, a member of the City College of New York's track team and Lebow's eventual successor, to be the chief timer. Steinfeld brought his girlfriend, Alice Schneider, along with him to race-planning sessions since she was into the then new technique of computer scoring. This computer connection, which was bristling with potential, turned into one more problem for the overburdened race director when Schneider brought in a male programmer to be responsible for the marathon's entry forms. The woman with whom the programmer had been living decided to throw him out of her apartment, and the programmer had left some two hundred completed marathon entry forms—including applications from some of the world's top distance runners—in his former lover's apartment.

Lebow politely asked her for the forms, but to no avail. Worried that this snafu could bury his marathon, Lebow appealed to her sense of reason, asking why those runners should suffer because of her broken romance, but she remained unmoved. Schooled as he was in the art of survival, the race director dropped all pretense of dignity and begged the recalcitrant record holder. Still she refused to give ground. With no recourse remaining, on the morning of the marathon, despite attending to a thousand last-minute details, Lebow had to set up a registration table at the Fort Wadsworth gym, and there, amid the prerace stretching, taping, and lubricating, the athletes completed another set of entry forms.

In planning his course, Lebow remembered having tumbled down the wrong road at a marathon intersection in Atlanta, and he wanted to avoid such a mishap at his own race. But how could he visually direct runners to stick to the actual course? A blue line became the route's identifying mark. In addition to its role in guiding runners, the blue line also announced to New Yorkers through their streets that the marathon was on the way. A truck normally used for street lane markings, equipped with a big paint drum at the back for spraying the road, was supplied by the New York City Highways Department. The painting had to be done at night in order not to tie up traffic, and since the line snaked through sidewalks where the runners passed, a hand-pushed truck had to be put into service to prevent sidewalk splattering.

Marathon Sunday drawing closer, Lebow's running club's West Side YMCA office was thrown into chaos with last-minute details. "Fred was running around like a chicken with two heads," noted British racing star Chris Stewart. Registrar Joe Kleinerman slept overnight on the club office floor, available to answer phone queries, rather than return home to his Bronx apartment.

As the number of entries rose to two thousand, an earlier cutoff date of October 12 was imposed. Eventually, five hundred applications were rejected. Lebow had achieved the diversity he sought, with runners from thirty-five states and twelve foreign countries. Underscoring the growing "everyman" quality of marathoning, 50 percent of the field consisted of first-time runners.

Fifty-eight women, the most ever for a marathon, were among the group. Demographically, the competitors were upscale and highly educated, including 317 doctors, lawyers, and scientists. Some 300 runners identified themselves as students. The participation of such educated runners reflected the new awareness of the cardiovascular benefits of running, and the increased leisure time available to this upwardly mobile class for marathon training.

The youngest runner was ten-year-old Jerry Pierce from Moncie, Indiana. The oldest was seventy-one-year-old Robert Earl Jones, father of actor James Earl Jones. One blind runner, Joseph Pardo, was entered in the race. Lebow's hype attracted celebrities such as marathon swimmer Diana Nyad and Kenneth A. Gibson, the mayor of Newark, New Jersey. Ted Corbitt, distance running's elder statesman at the age of fifty-six, signed up, as did former New York City Marathon winners

Gary Muhrcke, Tom Fleming, Norb Sander, and Sheldon Karlin, all trying to make history again.

Though marathon planning seemed to be succeeding, an alarm went off in the harried race director's dream on the Saturday night eight days before the race. His nightmare? No water was available along the course for thirsty runners. In the morning, the promoter remembered that he had indeed arranged for water stations in Manhattan, but not in the outer boroughs. Without water in Brooklyn or Queens, Lebow knew that his marathon would end in disaster, even endangering the lives of competitors. His challenge was where to find volunteers at this late date to man water stations. To the rescue came Joe Kleinerman, a thirty-five-year post office veteran, who supplied Lebow with a map of postal zones along the marathon route. Confident that his colleagues would sympathize with Lebow's predicament, he asked the race director to phone each postal station to explain his quest. In response to Lebow's calls, nearly all the postal workers volunteered to set up water tables. At a meeting the following Wednesday evening, all but one of the postal workers whom Lebow had phoned appeared for last-minute instructions on the manning of racecourse water stations.

Lebow was scared during those climactic days before the marathon. So many things could go wrong. Would the runners be able to make their way unimpeded through closed city streets? Would drawbridges that the runners had to cross stay shut? Would potholes suddenly surface? Would the police stop spectators from leaning out and blocking the runners? What if a fire broke out on the course?

Walking on the Verrazano-Narrows Bridge the day before the marathon, Lebow discovered that the expansion joints that held the bridge's surface together contained spaces big enough to grab an athlete's foot. Unless covered, many marathoners would be injured and a human pileup would follow, turning the marathon into a bloody fiasco. But the Bridge Authority lacked any covering material for the joints. Lebow had to quickly raise $350 for the thirty needed planks.

Total exhaustion was what Lebow and his troops felt in the last days before the marathon. All sorts of urgent issues popped up. No precedents existed for this untried event. Volunteers had no idea that this pioneering race would develop into one of the world's main entertainment spectacles. The immediate goal was simply that the runners not be confronted with obstacles along the route.

Sunday, October 24, 1976, at four o'clock in the morning, a jittery Lebow was driven from Manhattan to the Fort Wadsworth Staten Island staging area. A drizzling rain sharpened his feelings of isolation as he surveyed the desolate fields. By six, the buses transporting runners from the Manhattan pick-up point arrived—one less worry for Lebow. Although the Fort Wadsworth gym was unfamiliar to the runners, tension lessened for the race director as they bantered, stretched, rubbed themselves with Vaseline, and schmoozed about past races. Though the weather was overcast, Bill Rodgers said the forty-degree temperature created "ideal conditions for a marathon."

When the 2,090 competitors lined up for the first edition of Lebow's five-borough marathon, the race director had already made history. He had put together the largest marathon ever, an achievement made even more impressive by a route extending through one of the most congested cities in the world. Overshadowing questions about the athletic success of this five-borough spectacle was the social unknown. Would Lebow's production result in a happy ending, bringing unity and joy to a city so gripped by neighborhood divisions?

About the field, the *New York Times* reported on October 25, 1976, that there were "participants from all walks of life." No surprise, added the newspaper, because as "a truly democratic sport," marathoning "seduces" all types of competitors.

Few came with as poignant a story as Dick Traum, a thirty-five-year-old scientist who had lost his right leg in a freak car accident. Wearing an artificial leg made of steel, plastic, and plywood, with a rubber foot, Traum intended to become the first amputee to run a marathon. His running over the year had resulted in the media publishing "inspirational" stories about him, but Traum disliked the moralistic label. On the running course, he refused the image of victim or outsider: "I thought of myself as a runner, a peer among the other runners with whom I associate."

Traum was not deterred from competing by an accident that had occurred during his last long run before the five-borough race, a half marathon in Central Park, in which a bicyclist had slammed into him along the route, knocking off his prosthesis and sending it flying across the pavement. To prevent a recurrence, Traum brought along a support group, including his wife, Betsy, a brother-in-law following in a car and a friend riding alongside on a bike. In the car was a pair of crutches, just in case. "If I was anywhere within several miles of the end, I figured I could finish on the crutches," said Traum.

In order to make sure he would neither run through unsafe streets at night nor reach a deserted finish line, Traum and Lebow decided that he would begin the race at 7:00 A.M., three and one-half hours before the official start. He actually set out at 6:49 A.M. because the emotional pressure of trying to become the first amputee marathoner in history was too great. By then he had spent so much time anticipating the event that it was no longer fun. "It was nerve-wracking, and I just wanted to get the tension over with."

Jacques D'Amboise, a principal dancer with the New York City Ballet, also experienced the mild shock of competing in Lebow's five-borough odyssey. Although many professions were represented in the pack, dancers were not normally drawn to running because the sport strained muscles needed for stage performances. But at age forty-two, D'Amboise no longer worried about the youthful, classical ballet style that required the intricate use of the pointed foot. His rebuff in encouraging schoolboys to study dance spurred him to compete in Lebow's production. Turned away by an athletic coach at one school who told D'Amboise he didn't want a ballet teacher, and hurt by the rejection, the dancer said, "I want to go back and say, 'Listen, I just ran a marathon,' " so he sent off his entry in September, before he left with the ballet for a three-week appearance in Paris. During the trip, he trained by running the Parisian streets in the morning hours, and back in New York's West Side, where he lived with his wife and three children, he steadily increased his distance, working up to a twenty-mile run. He outfitted himself for the marathon in blue and yellow sneakers, white socks with yellow trim, blue track shorts, and a pink jersey. Unable to contain his excitement, D'Amboise approached the starting line on the Verrazano-Narrows Bridge doing cartwheels, kicking and stretching his arms in all directions.

Lebow hustled competitors to the bridge's toll plaza in order to make the 10:30 A.M. start, but he had no luck grouping the elite runners to launch the race as a pack. Slower runners penetrated the pack in the morning's disarray. A police motorcycle escort stood poised on the bridge, ready to lead the runners. Behind them waited a motley press crew in a pickup truck. Lebow, not sure how the race he constructed would turn out, was a bundle of nerves. Seated beside him in the van serving as the race's pace car was chief ham operator Steve Mendelsohn.

Percy Sutton fired the starter's gun, and under the overcast skies the throng of runners pressed across the span. Closely inspecting the course so that no obstacles blocked the path, Lebow was relieved that the plywood he placed over the bridge's expansion joints warded off any accidents.

Pekka Paivarinta, the twenty-seven-year-old Finnish Olympian brought to New York by sponsor Finnair, took the early lead. He had an early margin of five hundred yards over the rest of the pack, his brisk 4:45-minute miles through the first five miles having Lebow fantasizing to Mendelsohn of a possible world record. But the Finn's overeagerness failed to intimidate the others. "He did that before in Japan," commented twenty-nine-year-old Frank Shorter, who preferred running in a ten-man pack, together with Bill Rodgers, about four blocks behind Paivarinta in Brooklyn. He said later, "He died there and he died today."

Shorter was intrigued by the Hasidic Jews of Williamsburg. "I will never forget the look of bewilderment and sort of recognition of an older man with white sideburns, a hat and beard. 'Should I clap?' he asked himself. Slowly, he clapped and got involved with the race. I found this wonderful."

In case Lebow was getting lost in dreams about the excitement of records being set in this five-borough marathon debut, the barricades at the race's halfway point on the Pulaski Bridge between Brooklyn and Queens quickly disabused him. Despite Lebow's instructions, the barricades were set up terribly wrong. The police had lined the barricades across the roadway, not the walkway. Lebow feared that the athletes would be squeezed into too tight a space.

With the lead runners quickly approaching, a keyed-up Lebow took things into his own hands. This was not the time for polite niceties with the cops. He darted toward the mislaid barricades, repositioning them his own way. But the cop on the bridge was shocked by Lebow's chutzpah and wrestled the frenzied race director as he shifted the barricades. Screaming obscenities, Lebow was threatened with arrest by the aroused officer. Narrowly missing being jailed at his own marathon, Lebow succeeded in rearranging the barricades. As the cop angrily approached, the race director was pulled into the van at the last moment and fled into Queens.

By then, Rodgers had taken the lead, true to his marathon strategy: "I like to start easy, run hard for a while in the middle to shake the others, and then coast home." The five-foot, eight-inch, 130-pound Rodgers was wearing his signature white gloves, Greater Boston Track Club T-shirt, and a pair of borrowed soccer shorts. He had forgotten to pack running shorts for the occasion.

After Rodgers had been in the lead for a while, Chris Stewart, nearing the Queensboro Bridge, challenged him. In order to learn the strength of his competition, the Bostonian would break away and then run with his challenger a while to check out his running style, listen to him breathe, and see how strong he really was. If possible, he would talk to them. "That's what I did with Stewart," reported Rodgers. "I asked him his name and . . . then I knew who he was and that he had a fast marathon time. . . . I said to myself, okay, now I'm going to run a little bit harder and see what happens. Fortunately, he began to have some difficulty and fell back."

Though he planned ahead, Lebow was unprepared for the damage that the Queensboro Bridge's grating inflicted on the feet of his runners. Stewart emerged from the bridge with bloodied feet, no doubt contributing to the laboring noticed by Rodgers who, once in front again, relaxed, breezing toward Manhattan's East Side Drive. At the eighteen-mile mark, Rodgers whizzed past amputee Dick Traum, shouting, "Attaboy, Dick." Though the fast pace of Rodgers and the other front-runners had made Traum feel as if he were "going backwards," this compliment spurred him on. Rodgers's intimate greeting, said Traum, "had to be one of the most exciting moments of my life."

For Rodgers, the urban sprawl along the drive was far more harrowing than the bucolic route of his native Boston Marathon. He inhaled car exhaust fumes from cars passing parallel on FDR Drive. But the main irritant was the flights of stairs on the drive's sidewalks. "What kind of marathon is it that makes you run up stairs?"

Lebow's main worry by this point was that runners would stray off course. He was panicked by fears that the early morning rain had washed away the blue line. At the Willis Avenue Bridge, he waited on the Manhattan side while Rodgers crossed the bridge, entering the Bronx. What if the course marshals didn't appear and Rodgers continued into the Bronx interior instead of making a U-turn, returning him to Manhattan? Would the rest of the pack trail Rodgers deeper into the Bronx?

Fortunately, Rodgers ran right on course, trailed by Shorter and Stewart. Now, the pack swept past First Avenue, then Fifth, finally entering Central Park. Determined not to lose sight of Rodgers again, Lebow positioned his van only a small distance in front of the Bostonian.

Disarray plagued the finish line. Crowds pressed in everywhere. Ken Moore of Eugene, Oregon, a top finisher at the 1972 Olympics, was pulled off the course by a cop in the final fifty yards because he had no bib number. Vehicles haphazardly stopped immediately in front of the finish, forcing Rodgers to weave his way to victory. Despite all the chaos, Bill Rodgers's winning time of 2:10:10 set a 1976 marathon record!

Nearly a half hour later, Miki Gorman, a forty-one-year-old diminutive Californian who had not started running until the age of thirty-three, set history's second-fastest women's marathon time at 2:39:11. The five-foot, eighty-seven-pound Gorman reached the Central Park finish with the seventieth-fastest time overall.

In addition to receiving the Tiffany-made sterling silver trays donated by the Rudin family, Rodgers and Gorman were crowned with laurel wreaths handmade by Jane Muhrcke, wife of the winner of the first-ever New York City Marathon, Gary Muhrcke.

Indicative of the world-class entries Lebow had attracted, 312 men and 2 women finished in less than three hours, and 1,192 men and 30 women in less than four hours.

Robert Earl Jones, the seventy-one-year-old actor and father of James Earl Jones, running his first marathon, surprised himself by crossing the finish at 5:30 P.M., in seven hours. "I'm so happy," ˙ ˙
who had played Robert Redford's mentor, Luther, in
Award-winning film *The Sting*. "My head was clear, and I
just needed another pair of legs!"

Some four hours into the race, dancer Jacques D'Amboise, the veteran of so many stage bows, not wanting to disappoint the hundreds of cheering spectators crowded around the finish line, took his final strides with a triumphant smile on his face and his arms stretched wide, turning from one side of the path to the other! Minutes later, sitting exhausted but happy in Tavern on the Green, he paid Lebow's enterprise the ultimate compliment, announcing, "That was so much fun I'd like to run another."

Athletically, Rodgers gave New York an even stronger compliment, calling the course "a little tougher than Boston. Boston's basically downhill, although, it has those hills. This course had a few hills and fairly tough terrain. It was like running cross-country." But Rodgers's victory glow dampened a bit when he discovered one of the hard facts of New York City life. The 1973 Volkswagen he drove down from Boston, which he'd illegally parked, had been towed away. Lebow gave him the one hundred dollars to get his car out of the impound lot, hoping that Rodgers would not sour on the city and decline future race invitations because of his missing car. Grateful for the kindness Lebow showed, Rodgers observed of getting his car back, *"That* would never happen in Boston."

In spite of the records set at this inaugural five-borough marathon, it was Dick Traum more than any other runner who captured the heart of the crowd. Aiming to complete the race in eight hours, Traum crossed the finish in an impressive 7:24. "No way was I going to stop," said Traum. "The last quarter mile of the race, when the course was packed with spectators on each side, they roared as if I were running down the football field with the ball, headed for the winning touchdown. The difference is this didn't stop after fifteen seconds, but went on and on for what seemed like forever." "I wouldn't believe a person with a handicap could work up the nerve and strength to compete," said one spectator to reporter Harry Stathos of the *New York Daily News* (October 25, 1976). "It said something to all of us. It says our troubles aren't so great. If he has enough stamina to do that, we have enough stamina to do what we have to do."

Traum's achievement also received the greatest amount of applause at the Road Runners Club awards ceremony at Lincoln Center's Avery Fisher Hall later that evening, and his success laid the foundation for his founding the Achilles Track Club for disabled runners, uplifting the lives of thousands. But in evaluating his own life's high, Traum claims it was Lebow's first five-borough race that stood out: "If I had one day in my life to live all over again, it would be my first marathon."

The improbable race staged by Lebow that Sunday afternoon in October demonstrated his ability to stir the media pot. In two articles on the front page of its second section, the *New York Times* the next day, October 25, 1976, described the long run through the city streets:

> Choirboys cheered outside a church in Brooklyn, just before the 11:00 A.M. mass. A woman passed out complimentary oranges on East Fifty-ninth Street. Motorists and taxis gave ground without a grudge. . . .
>
> The race embodied the city's character, good and bad. Some spectators watched out of curiosity, unfamiliar with the mystique of long-distance running. Others enjoyed the neighborhood flavor of the race, an event that some skeptics said could not be held outside the controlled confines of Central Park.

Notably, at no point was Lebow mentioned by name in the *Times* account. The media focused on the event rather than Lebow's designs as its producer. Though New Yorkers could not avoid taking notice of Lebow's first festival, simply based on the traffic congestion that it left in its wake, the race director cleverly promoted it as more than a sports event. Instead, he glorified the marathon as a healthy enterprise, especially for his core constituency, the fitness-conscious, well-educated baby boomers.

Respecting academic expertise, even though he himself never completed high school, Lebow arranged for a four-day conference beginning the day after the marathon. It dealt with the health aspects of strenuous exercise and marathon running. The prestigious New York Academy of Sciences sponsored the event, drawing some four hundred doctors, researchers, and running buffs.

Dr. Thomas J. Bassler, a California pathologist who completed the New York City Marathon earlier that week in some four hours, gave marathoning the health certificate Lebow was looking for. He declared to the conference in the Barbizon-Plaza Hotel that any competitor who built up his stamina over a period of time to the point where he could go the marathon distance "would never die of a heart attack." As proof, Dr. Bassler noted that at least five heart patients who had undergone double coronary-artery bypass surgery only four months earlier had run in the New York City Marathon, finishing in about four hours.

Despite such enthusiastic endorsement, the *New York Times* reported on October 28, "His views were greeted with skepticism by many of the medical specialists present." Rather, noted the *Times,* "the recent avalanche" of middle-aged and older joggers and marathoners had not given researchers enough time to assess either "the lasting health benefits or risks" resulting from such strenuous exercise.

Dr. Terrence Kavanagh of Toronto's Rehabilitation Centre, who had completed Lebow's marathon in more than four hours, offered a more modest argument for the benefits of exercise for persons with heart problems. In his exercise coronary-rehabilitation programs, Dr. Kavanagh had tested 780 patients for seven years. After stress tests for each patient, he found that persons over forty-five built up their heart-lung capacity gradually to the point that they were able to run three miles at a speed of twelve minutes a mile, five times a week. Those under forty-five covered three miles in thirty minutes, five times a week. But only a small percentage of the group engaged in marathon-distance runs.

Age longevity, however, should not serve as the motivator for running, argued Dr. David L. Costill, director of the Human Performance Laboratory at Muncie, Indiana. Sounding themes similar to Lebow's vision of running as a lifestyle enhancement, Dr. Costill said, "What you really want from exercise is to improve the quality of your life rather than to make you live longer."

Despite the bold beginning of his premiere five-borough marathon—the record numbers of runners and spectators—Lebow remained unsatisfied. True, he basked in the glory of conquering the city and breaking into print. But he could not relax for too long. He must further prove himself. He was still the Holocaust survivor. So in hindsight, he considered the 1976 marathon "the worst organized" he had

he Fort Wadsworth staging area was chaotic, the finish line th characters who did not belong there, the communica-n inadequate, the methods for scoring runners primitive.

No reference, however, was made to the lack of street theater, a tact he pursued in later years in mainstreaming his marathon party into pop culture.

Lebow's critique was objectively well taken. He had always wanted to promote a spectacle, and in the years ahead his race crystallized into just such an incredible show. What originally cost sixty thousand dollars to produce would escalate into a race costing millions. Two thousand runners mushroomed to thirty thousand, and the crowd grew from a half million to two million.

Indicative of how the die was cast for his people's race was the conversation at the Barbizon-Plaza Hotel between running icon Dr. George Sheehan and *Boston Globe* reporter Joe Concannon. Dr. Sheehan's message to America was that running represented more a lifestyle than a sport. So impressed was he with Lebow's grit in staging his five-borough debut that he prophesied New York would soon overtake Boston as the nation's premiere marathon. Little did Dr. Sheehan guess how much marathoning was destined to change when *hyped* by a *hustler* who was always in search of shtick!

3

King of New York for a Day

PUSHING HIS WAY THROUGH the cordon of elite runners primed to spring across the Verrazano-Narrows Bridge, the scraggly bearded Fred Lebow was searching out trouble at his marathon party. Bullhorn in hand, his eyes tracked from left to right, seeking to pick off any interlopers who had snuck into the elite ranks for a head start on the 26-mile, 385-yard course ahead. Quickly, the astute-eyed race director spotted a runner without the proper number. "You hot-dogger, get back," roared the heavily accented race director. "You won't last to the other side of the bridge. I know who you are, you hot-dogger. Officers, remove that man," ordered Lebow. "Officers, please move your vehicles. The race begins in five minutes."

For Lebow, Marathon Sunday, the one day around which his entire year's calendar revolved, was his moment as king of New York. This slightly built, disheveled-looking impresario was producing the biggest marathon party in the world, the Big Apple's spectacle celebrating life.

Driving through the city's five boroughs in his white, sponsor-provided Mercedes convertible—the twenty-seven-thousand-strong pack of runners closely behind him, pounding away with distant looks on their faces—Lebow barked commands, waved to the crowds, ordered the accompanying press vehicles to stay in tow, and fired off queries to chief ham operator Steve Mendelsohn seated at his side. In this moment as New York's ultimate celebrity, Lebow's persona was more that of a field marshal leading his troops into battle than that of a race director or star. Himself a marathoner (belonging to the middle-of-the-pack variety), Lebow knew that for every runner, going the distance meant a rendezvous with glory.

Lebow's climactic day of the year was already veering toward mayhem, even before the race had begun. Like the fabled Brigadoon, "Marathonville," the city Lebow reconstructed at Staten Island's Fort Wadsworth staging area each year, came to life for only the few morning hours of Marathon Sunday. As usual, he had laid siege to the area at 4:00 A.M. A small army of volunteers had already erected the tents, the signs, the tables displaying sports drinks and bagels, the banners, the portable toilets, and one of Lebow's favorite gimmicks, the world's largest urinal.

Making the rounds before sunrise, Lebow sampled the hot chocolate for its heat level, straightened barricades, inspected the tautness of the balloons overhanging the bridge, parried journalists, phoned television meteorologist "Mr. G" (Irv Gurofsky) twice for last-minute weather reports, tossed discarded drinking cups that were lying on the ground into the garbage, and checked on the flow of runners being bused to the staging area from the steps of the Fifth Avenue branch of the New York Public Library.

He was always conscious of the arriving athletes as they prepared for the race by stretching, greasing, hydrating, urinating, and jumping up and down in group exercise warm-ups; as they bantered about races run, injuries overcome, and hoped-for finish times; and as those who were oblivious to the noise in Marathonville skimmed the Sunday *New York Times* or napped in a corner.

Above the two-mile-long Verrazano-Narrows Bridge droned nine helicopters. Boats in the bay shot streams of water in the air. Music on the loudspeakers energized the pack, and announcements in a variety of languages told the runners where to line up. Politicians declared their admiration for the marathoners, welcoming them to New York City.

Lebow, in his Transylvanian accent, urged the athletes to drink at the water stops, to enjoy the city's sites along the way, and to celebrate crossing the finish line by dancing later that night at Roseland. Jittery runners were given last-minute counseling by mental health therapists of the Psych Team, assuring them they had the emotional wherewithal to finish the race.

As the drumbeat of the start beckoned, the runners inched up the sloping path abutting the bridge, the discarded sweatpants and jackets that had shielded marathoners from the prerace chill littering the entry area, Lebow in control, preparing to take his lead in the pace car as soon as he was sure the start had gone okay.

The night before, in festive spirits at Tavern on the Green, they carbo-loaded for Lebow's party. Stout and skinny, old and young, self-styled muscle men and placid-faced novices, they represented every possible profession, the fifty states, and nearly one hundred different nations.

Despite the formidable distance that lay ahead, the tableau at the start consisted of runners appropriately attired for Lebow's theatrics. Although it was the T-shirt that epitomized the party spirit, some dressed in such silly costumes as a clown, a rhinoceros, a waiter, a groom. They treated the race more as a fun fete than a grueling, enervating hurdle. Across the marathon's 26-mile stage, they were performing for 2 million roadside spectators.

From its beginning in 1970 as an obscure event staged totally in Central Park, with its 127 serious runners forcing their way past bicyclists, dog walkers, and Sunday strollers, to its broadening in 1976 to encompass the city's five boroughs in honor of the nation's bicentennial, with some 2,000 starters making their way along the exciting new route, Lebow's marathon had grown into a show that, by the late 1980s, drew some 30,000 starters and added $100 million to the city's treasury. As the race grew in size, it was transformed from a purist athletic event into a festival, Lebow's flair for the dramatic casting the New York City Marathon into an entertainment outing, a 26.2-mile block party! It showcased the Big Apple both to athletes and to television viewers as an exciting vacation spot. No wonder the city treated Lebow as if he were its king!

Behind the marathon's hoopla stood the mundane task of successfully transporting 30,000 runners some 26 miles through the world's most frenetic city. Trappings for the 1987 marathon, for instance, included 204 buses to transport runners to Staten Island, 440 portable toilets, 1 million paper cups, 88,000 safety pins, 27,000 Mylar blankets, 4 tons of ice, 7,000 race-day volunteers, 30 medical units consisting of 1,760 medical volunteers, more than 2 tons of bagels, and much more.

On the surface, Lebow seemed an ingenious version of the Catskill Borscht Belt entertainer in sneakers, a picture that served him well even though it so badly understated his role as visionary and promoter of

New York's huge one-day festival, and of the running movement as a whole. In his brief shining moment as king of New York for a day, the nondescript-looking race director, who became more recognizable than the flamboyant show he created, was greeted with shouts of "Hello, Fred!" as his cortege sped by. Energized by his own hype, Lebow roared into his bullhorn, "Cheer them on," as the sweaty procession dashed into each neighborhood.

Entering the Hasidic section of Brooklyn, he commanded in the Yiddish of his childhood, *"Lommen heren!"* (Let's hear it!). The initial attitude of disinterest among the Hasidim toward the marathon gradually evolved into one of bemused support; their hostile stares gave way to offers of sliced orange wedges for the runners' nourishment, and on one exceptionally hot Marathon Sunday in 1984, when the race director was worried about the possibility of his runners dehydrating, the handful of Hasidic roadside spectators returned with seltzer (!) in response to Lebow's shout of *"Die laufer darfen vasser"* (The runners need water).

Exiting the Bronx for the final assault into Manhattan, he ordered, "Let's hear you, Harlem."

Lebow's grand finale in the race took place at the Central Park finish line, where, furiously waving in his runners in windmill arm sweeps, he capped his role in the show he created. "Fred was the only race director I knew who waved like crazy, trying to pull you in," said Frank Shorter. "He was so animated and excited. He couldn't sit still at the finish line. He was having so much fun, because he cared about the performance. He cared about you. He wanted everyone to get out of themselves as much as possible." So that runners could savor memories of his party in the comfort of their own living rooms, one year he even resorted to selling "a piece of the Marathon." In a flyer to his running club's members, he offered banners that had been suspended from light poles along the route, at a cost of one hundred dollars each.

The value of human striving was an unstated theme of Lebow's marathon. Each runner served as his own competition. Or, as running philosopher Dr. George Sheehan put it, to know one's self is to test one's limits. For Lebow, the marathon symbolized more than thousands of sneakers whisking along the Big Apple's pavement. The marathon was a metaphor for life, with the end goal being reaching the finish line. In preparing each new version of his marathon show, Lebow himself embraced this theme of striving with the question, "How could I top last year's race?"

Lebow's "subjects" for the day—his marathoners—were "Everyman" and "Everywoman." He attracted many unlikely competitors through the magic of a street party in the city with the world's highest marquee recognition, and for each of them a secret dream spurred this seemingly crazy 26.2-mile fete. "This year in New York, we had 27,749 finishers," noted Lebow in 1993. "I'd say there were about 27,749 [different] reasons why people ran."

But in Lebow's vision of a people's race, the under-three-hour finisher held no more status than the six-hour schlepper. He paid top athletes to compete because he wanted his race to be taken seriously in the running world, and, indeed, records were set on his course. But another motive for signing up these athletes was so that the ordinary "plodder" could feel that he was playing on the same field as the greats.

In putting a human face on marathoning, Lebow not only transformed the lives of his runners, but also redefined himself as well. Holocaust survivor . . . teenage diamond smuggler . . . yeshiva dropout . . . television salesman . . . nightclub owner . . . knockoff-clothing designer in New York's garment center—these were Lebow's earlier identities. By accident, he took up running and wound up reinventing himself once more. As a race director promoting his populist vision of a distinctive New York experience, his persona became that of a dealmaking showman, hyping a physically straining race as if it were, and to turn it into, a fun challenge.

More than a running icon, Lebow in many ways defined the American fitness movement in the last decades of the twentieth century. He was not an ivory-tower entrepreneur, but always out in the field promoting his vision that running is fun and marathoning hip. He worked seven days a week, but because of his zeal he never compartmentalized his schedule into business time and personal time. Even outings to other running sites became missions in searching out shtick to bring home to his own marathon party.

Exploring Lebow from the theme of transformations raises challenging questions as to the career of a modern-day sports entrepreneur. Independent of his reputation as king of the road, a lesson to be learned from Lebow's life is how an impassioned advocate can seize the moment with a dream: "One beautiful spring day, I was in my office early in the afternoon, and on sudden impulse, I left, went up to Ninetieth Street, and started running. It was wonderful, and I told myself that if it was so important to me, it would be immoral not to deliver the message to others."

Who was this gritty promoter who made the crazy idea of a 26.2 miler part of world popular culture? How did Lebow, completely unschooled in mass marketing, change New York City's tempo, closing down its streets for a spectacle in sneakers? What shenanigans did this Transylvanian American use to wrest the keys of the city from politicians and deal with the running world's governing bodies? How did his chutzpah help him squeeze money from sponsors? What was the shtick he used to transform an obscure race of some 120 starters in Central Park into the greatest footrace in the world, and how did he manipulate the media to get the publicity he needed? How did he shrewdly assemble an international entourage of runners and amass a crew of thousands to make sure everything went smoothly, and a crowd of 2 million spectators to cheer on and energize his motley procession of 30,000 streaming through New York's crowded streets? And why were his runners basking in glory—instead of screaming in pain—in spite of the callused toes, strained Achilles tendons, sore knees, and exhaustion they dealt with at the end of every marathon? How did Fred Lebow get to be king of New York for a day?

"Running" the Show

4

Who Was This Gritty Promoter?

THE MORNING FOLLOWING each New York City Marathon was always a time of letdown for Lebow. No more spearheading the charge through the city streets, no more cajoling the media, no more accolades from crowds. "What happens, and it has happened to me, is that you have this crescendo, and then it's over, you've lost your desire to conquer. For a lot of us, there's more joy in seeking than attaining," he explained.

In wry tones he would describe this "self induced depression," saying, "I always feel sad on the Monday after the marathon. I call it 'post-marathon depression,' " but later in the week, when the videos of the race would arrive, he would resume the posture of a garment-center designer planning his new season's dress styles and get to work on his private dreams about the mix of merchandise and shtick he would need to dazzle the customers at his festival the coming fall. He would be driven by a perennial desire for accomplishment and focus on his goal of coming up with new marvels for his one-day party through the streets of New York.

Who was this man that he should he go through all the ups and downs, and all the effort it took, to share his excitement of running with others? Why not simply enjoy the sport himself instead of laboring so determinedly to stage his spectacular marathon festivals? Did he truly enjoy his quest for encores, or was his "people's parade" merely a sop for fitness and camaraderie?

As a runner, Lebow's course performance put him somewhere between the middle and back of the pack. In the sixty-nine marathons he ran, never once did he finish in less than three hours and fifteen minutes. In the first New York City Marathon he held, in 1970 in Central

Park, Lebow came in forty-fifth out of the fifty-five finishers. Running experts described his running essentially as shuffling. According to Kathrine Switzer, "Fred was a real no-hoper as an athlete." Dick Traum, founder of the Achilles Track Club for handicapped athletes, noting that Lebow lacked the wiry build of star runners, explained, "He had a Jewish body."

He also had a Jewish name, Kathrine Switzer reminded him as they brainstormed how to promote women's long-distance running one afternoon in Central Park in the early 1970s. "Fishl, Fishl, that's a beautiful name," she said. "Why don't you use it?" Lebow answered dismissively, "Oh, it's hard to pronounce and it's not an American name."

A hint to who this gritty promoter was, personally, can be found in this short conversation—a key answer to the questions of why and how he did what he did being found in his formative years as Fishl—from his Orthodox Jewish home in pre–World War II Romania and his encounter with the Holocaust to his forced journey to freedom and the chosen home he would make as an American. The child named Fishl had been taught the value that, rather than lead a status quo life, a Jew must continually *shteig*, which means "to climb, to strive," in order to justify his very being. Motion, striving, became a metaphysical responsibility. To not climb, according to this Orthodox Jewish teaching, was considered a dereliction. Though Lebow, in the social disarray of post-Holocaust Europe, gave up most of the Orthodox Jewish rituals, the ideal to *shteig* had been so embedded in him from such an early age that he could not undo it.

"Trying was Fred's specialty," noted Kathrine Switzer. "Fred didn't care that he had little ability to run faster, he had the stubbornness to run longer." This imperative to *shteig*, coupled with his Holocaust experience, laid the foundations for Lebow's marathon vision and fostered the very traits that would enable him to create his masterpiece theater. "Fishl's entire childhood was filled with fancy footwork," wrote Switzer. "Their home was taken over by the Nazis and their lives centered on avoiding Nazi persecution. Again and again, in fact, he owed his life to his ability to make the effort."

Lebow once commented to chief marathon ham operator Steve Mendelsohn about the United States' exposure to World War II, "You have it rich and comfortable in America. Americans don't have any appreciation of what happened in World War II, not having lived under Nazis," and he would occasionally mention the Holocaust in passing. On a personal basis, though, he would rarely share any memories of the war years. This caused those who knew him to conclude that there was a deliberate avoidance. "He hid what happened during the war," said his longtime Road Runner Club associate Vince Chiapetta. And although Laura Leale remembered discussions with Lebow about religion, his reluctance to discuss the Holocaust was noteworthy, as she observed: "I believe he suppressed a lot about his childhood. . . . There had to be something there in his memory that caused him great pain. He didn't really face the past or want to be open about the past." She suspected that the years he was separated from his family following World War II took a big toll.

Hard knocks as a Jewish youth alone in postwar Europe shaped Lebow's dream in two respects: First, it contributed to his need for a spirit of inclusiveness in his marathon festival. Elite "categories" and any sort of "exclusionary standards" held a hollow ring to someone who had been forced—because of religious persecution—to maneuver throughout his formative years just to stay alive, so Lebow toiled to include as many nationalities, races, levels of running ability, and runners of both sexes as possible. And second, though his Orthodox heritage represented a source of inner conflict, his Holocaust experience served an important role in forming the entrepreneurial spirit and adaptability needed to build his marathon empire, and equipped him with such basic survival strategies as flexibility, the need to take risks for self-preservation, and the ability to make the most of any situation, as he did when he created, and then went on to learn skills from, his premarathon garment-center career.

Lebow was a remarkable study in contrasts. At times he was disarmingly direct, informing running official Jeff Darman, for example, that his wife was so attractive, he would ask her for a date were she single. At other times, he was aloof, abrupt, or evasive. Alice Schneider, the wife of Lebow's alter ego, Allan Steinfeld, and head of his club's computer services, said, "Many times I would talk with him, but he wasn't really interested. He asked me a question. I would answer him, but he didn't really want to know."

His charm was often selective, focusing at bottom on putting the best spin on his marathon theater. To those useful in advancing his design, he was solicitous and entertaining. To others who he felt impeded progress, the tacit message was, "Don't waste my time." Laura Leale, Lebow's public relations associate, described Lebow's dual messages: "He could be attentive, loving and caring. He could also be mean and insulting."

Although he could obsess on promotional strategies, such as the design of a T-shirt or a race banner, one constant in his communication style was a short attention span. When he needed to win a power play or to charm a supporter, Lebow's attention was indeed riveted. But his mind was clearly elsewhere, following the Yiddish expression "Mein kop is in di himlen" (My head is in the clouds), when his companion told him things he already knew or that he considered useless.

Kathrine Switzer, women's winner of Lebow's 1974 marathon and later a sports commentator, was exasperated with his attention deficit. "He would be thinking different things at any part in the conversation. If I said something, he would go back to something else. I'd say, 'Fred, you pay attention to this.' I'd ask him to repeat it after me." Despite his calculating bent, Lebow did suffer from a genuine absentmindedness.

Beneath a deceptively playful exterior, Lebow was an acutely realistic student of human nature. It was that savvy that equipped him to march victoriously into each of his marathon pageants with new stunning deals outclassing would-be marathon competitors.

An expert at body language, he sized up others based on subtle physical messages. He also sent clues to his own thinking through physical signs. "If Fred didn't like a topic we were discussing," said Dick Traum, founder of the Achilles Track Club, "he would look somewhere else."

His mind seemed to be in a state of constant self-absorption, estimating how much time he had to make a decision, calculating where power lay in a situation, evaluating where new shtick could be mined for his races. "He was always in the midst of something, or in the midst of stirring up something," said Anna Noel-Mayberry, organizer of the premarathon pasta party in the 1980s. "With a twinkle in his eye," she said, "Fred would stir up the pot to get the juices flowing."

Lebow's intensive promoting of his marathon contrasted sharply with the casualness with which he approached so many personal details of his life. Unlike the razzle-dazzle with which he designed his marathon, he was not personally concerned with the flamboyant trappings of New York success. Putting a humorous spin on his unpretentiousness, the race director in 1982 commented, "I'm basically a very simple person. I don't even have an unlisted phone number."

Although he may have felt a macho swagger in his signature running outfits, it was only as part of the theater he was creating. His own clothing held limited interest for the promoter. T-shirts were worn as messages of his vision. Girlfriends did much of his shopping for clothing, supplementing what marathon sponsors provided. Paula Fahey said he had never owned a pair of blue jeans until she bought him one. Not one to regularly shop, Lebow was also out of touch with the cost of men's clothing, she said. "He loved wearing a tuxedo," said a later girlfriend, Heather Dominic. Though a departure from his standard running attire, his tuxedo still projected an image of running heroics—he completed his tuxedo outfit with running sneakers and his signature cap.

The runner-director's taste in food was simple. He believed nutrition was "very important," but he was too sober-minded to place stock in fads such as vitamin overdosing. "I know one runner who tosses down thirty vitamin pills at a time," he wrote, "yet he looks so unhealthy, like a pale vegetable. You can't live off vitamins." What Lebow lived off mainly was bread, fruits, and vegetables. "He loved bread," said Paula Fahey. "When he would smell bread, he would remember being a kid." He claimed to eat meat "only two to three times a year." Not really a vegetarian preference, his reluctance for meat stemmed from the kosher dietary requirements of his Orthodox childhood.

Laura Leale, who as his public relations associate was in daily contact with Lebow, noted that "in his own way, [Fred] tried to keep kosher. He was neurotic about his eating, and he had this neurosis about keeping kosher. We had an older woman at the club who used to bake birthday cakes. He wanted to know what was in it—was it lard? I don't think Fred trusted her when she said there wasn't any lard." Publicly, he claimed to be a vegetarian, but he was really keeping kosher following his own personal formulation. As Allan Steinfeld noted, "Whenever we would go anywhere, he would always order a vegetarian plate. Actually he kept kosher." Kathrine Switzer recalled that once, at a track-writers luncheon at New York's Mamma Leone's restaurant, where the reporters were all served pasta and meat sauce, Lebow conspicuously asked for an order of scrambled eggs. Moreover, after accompanying Lebow to a reception at a temple following a race in New Jersey in 1980, Patricia Owens, the elite-athlete coordinator at the time, observed, "I saw him eating meat and chicken . . . [and said,] 'Fred, I thought you were a vegetarian.' He said, 'It's okay here because it's kosher' [and] I was almost speechless. I never saw him eat meat at any other function." Even at Jewish-sponsored events, Lebow refused to eat meat until he was certain it was kosher. In April 1992, for example, at the scientific awards luncheon of the Israel Cancer Research Fund at New York's Grand Hyatt, the group's executive director, Milton Sussman, noticed the race director walking around the ballroom, avoiding the buffet, and asked, "Fred, why aren't you eating?" to which Lebow replied, "Milt, I only eat kosher food, and I don't know what you have here." "He started to eat once I assured him that all our affairs are kosher," Sussman confirmed. Lebow's colleagues have almost no memories of his having eaten *treife* (nonkosher) meat or shellfish, and since he never cooked in his apartment and rarely attended functions where kosher meat was available, the upshot was that he rarely ate *any* type of meat.

A food indulgence for Lebow? "My current favorite is a fish cake and French fries at McDonalds. I top it off with a piece of poppy seed cake from a deli."

With his girlfriends, Lebow made the rounds of Manhattan restaurants, ordering pasta, vegetarian, fish, and dairy dishes. Heather Dominic, who idolized the race director, held onto the cards of the eating establishments where he ate—the Cream Puff Cafe for cake and coffee, Zuchini's for soups, Portico Ristorante for pasta, and EJ Luncheonette, a favorite following Sunday's Central Park races.

Lebow's sparsely decorated studio apartment in the East Seventies also underscored his spartan lifestyle. Furnished in muted tones by club staff and volunteers, the apartment basically served as a place where he slept, stored T-shirts, and brought women guests. With his penchant for eating either at his office or at restaurants, the apartment never became a site for home-cooked meals. The main foods consumed at home were fruits and nuts. So unfamiliar was the running entrepreneur with his way around his own kitchen that he could not answer Paula Fahey when she asked whether his oven was gas or electric.

Lebow's disheveled office desk contrasted with the sharp sense of detail with which he planned his marathon party. "He didn't know where things were," said Leale, referring to the clutter of news clippings, used paper cups, photos, books, magazines, letters, and memos. *Tschoshkes*—those little knickknacks, mementos, gadgets, and "things"—spilled over to nearby bookcases. "People would send him things all the time," she said. In late afternoon, Lebow often played country music or the songs of opera performers such as Pavarotti for relaxation.

For all the simplicity in this entrepreneur's day-to-day life, two vanities stood out: emphasis on his physical appearance and the refusal to admit his true age. But both these characteristics, known to his running club associates, radiated amusement rather than cast a shadow on the way he promoted his vision. They saw these ego boosts as eccentricities of the showman they admired.

Lebow's concern with looks focused on fussiness with his face. The decision to grow a beard, far from being haphazard, was designed to enhance his celebrity status. "I'm ugly without my beard," he once told garment-center associate Maurice Dickson.

To hide the aging process, Lebow tried not to be seen in public wearing eyeglasses. When Kathrine Switzer was in London with Lebow at a meeting of the Association of International Marathons, she passed him a note. "He put on reading glasses, and I stared at him." Citing the eyeglasses, Lebow wrote back, "Do they make me look old?"

His club's magazine also advanced lies about his age. In a 1988 tongue-in-cheek article forecasting "Marathon 2000," Lebow was described in the future period as "the sixty-three-year-old former race director." Considering he was already fifty-six, and the millennium was twelve years away when the article was written, something didn't quite add up!

During what was intended as a fifty-fifth birthday party for the race director, held at his running club, associates smiled when he insisted that he was only fifty years old. "Fred's birthdays were the only place where you kept getting younger," observed staffer Victoria Phillips.

Although in his gritty way Lebow's main focus was promoting his marathon party, and more broadly the running lifestyle, women ranked as convivial secondary players in his life. True, he did not embark on hyping his urban theater in order to spur his social life. But as a consequence of his celebrity, his career as race director was densely packed with women friends. He left a legacy of pleasure and heartbreak with these women, none of whom was victorious in taking away his bachelor status.

Some women were drawn to him because of his reputation as a running impresario. He himself had a proclivity for women runners. Women enjoyed his playfulness and lighthearted wit. As a lifelong bachelor wary of threats to that status, there was no one type of relationship that Lebow cherished. All his relationships, though, existed in the immediate present. Whenever a woman pressed for a possible future, she ran off course because the main thrill for this unabashed race director remained the New York City Marathon.

Rolf Waldeis, a Mercedes-Benz marketing executive, witnessed Lebow accompanied by any number of beautiful women both at running events and at Mercedes-sponsored symphonic performances where the race director dressed in tuxedo and sneakers. Waldeis was not surprised with this eclectic dating ensemble. "I took him to be a European man," said Waldeis. "It was not a big deal to have various girlfriends." At his running club, staff gossiped about "Fred's Fifis," the generic term for Lebow's girlfriends. A Rolodex on the race director's desk held the phone numbers of prospective dates. The ephemeral nature of Lebow's commitment was a given in his relationships. Running commentator Jim Ferstle said, "He was not being dishonest with them. He didn't sell them a bill of goods that we'll get married someday."

Lebow was not at a loss for feminine company in his international travels. David Katz, director of the finish line at the New York City Marathon, was once asked to supervise the finish line at a marathon in Africa. Lebow showed up at the race with a beautiful woman who, when asked by Katz how long she had known Lebow, replied, "Oh, about a week."

In wrangling a date, Lebow's lack of knowledge of a foreign language was no deterrent. To unsuspecting women, he simply pretended he knew their tongue. Ellen Finn, Lebow's elite-athlete coordinator in the late 1980s, accompanied him to a reception at the Polish Consulate in New York City where the race director was feted for encouraging Polish runners. Lebow was more focused on the two attractive women standing nearby than on the ceremony. During the speech making, held in Polish, an earnest Lebow took notes, translating for the women. The only problem, according to Finn, was that Lebow knew no Polish. Yet somehow, after his linguistic display, the women appreciatively gave him their phone numbers.

Running events were the main locale of his public activities with women, but Lebow also escorted them to dinners, shows, and sponsor parties. They considered him a talented dancer. In relaxed moments, he sang classical pieces for them both in his office and in his apartment.

Though markedly Jewish in persona and the product of an Ortho-dox Jewish upbringing, religion did not figure prominently in his rela-tionships with women in most of his New York years. As with his modified kosher eating habits, Lebow kept whatever Jewish feelings he had largely to himself. "I never felt a strong sense of his interest in Jewishness," said girlfriend Paula Fahey. "It was more a lifestyle than a religion."

Lebow brought to his romances the same adaptive and pragmatic traits that he used to transform his marathon. Showmanship, humor, manipulativeness, charm, and diplomatic tact, features ensuring the success of his marathon party, helped his relationships with women. A masterful communicator, he listened intently to women in whom he was interested, and confidently filled conversational gaps through a plentiful catalog of stories and anecdotes.

Rather than aggressively marketing himself, Lebow realized that at times the best romantic salesmanship meant refraining from self-promotion. He perceived that the most headway would result from lis-tening, observing, and finally presenting himself to the women he sought as a sympathetic ally. Once he gained their trust, their love would follow.

"He treated women the way he treated the board," said club treas-urer Peter Roth. "He told them what they wanted to hear." Roth saw how Lebow used this tack when he "walked up to a very attractive blond" runner who was with her child. "Tell me, what is it like having children?" asked the straight-faced race director. "I'm considering it myself."

Others in Lebow's circle saw his interest in women extending beyond the elemental need for companionship. Anna Noel-Mayberry, who coordinated many of the race director's premarathon pasta parties, claimed that women satisfied an ego need. "He loved pretty things falling over him," she said. Young women particularly fascinated the race director. As he aged, his more long-term girlfriends were younger and younger. Some thirty-five years separated Lebow and Heather Dominic, who was his last serious girlfriend.

But looks and youth alone did not determine the Fifis whom the race director sought. His big moves were in pursuit of challenging, independent women. Laura Leale remained convinced that he was "a chauvinist" who believed that "men know better." But, she conceded, "He respected smart, attractive women. He was really taken with a smart woman."

Lebow the diplomat turned away from definitively breaking up with women, much the same way he refused to abjure players who disappointed him in his marathon party. Instead, he maneuvered women in whom he was no longer interested into situations where they finally concluded they had no choice but to end the relationship.

With those women who had offered to work as volunteers in his marathon, he also followed a strategy of patient diplomacy. He was never one to burn his bridges with women, especially pretty potential volunteers. In his book, he described the case of a woman volunteering to put on a postmarathon pasta party. With her long, curly black hair, white minidress, and black boots, she caught the race director's eye. But Lebow had already engaged another woman for this party. Looking toward the future, however, he pragmatically concluded to keep her on file—he might need someone with her enthusiasm and brains at a later date.

Despite his female conquests, Lebow hesitated intoning the words, "I love you." Paula Fahey, among his most serious girlfriends, said that the race director "didn't believe" in the notion of romantic love as portrayed in American pop culture.

Given his devotion to his marathon vision, colleagues did not fault Lebow for never marrying, despite all the Fifis in his files. How could this impresario, they asked, so committed to promoting running, maintain the conventional schedule of a married man? "Marriage did not suit his priorities or lifestyle," observed Ellen Finn, elite-athlete coordinator at Lebow's club in the late 1980s. "He was married to the club."

According to Lebow himself, as quoted in a *New York Post* article from November 11, 1992, "Marathon Man Holds Hope for Another Run," he hadn't married because he "never had time or an impulse." In the same article, he said, "The smartest thing I ever did was that I didn't get married. I've saved myself six divorces. . . . I'm difficult to live with because . . . I'm consumed by running."

How much Lebow's experience during the Holocaust, and his subsequent roaming around Europe, played in his not taking the risk of marriage can never be known, but it was because he was buoyed by his Holocaust-survivor optimism, independence, and can-do spirit that he was able to take creative risks in staging untried fun races such as the Wall Street Rat Race on income-tax filing day, April 15, and a one hundred-mile race for ultramarathoners, round and round Shea Stadium's track. Though his primary dream was fanciful—closing down the streets of the clogged Big Apple so that a hodgepodge of ordinary plodders could go the distance—he executed it with pragmatism and doggedness. "There were sixty-five different ways I had to tell Fred, 'No,' " said Frank Shorter.

Lebow's doggedness sometimes made enemies. When he was voted the most powerful figure in long-distance running in a March 1988 *Road Race Management* survey, one respondent stated, "[H]e's a pain in the ass when he's against you."

As is often the case with Holocaust survivors, Lebow was able to divorce himself from long-term bouts with self-doubt, fatigue, anxiety, and depression. Kathrine Switzer noted, "Compared to what he went through as a kid, he could handle any adversity." Lebow shared this type of confidence when he advised girlfriend Heather Dominic, "If you ever want to go in any place, and you aren't sure whether you'll be admitted, walk in like you own it."

"Fred stories"—yarns about his deal-making prowess—abounded. When four surly teenagers, dressed in leather jackets, threatened let Lebow's one-year-old five-borough marathon pas Brooklyn turf, they were disarmed by his confidence a ing. After asking them to wait, Lebow returned with a b from the pile stored in his office. For Lebow, giving aw similar to the president's handing out pens. Relieved that they accepted the T-shirts, Lebow inquired as to the name of their gang. When their leader insisted they were not gang members, only guardians of their neighborhood, Lebow, whose negotiating smarts always identified with an adversary, saw he had the wedge he needed. "Watch your turf for us, because you can protect it better than anybody else," he urged, and then, to make it official, he appointed them special block leaders. Sweetening the deal, he brought out thirty of the white windbreaker jackets worn by course marshals, and after an hour of macho bantering, Lebow and his block guardians were laughing like old pals. He assured them they had saved the marathon for all of New York City. He shook hands and never heard from them again.

In the thick of battle as race-world entrepreneur and deal maker, Lebow would publicly present a minimal Jewish image. But even though not the type given to deep introspection about life's ultimate issues, the savvy promoter's Jewishness was always part of his self-definition. When his boyhood friend from Arad Rabbi Stauber asked once, "How did you get into the running business?" Lebow, with a self-depreciating observation that running represented a metaphor for the often-forced wanderings of the Jewish people, answered with a question of his own: "Tell me the truth, Chaim. After all, when did we Jews ever stop running?" As *New York Times* sports columnist George Vecsey expressed when discussing Lebow's spiritual side, on October 10, 1994, "He always knew who he was and where he came from."

The heart of Lebow's Jewish connection on the marathon route was the Hasidic community of Williamsburg, located at the ten-mile mark along Brooklyn's Bedford Avenue. Whatever color the Hasidim added to the marathon itself, the trip through Williamsburg held personal meaning for Lebow. Williamsburg represented a throwback to the culture of his childhood. "When we went through Williamsburg, he had a heightened sense of excitement," said Steve Sultan, a photographer who rode with Lebow in the pace car for many years. "He was invigorated." Yet on a deeper level, Williamsburg underscored the pain that this cosmopolitan bachelor must have felt in having distanced himself from the insular lifestyle of his family and his past. According to the *Times*'s Vecsey, "It took me years to even sense Fred was spooked by the impassive stares of the Hasids, almost as if they were judging him."

In his Jewishness, Lebow was set apart from most American-born Jews because of the strictly Orthodox Judaism of his childhood and his World War II Holocaust experience. On the other hand, he was like most American Jews at the time because he no longer observed most of the Orthodox rituals. While his book, *Inside the World of Big-Time Marathoning* (1984), does not give an actual date, it appears as if he made the decision to abandon Orthodoxy hand in hand with the decision to change his name from Fishl Lebowitz to Fred Lebow sometime in the early 1950s.

For sure, by the time he reached New York as a thirty-year-old man in 1962, several years before he became involved with his marathon vision, he had already stopped leading the life of an Orthodox Jew. But although Lebow did not choose to wear his religion on his sleeve, he did often interact with Jewish staff members, runners, and others connected with his marathons in a decidedly Jewish way, and he had an inborn sensitivity to their particular needs. As he took the New York City Marathon from obscurity to world renown, many of his main associates would be Jewish. Perhaps significantly, none of them shared his European upbringing, so whatever dissonance he may have felt between his Orthodox heritage and his commitment to road running was experienced by him alone. He never denied his Jewishness, and he even continued to observe certain of its rituals, but he saw himself as having developed beyond the religious restrictions of his youth.

The dichotomy between his religious childhood and his New York lifestyle was revealed the day after the 1982 marathon, in a three-hour interview. Lebow's glibness deserted him only once, when he was asked about his family and religion: "It's a difficult question," he said, his hands shielding his mouth. "I don't believe everything we do has childhood beginnings. Once we reach adulthood, we develop our own philosophy, our own likes and dislikes."

In addition to keeping kosher, albeit his own modified version of kosher, Lebow's philosophy included observing the main Jewish holidays: he fasted on Yom Kippur, the Day of Atonement; held a Passover Seder and lit Chanukah candles with his running club associates; and on other holidays often drove up to the home of his sister Sarah Katz in New York City's heavily Orthodox suburb of Monsey, but whether for the religious observance or for Sarah's food is unclear. Lebow's younger sister specialized in preparing Lebow's favorite childhood foods, particularly those based on potatoes. Brian Crawford, a close non-Jewish friend from Cleveland, often accompanied Lebow in these holiday visits, and Katz and Crawford developed such a close friendship that Lebow would tease girlfriend Paula Fahey, "Brian was a better practicing Jew than me!"

On the surface, Lebow's devotion to running was what separated him from a close relationship with his siblings. Hyping his marathon and other races became Lebow's singular focus, taking precedence over everything else. Whenever he had to choose between family functions he knew he would enjoy or promoting his marathon creation, the marathon won out. "To create a success . . . [and] fulfill the visions that I had, I had to make a sacrifice," the race director confessed. And it truly was a sacrifice, so whenever an opportunity arose where no conflict existed, Lebow cherished the moments spent with loved ones.

Despite his obsession with running, philosophically such a singular commitment should not have estranged Lebow from his family. Running was not an action forbidden by the Torah, his family's behavioral guide. In fact, Jewish teachings stress the need to keep one's body, as the repository of the divine soul, in good health. It is only when rigorous physicality becomes narcissistic that it is seen as a problem. Orthodox Jews regularly competed in Lebow's marathon, even in the race's relative obscurity in the Central Park early years.

Rather, it was in the process of adding glitz to his marathon that Lebow dropped many of his family's defining religious observances. He gave up Sabbath observance, rarely prayed, and, lifelong womanizer that he was, almost never formed relationships with Jewish girlfriends. Why should overly restrictive rules, such as refraining from work on the Sabbath, reasoned Lebow, thwart his marathon vision? Although he once exclaimed, "Religion, who needs it," those of his colleagues who, like Laura Leale, were attuned to spiritual types of issues recognized "the inner conflict" between his Orthodox family upbringing and his hedonistic lifestyle. Since his family's religious passions were no less consuming than were his for his urban street theater, relations between them cooled. He even told intimates such as ABC commentator Larry Rawson that he was the "black sheep" of his family.

From Lebow's public standpoint, what the *New York Times* described as his "troubled relations" with his family stemmed from their having totally dismissed the running lifestyle. During the interview he had sadly told the newspaper, "It's almost as if I come from a different family. You know, not one of them runs," totally dismissing *his* separation from their Orthodox upbringing. Still, he did have varying degrees of contact with family members, including brothers Michael Lebov of Chicago, Simcha Lebowitz of Brooklyn, Morris Lebowitz of Cleveland, and Shlomo Lebowitz of Tel Aviv, and sisters Sarah Katz of Monsey, New York, and Esther Greenfield of Haifa.

Sarah, a nursery school teacher, was the sibling with whom Lebow was closest. She challenged press accounts showing a self-promotional side to her older brother. Instead, she emphasized his modesty and loyalty to their parents. "Sometimes I see an article and I want to punch somebody," she told the *New York Times*. "I can't believe that this is my brother. Anybody who says it's for the power, they don't really know him. That tremendous drive, in the beginning it was mostly for my parents, just to make them happy. If he didn't become a rabbi, he would still show them he could be something." Yet she doubted the value of Lebow's running agenda herself. "He has such big ideas, but all of this, what does it amount to? In the end, I'm not sure how much he'll have." She agonized over her brother's remoteness from his devout family and his notoriety in a culture where the family never traveled. "If he would make a million dollars maybe I would understand, but he hardly has enough to live," she said.

Despite such criticism from his Orthodox siblings, Lebow clearly held them in affection, particularly Sarah. He regularly invited her to the marathon, his club's awards dinner, and other ceremonies. Their affection for him was also clear, as Sarah's quotes often showed. She once shared, lightly, "One of my brothers said, 'I knew [Fred would] be a runner because he always ran away from chores!' " And on a serious note, she praised her brother, claiming, "[Religion] is still so much in Fred's heart, but he can't show it. Even though we don't see him much, I tell my children to learn from him—inside he is so honest and so modest."

When Lebow dropped his religious observance, he did not drift into spiritual complacency. Once he got his bearings in New York, work as a garment-center knockoff artist provided his income, but it was from the running lifestyle that Lebow drew his conviction of personal worth. According to John Chodes, playwright and biographer of one of Lebow's heroes, ultramarathoner Ted Corbitt, "Lebow always the missionary, the zealot, the fanatic came to believe that running was an ultimate truth of life. It turned hostile, vicious people into pussycats. Running took away hate and anger and made people love each other." It was Lebow's belief in the "religious element" of running, according to Chodes, that "forced him to work like a madman."

After finding his niche in running, Lebow's pragmatism converged with his enthusiasm for putting on a show. But how do you attract crowds in New York? By staging an exciting show and letting people know what was playing. Once his stage was transformed into a more scintillating version of the austere marathon, using his New York brand of self-depreciating humor he would hold out a heap of inducements for joining his party. No illusions about sponsors, city politicians, elite runners, or the media would stand in the way of this highly driven impresario. "I don't deny I'm driven," Lebow said. "I sympathize with driven people, whether in business or doing something destructive like alcohol or drugs. I know that passion can be misdirected and I'm thankful that my passion directed me to this end or who knows what would have come of me."

In the late 1970s, Lebow's "New York aggressive" style, coupled with "middle America's" wariness of New York City domination in general, would contribute to harming his agenda at national road-running councils. But the only time he felt his "Jewishness" might have truly harmed the New York City Marathon itself was in its early years, when the five-borough route was laid out. Steve Wald, who was then on the New York Road Runners Club Board of Directors, recalled Lebow's reaction when he encountered opposition to the 1976 event passing through certain New York City neighborhoods. "Fred said to me, 'Do you think it's because I'm Jewish? Is it anti-Semitism?' " Wald was amused when the heavily accented race director asked, "Do you think they know I'm Jewish?"

It could also be seen as somewhat amusing when, despite the fact that he had lived in the United States since the 1950s, it was Lebow's Jewish persona that stood out in terms of how he was identified by others. Dick Traum told how this phenomenon surfaced in connection with the 1983 Beijing Marathon. Lebow had been given a front-row starting position for the race because of his renown, but because of his slow start, he was knocked down and his shoulder dislocated. Along the course a Chinese farmer was able to repair the shoulder, but by that time the race was lost. In spite of the fact that he had been given VIP treatment because of his role in the running world and as director of the New York City (America!) Marathon, the headline describing Lebow's debacle in the Chinese newspaper read, "First Jew to Run Marathon Finished Last."

It was not at all amusing when a competing race director, during a heated battle for primacy, made it very clear that he knew Lebow was Jewish by making a not-so-indirect anti-Semitic remark, referring to Lebow's years in the garment industry. Considering Lebow's excellent reputation for honesty, hard work, and dedication—during his years in the garment industry and later in the running world—the remark was especially off base.

Lebow had never forgotten the chance he was given in the garment center to develop his "knockoff" skills. Berg & Berg Knitting Company owner Martin Schloshberg related that, even after Lebow's rise to international prominence, "Fred *always* called me 'Boss.' No matter how busy he was he always called back." Among the highlights of Schloshberg's memories was the birthday party held for his wife, Andrea, at New York's St. Regis Hotel in 1985, where the already famous knitter-turned-race director was the hit of the affair—dressed in tuxedo and running sneakers.

So convinced was Lebow of his vision, said Marathon Center coordinator Larry Wydro, that "if Fred had an idea and you didn't agree, he assumed that you didn't understand the idea, and he would keep explaining it. Everybody thought he was crazy when he came up with the Fifth Avenue Mile . . . the idea of closing Fifth Avenue for an afternoon. But if he knew it was the right thing to do, he would keep pursuing it."

Such obsessive commitment strengthened the race director's hand in selling his vision, said Peter Roth, treasurer of the New York Road Runners Club, who also expressed the sentiment that "Fred didn't do anything to discourage people's preconceptions . . . that he would walk over his mother's grave if he had to do it." Lebow's agent, Barry Frank of the International Management Group, was very taken by Lebow's conviction: "I never saw anyone so committed to an idea, as Fred. He was so dedicated to what he did [that] I wanted him to succeed. Fred was not a big client, not [even] among the top thirty of my clients. But when you see someone who cares that much, you want to help."

But was Lebow *original* in his populist vision of bringing tens of thousands of "everymen" through the glitzy streets of New York to cross a finish line? To be sure, running had started to define the leisure culture of the city by the time Lebow came on the scene in the 1970s, the way baseball did a generation earlier, and theatrics to lighten the physical toil of running a marathon were already taking place in competitions outside New York during Lebow's earliest years as a race director. Nina Kuscsik remembered participating in a marathon in Honolulu where they gave out buttons saying, "I support fast women!"

So if he wasn't all that original, what was it about Lebow that distinguished him in the development of the marathon vision? His unrelenting drive . . . his caring persona . . . and the chutzpah behind his dramatic flair! As Switzer, a running promoter herself, noted, "He has a hundred ideas a day. Ninety are off the wall, but you've got to pay attention because the other ten are brilliant." And she should know, because it was her mind that Lebow often picked. "Sometimes Fred would call me out of the blue. . . . I'd always be flattered even though he was probably calling twenty other people. He would say, 'I got this great idea for a mile race down Fifth Avenue [and] I said, 'Brilliant. Where [would] you have the finish line?' " After thinking for a moment, Switzer suggested Tiffany's, and Lebow congratulated her back, "Brilliant!"

Lebow was not original in the sense of creating new ideas where none ever existed, but like the knockoff-dress designer he was, he had an enormous talent for taking someone else's idea and making it glitzier . . . making it work. The notion of the Fifth Avenue Mile, for example, stemmed from the indoor Wanamaker Mile, and the New Year's Eve Midnight Run had its origins in the Latin American festival scene.

But whatever its origins, there's little doubt it was this man—born Fishl Lebowitz in Arad, Romania, and renamed Fred Lebow as he settled in America—who made the New York City Marathon an event hailed worldwide. And as his personal fame began to outsparkle the show he had made shine, the image of the feisty, eccentric-looking race director irrepressibly waving from the pace car became synonymous with the event.

"It was a very appealing image," said Steve Wald. "The little bearded Jew standing up in the convertible. People knew he was basically a volunteer sort of guy, involved, not aloof, unlike the greedy millionaire athletes and promoters in the sports world." And this is who "the gritty promoter" was.

So when it comes to evaluating Lebow's vision—and, in a way, his life!—the question of "originality" is perhaps less important than his drive and steadfastness in producing exciting urban theater. Thousands of couch-potato types were persuaded by Lebow's vision to go the distance in a marathon . . . or to at least start running. To accomplish this goal took both an awareness of social trends and a continual commitment to hunting for and creating shtick to garner exposure for his marathon and the road-running style of life. It took the need to *shteig*, to climb, to strive. It took a lot of trying, a lot of stubbornness, and quite a bit of fancy footwork. It took a clever and entrepreneurial spirit, flexibility, the ability to take risks, and the ability to make the most of any situation and learn from it.

Would an education in mass marketing have helped?

5

Unschooled in Mass Marketing

With his chutzpah and drive, all he needed was his vision and the right stage!　IN 1969, MARTIN SCHLOSH- BERG, owner of Berg & Berg Knit- ting Company and Lebow's boss at the time, had been unable to foresee "the knitter from Brooklyn's" po- tential for fame. Nevertheless, he took his employee's advice and started running. The executive who, prior to Lebow's entreaties, had seen himself "becoming a sedentary person" was grateful to his em- ployee for "changing my life." On a sunny Sunday that year, Lebow had persuaded Schloshberg to jog three miles with him down Second Av- enue, and his exhausted boss made it back home, showered, and went to bed. Schloshberg confessed, "Monday morning I went to work and felt so terrible [I screamed to my knitting machine mechanic,] 'You killed me,' " and Lebow smiled and answered, "Good. I want to do it again."

Maurice Dickson, another of Lebow's supervisors from his gar- ment-center years, admitted, "We all thought he was nuts, but we knew he had something big. We would joke with him, 'Who needs you to run?' " He would answer, insisting, "Everybody's going to be running one day."

What were the sources of Lebow's vision? When he was introduced to running in the mid-1960s, "[he] remember[ed] thinking, what is it that I've suddenly discovered? Am I the only one who feels this way? Is there something wrong with me? . . . because I hardly saw anyone else running." Why did the phenomenon of running elicit such exuberance in Lebow? To explain his excitement in the context of physical factors— heightened energy, weight control, "runners high," and such—is too simplistic and misses the spiritual pull that running held for him. "It wasn't until Fred discovered running that he discovered the hero within himself," observed Kathrine Switzer, women's winner of the 1974 New York City Marathon, running publicist, and race organizer. "Fred knew something that most people don't: Fitness is also a belief, in your heart, of your personal triumph."

How did that exuberance evolve into the vision of a marathon as street theater, and what elements from his personal life contributed to this vision? The answers to these questions shed additional light not only on the life of Lebow, but more broadly on the forces that drove the hundreds of thousands of competitors in the New York City Marathon and marathons around the world—five-minute milers and fifteen-minute walkers alike—to test their limits at his festival and its many spin-offs. Lebow's vision represented the disparate parts of his own love of running, despite his mediocre abilities: his youth in Europe from which he drew the themes of striving and inclusiveness, his savvy promotional skills, and, finally, the locale of New York City, ethnic mirror of the world and bastion of innovation.

On New Year's Eve, December 31, 1978, golf coach Dick Metz and his date had their costumes all laid out for Fred Lebow's New Year's Eve midnight masquerade run in Central Park. The only problem was that they were both formally attired for dining at Raoul's Soho Restaurant, where they were ushering in 1979. So as not to lose the holiday spirit, Metz ordered a limo to transport them from the festive restaurant to join the revelers in sneakers at the Central Park start, and to save time, "we changed clothing in the limo" during the ride uptown.

After Metz covered the first four miles himself—"my date wasn't much of a runner," he admitted—the costumed couple ran the last mile of the carnival-laden park together, then dashed back to the waiting limo where they changed again while being transported back to the restaurant for a proper dessert, drinks, and a final New Year's toast.

Only in a Gotham whose culture was given to entertainment and shtick could such high-end theatrics take place. The props were there, waiting to be manipulated by Lebow's glitzy vision. For this showman, New York's chic stage was more than the streets or the ethnic neighborhoods through which his marathon parade streamed. It meant the media, the banners, the crowds, the flamboyance, the city's affinity for new thrills, and the global familiarity that its name inspired.

Both the city and the race director were masters at their game. The willingness to take risks and to innovate, the impatience, the need to always be right, the refusal to stop trying—these elements defined both the spirit of the city and the style of the running entrepreneur. Sports and entertainment were fused, with a relentlessness that hung free of traditional racing norms.

In his vision, Lebow was not only promoting the notion of the marathon as a show. He was also promoting New York City as the site of the party—his race was a New York City happening. He celebrated the city as much as he did his runners. Bill Rodgers, four-time winner of the New York City Marathon, in describing Lebow's use of the city streets, noted, "Fred's genius was in realizing that he had the greatest stage in the world and in opening it up to average runners."

Because of its prominence, New York City was the ideal base from which this race entrepreneur could reform American culture. The ingredients he would need to make his sport big-time were simply easier to come by in New York City—ingredients such as mass participation, corporate sponsorship, television coverage, voluble crowds, six-figure prize money. The New York stage, he realized, would bring him into close contact with the parts of corporate America he needed: the sponsors whose cash he would seek and the media whose attention he would subtly manipulate were based in the same town as his race, making it easier for the racing impresario to personally ply his salesmanship with these players at prearranged meetings and at sponsors' promotional events. In addition to these convenient "office" arrangements, the race director would literally run into sponsors and journalists at the seat of his power, the turf of Central Park. He saw that linkage to the city's political leaders would make it easier to wrest the keys he needed to such municipal services as police and traffic control. With political support he would be able to publicize his running movement and bring celebrity to himself and his show—the city's mayor always appeared at the starting line and at the finish to congratulate winners, and lottery drawings for special marathon entries were strategically held on the steps of city hall. Demographically, he had the benefit of a budding constituency. No city in America had the large number of singles that New York had, and these singles would form the backbone of Lebow's Central Park running empire.

Lebow, like many New Yorkers, had a need to know. The city's cut-ting-edge quality made it a learning experience for this race promoter who was always in the process of intelligence gathering for new shtick for his party. His inquiring mind applied sophisticated promotional experiments taking place in the Big Apple to his own show.

Apart from the cheering, he saw that the race could serve as an educational experience for New Yorkers, increasing their awareness of their own city. Yuppie Manhattanites, many of whom were psychologically removed from the outer boroughs, became more familiar with those neighborhoods after viewing the race on television. Scenes of runners threading their way through Brooklyn's melting-pot neighborhoods drew Manhattanites into a new sense of community with the other boroughs.

When asked in 1988, at the height of his career, "What do you see as your biggest personal contribution to road racing?" Lebow failed to cite the hundreds of thousands of finishers in his marathon, the rise of the world marathon movement he pioneered, or the celebrities or presidents who by then regularly ran. Instead, he answered, "That I ran a 10K last Saturday in 44:58. . . . To me that is far more important than having 20,000 people finish the New York Marathon."

His own running mediocrity helped formulate Lebow's vision, and three purposes were served by the resultant transformation of marathons from austere athletic competitions to "entertainment happenings": First, the show environment helped emotionally equip the ordinary runner to overcome the physical and psychological rigors of the marathon distance; television broadcasts reflected Lebow personally reaching out to this ordinary runner. Second, the marathon festival was designed to have an impact on the crowds lining the streets—the exciting street theater attracting large crowds of people that Lebow could recruit to running, and perhaps to marathoning. "He wanted someone who was a spectator one year to enter [the marathon] and to be part of it [the next]," said Nina Kuscsik, women's winner of the 1972 and 1973 New York City Marathons. And third, the rollicking show drew more media attention, which validated, for *all* the players in his production—the runners, sponsors, volunteers, police, and crowds—the decisions they individually made to participate.

How did the marathon party Lebow envisioned develop? What wa the impact of demographics, particularly the emerging baby boomer generation? How integral was New York City, the arena for his show, in bringing the promoter's vision to reality?

Before Lebow's marathon vision developed into that of a people's race, his goal was much less grandiose. He simply wanted to direct a well-run, competitive, successfully executed contest. But Lebow came on the scene at the same time the running fitness movement took off. Best-selling books by George Sheehan and James Fixx appeared in the late 1970s, extolling the health virtues of running. Their books, and other media references, validated the intellectual and health benefits of a marathon, and a demographically accessible public like Manhattan's West Side population stood ready to sprint to this new theater.

When Lebow's vision began to take shape, the sports identity in New York City began focusing on the individual runner rather than the neighborhood team. The West Side single became the new version of the urban man or urban woman. In their aloneness these boomers now had an outlet—the running scene—where they temporarily banded together with others while retaining their personal identity. By forming this new running culture in the city, Lebow was producing a sense of community where none existed previously. Baby boomers not only had the money and leisure time to participate in Lebow's vision, but were now able to also embrace it on a deeper level, from a values standpoint. "Boomers," wrote *Newsweek* columnist Joe Klein on March 18, 1996, "were, and are, a generation afflicted by the luxury of choice." For these overwhelmingly secular boomers, facing the challenge of testing their bodily limits in a medically validated marathon posed an exciting prospect. The boomer lifestyle, unlike the communal and sacrificial ties of earlier generations, was primarily self-centered, allowing one the luxury of training to "go the distance" in a marathon without feeling selfish about depriving others of one's time. Fred Lebow enticed these boomers with two sales pitches for his party: first, the drama or theatrics of performing in the ethnic web of New York City, and second, the ex-

ng the limits of both the human body and the human
al and spiritual validation of one's very being.

to discourage these commonplace runners, Lebow
hing the marathon itself was indeed a victory in and of
ompetition for each runner was his or her own poten-

tial and not the more speedy athletes on the course. "You compete against yourself and can always do better in the next race," Lebow said to encourage them, "so you're always a winner."

Since Lebow's runners did not reflect the ethnic makeup of New York City, he tried broadening his population. He acknowledged the problem in a reference in his club's 1983 magazine, where he was quoted as being "concerned that New York Road Runners Club programs were primarily for the benefit of white upper-middle class athletes." As a result, the Urban Running Program, designed to widen participation, eventually grew to some eighteen thousand kids between the ages of three and seventeen, and in the spirit of Lebow's shtick, program head Angel Nunez also set up meets at nearly thirty city homeless shelters.

Lebow's enhanced vision—his marathon festival—was continually a party in the making. Scoreboards on First Avenue, carpeting on the bridges, more handsome grandstands, more visible clocks at the Central Park finish, improvements in the pressroom, additional displays at the Expo—these were the types of technical refinements Lebow continuously introduced, but it was the glitz he rhapsodized about when evaluating his vision. When Henley Gibble and Tom Carter of the Road Runners Club of America's *FootNotes* magazine remarked to Lebow, "You've always had a vision," the race director replied, "Yeah, but I think I'm so frivolous. I just *like* flags, music, bands, banners, you know, the hoopla. Yeah, I like the hoopla."

He offered the vision of his show with a light, ironic touch: "We're going to have about a hundred masseurs and masseuses besides cots at the finish line," he told the *Miami News* on October 22, 1983. "I got the idea recently when I ran the marathon in Berlin. I had two of them working on me at the same time. It was great. . . . In fact, I enjoyed it so much I went to three different tents." This pragmatic pursuit of fun defined Lebow as he transformed the nature of the marathon. Such dour trademarks as "the loneliness of the long-distance runner"—and the glorification of pain and excessively rigorous training techniques— would not bring people to his event. The spin, he knew, must be one of happiness, not gloom, if new runners were to make the effort. By 1977, in just its second running, Lebow's five-borough party had become the world's largest marathon, with 4,823 starters and 2 million spectators in the streets cheering the column of runners.

By broadening his running public, Lebow signaled the conceptual shift he sought toward the nature of distance running. "Fred was the antithesis to the image of the purity of running," said running commentator Jim Ferstle. "Before Fred, runners had almost an Aryan approach to life—'We zealots will have good health, live longer and have more self-fulfillment than the rest of you. We are pure because of that.' [But] when Fred came, alarm bells went off. . . . Here comes this barbarian who will line his pockets with gold and turn the sport into a crass event like pro-wrestling." The seasoned competitive runners were not opposed to Lebow's more populist notions simply because of an elitist approach to who runs in a marathon; they were seriously afraid that with an influx of marathon competitors, the course, particularly at the starting line, would become more crowded. An infusion of grassroots runners, argued these veterans, would compromise their own performance. "Elite runners don't have problems in the race. Their drinks are laid out in advance along the course," said David Patt, executive director of the Chicago Area Running Association. "It's the competitive runner who doesn't want to be caught in a big crowd with the fun runner. People complain over losing twenty seconds at a crowded start. It was Fred's challenge to keep it a quality event, as this new element entered the marathon."

Maintaining this vision of running as both fun and fulfillment called for Lebow to continuously perform on his own stage—a showman's role the race director definitely enjoyed—whether it was kissing Elsie the Borden cow at a press conference; running across the Brooklyn Bridge during a New York City transit strike; bantering with King Kong during the Empire State Building Run Up; deliberately running through the streets of Manhattan from appointment to appointment as passersby took note, often asking for autographs; or, finally, appearing in public almost always wearing his sneakers, running clothes, and race cap, as "the marathon man" personified. "He was like a Russian Jewish dancer with the message, 'you have to pay attention to me,' " said Judith Woodfin, who in her position as vice president of marathon sponsor Hertz drove Lebow in company lead Jeeps twice in the early 1980s. "He had a charm, not physical or masculine, but based on a vision. If you believed in the vision, you got involved."

Competition on the course was central to Lebow's vision. He

wanted to create fanfare. As such, the race director preferred the idea of a contest over the concept of simply featuring the fastest runners because the media found greater theatrics in the competitive angle. His vision of competition was global rather than national. Symbolically, for the race director, an international field represented a larger pool in which to showcase the best competitors . . . a world-class event required world representation. The magic of a marathon traversing New York City's ethnic neighborhoods—with runners hailing from Austria to Zimbabwe—provided the unity that was so much a part of this uprooted Holocaust survivor's vision. His party's international flavor was yet another of the achievements he cited in measuring his success.

Sensing that women were an untapped running constituency, his marathon would provide the first instance in which female runners competed on the same basis as men. Slow runners, racewalkers, wheelchair athletes, amputees, and the blind also grew infatuated with the challenge of Lebow's urban theater. Although promoting his marathon was his main ambition, he focused on broadening running participation of all types with a seemingly inexhaustible supply of zany race schemes, including a race up the steps of the Empire State Building and, in order to not abandon those in jail, the Rikers Island Prisoner Olympics. Not simply conceiving crowd-pleasing races, Lebow used his shrewd chutzpah and self-depreciating humor to win political approval for these events, to stage them, to spin them. He schemed to get his races into the news, knowing that in this media-driven culture, the running lifestyle faced competition from many other leisure-time pursuits.

Despite his lack of a formal education in marketing, Lebow delivered his vision of the marathon party in such a way as to inspire others to try to stage similar productions. When he first heard about the New York City Marathon, after its third year, Chris Brasher, one of Britain's star steeplechase athletes, proclaimed, "[T]he prospect of putting one foot in front of the other for 26 miles 385 yards of boring road filled me with foreboding. I could run the distance on the glorious hills of Britain, but to do it on the roads, watched by three cows and a dog, was surely the height of masochism." Still, he ran the marathon in 1979 and returned home so struck by the production that he asked, via an article in the *Observer* on October 28, whether London could stage such a festival. Brasher's article described the humanity of Lebow's vision as symbolic of the American dream:

> To believe this story you must believe that the human race can be one joyous family, working together, laughing together, achieving the impossible. I believe it because I saw it happen. Last Sunday, in one of the most violent, trouble-stricken cities in the world, 11,532 men, women and children from 40 countries of the world assisted by one million black, white and yellow people, Protestants, and Catholics, Jews and Muslims, Buddhists and Confucians, laughed, cheered and suffered during the greatest folk festival the world has seen. And at the end of it all the story was written in their faces—faces of contentment and happiness. I'm sure that it was written in my face, because I was one of these thousands who won the New York City Marathon. For more than 10,000 of us who finished, it was a great personal victory over doubt and fear, body and mind. And for most of us, we won only because one million New Yorkers came out of their homes and holes to feed and water us, to make music and brotherly love and to be Good Samaritans to all who felt like dropping by the wayside.
>
> There is only one explanation for this amazing phenomenon, and it has its roots in the heart of America. That great nation was founded on man's desire to improve himself, to claw his way up the mountains of achievement. . . . At the eight-mile mark I overtook a dinner-jacketed waiter carrying a tray with a bottle of Perrier, steady as a rock. He can't be running the whole distance, I thought, but he was, and he did. . . . Grete Waitz, the lithesome Norwegian who was to break the women's world best with the incredible time of 2:27, took shelter between two parked cars and got rid of her excess fluid that way. *I* waited until I reached the Bronx and then dived into the Blue Dragon bar— the only man in history to enter these portals and not ask for alcohol.

As Lebow's marathon grew into the world's most prestigious footrace, other race directors would turn to him for advice. He was sought after not only because of the prominence of his show, but also because of its pioneering spin. "There were only a handful of people in the sport who could talk in terms of a vision," noted Jeff Darman, former president of the Road Runners Club of America, regarding Lebow's conceptual skills.

Asked during one interview about the advice he would give, Lebow, talking about the party aspect of his show, said, "We have to make these races more than sporting events. We are now social and entertainment directors. It took me years to realize this." And a party his show had turned into, indeed, not at all like his experience at the blue-collar Cherry Tree Marathon in 1970, where the only thing partylike was a postrace drink at a nondescript bar and grill in the Bronx's remote Van Cortlandt section. As the marathon Lebow envisioned evolved, the party—or, more accurately, the stream of parties—had become integral to his production.

But marathon officials didn't always follow all of Lebow's precedents. Chris Brasher, who had gone on to found and direct the London Marathon, admired the humanity and excitement of Lebow's party, but he also "learned what not to do" by studying the New York race. Brasher claimed that, unlike Lebow, for his marathon they "[tried to avoid] connecting with everything the last 24 hours before the race. We delegated more than in New York. Our people made decisions on the spot. Fred always took too much on his shoulders. It was always a point of pride that he didn't go to bed the night before the marathon."

Did the New York promoter worry about competition from all the upstart races that looked for his advice? No, asserted Darman: "Fred didn't get jealous and didn't worry about better races. The stronger the sport is, the stronger he would become, because he was sitting on number one." Dedicated to the running lifestyle, Lebow's promotion of marathoning both in the United States and globally seemed natural. Observers viewed Lebow's festival as a guide for their own productions, and he frequently traveled to fledgling marathons to offer advice. Internationally, he was the motivating figure in founding the Association of International Marathons.

Before Lebow began his visionary campaign, marathons held a forbidding mystique that put them in the grasp of only the most fearsome of runners. But "[i]n running it doesn't matter whether you come in first or last," he said. "Marathoning is the only sport where the average person can compete along with champions. Susie Q can't play tennis with Martina Navratilova, but she *can* run in the marathon with [international running stars like] Grete Waitz." It was in order to persuade the Susie Qs of the world that they could muster the heroics to run a marathon that Lebow's foresight led him to turn his marathon event into a nonstop party. His shtick did make the public take notice of his street theater, but it was not the party itself that was the product he sought to promote. Most simply put, his dream, as always, was to transform the sport of running into an endeavor for "Everyman" and "Everywoman," with the marathon being merely the high point of achievement. Better to downplay the element of sweat, he thought, and highlight the glory of participating in a festival in motion.

In this spectacle of sneakers through New York's five boroughs, each runner searched in his or her own way for some measure of self-validation. Gradually, even grandparents and people stricken with various disabilities joined the party, swelling the ranks of cheering spectators and adding to media accounts of the truly heroic "common runner." The heroics of these ordinary runners in straining through his course were all the more reason for Lebow to take them seriously in his marathon vision. To themselves, they might be dreamers, but for Lebow they were customers: "Of supermost importance to me is considering the runner as a customer. He is always right. If he comes to the race at the last minute and demands his T-shirt in his right size, then he should get it. He has the same expectations for split times, water and refreshments. The days of packing up the finish line and leaving when the last runner crosses are gone."

As more and more people—of all backgrounds and capabilities—got Lebow's message, its "rightness" was reinforced for the visionary himself, as well as for the world. For some very special heroes, it was obvious that their participation would not be devoid of severe pain and anguish as they worked their way to the Central Park finish, no matter how exciting and supportive the party atmosphere might be, yet try they would and so very often succeed. These runners' dedication to the goal Lebow had envisioned and "sold"—and Lebow's dedication to his sport and his runners—was not merely "the heroics of ordinary" people. Lebow's party would go on to let the whole world know about some of its *extra*ordinary citizens!

The picture of Fred Lebow as an ingenious version of the Catskill Borscht Belt entertainer in sneakers would hardly do justice to Lebow's contributions to the running movement. More than any other figure, he was responsible for adding the urban marathon, refashioned as a party, to the landscape of American popular culture, and for getting the "ordinary grassroots" runner out on the road.

Ever the creative and imaginative visionary, Lebow's marathon vision was not one chiseled in stone, but one that reflected the realism of the survivalist he was. He altered his vision as his party became more popular. He compromised the vision in response to political pressures, and redefined it in his final years as he was coming to terms with his own mortality. A fixed principle for enduring the Holocaust had been survival at any cost. With a similar mind-set, Lebow maneuvered, twisted, adapted, and seized opportunities to keep his New York City Marathon preeminent. Change direction where necessary, develop new publics, stay open to cutting-edge reforms, always look over one's shoulder for lurking danger—these were the survival strategies Lebow brought to his vision.

Rather than navigating his festival to greater heights based only on his preconceived notions of entertainment, Lebow carefully sampled public opinion. What more authentic way for the race director to discover the public pulse than for him to ask questions, his own version of random opinion surveys? "People were not just people for Fred," said girlfriend Paula Fahey regarding his proclivity to question onlookers at running events. "They were sources of information." After soaking up their views, he knew better what to hype, which sponsors to solicit, how to entice the media.

For this race director, trips to other marathon sites were actually research excursions. "Fred took notes when he came out here," said Marie Patrick, executive vice president of the City of Los Angeles Marathon. "He came here to learn." Los Angeles offered Lebow lessons in hype and hospitality. Lebow's marathon differed from the West Coast race inasmuch as his production stemmed from his running zealotry and an organized running club, whereas "[w]e're not running people," said Patrick. "We were in the event business."

For all of his revolutionizing of marathoning Lebow was not much of a sportsman, limiting himself to distance running. Previous to that, he had played tennis. He did not become a track and field fan until 1985. He attended his first pro basketball game only in 1989, and his first baseball and football games in 1990. As Fahey, who once accompanied Lebow to a football game in Miami, reported, the race director refused to go alone with her to the stadium. Instead, he joined a group van ride because he wanted to pick up information from the other passengers to apply to his own promotional schemes. At the game itself, Lebow was hardly interested in what was taking place on the field. Rather, he focused on the sports production process—how the arena was set up, arrangements for scalping tickets, the delivery of pizza to fans, actions exciting the crowds. Lebow pumped those seated nearby for answers to his many queries.

The race director's capacity for listening and observing reflected a self-trained analytic intelligence. At promotional events he graciously gave full attention to anyone he spoke with. But he trotted out this sympathetic persona mainly to win support for his show. If Lebow saw that his empathetic pose failed to do the trick with doubters, he turned to a different tack. Anger and excitability became the new language of persuasion. "At board meetings, Fred in a flash became angry," said club treasurer Peter Roth. "Those of us who knew realized that he was using anger to manipulate us."

Charles McCabe, Lebow's Chemical Bank (formerly Manufacturers Hanover) sponsor, stood by stoically while the race director in making a point angrily kicked wastebaskets in the bank's office. Lebow threatened Tavern on the Green's manager, Walter C. Rauscher, that he would move the finish line a few blocks north unless he followed his site-layout ideas. "Now you're part of a world class event," the race director warned Rauscher. The restaurateur, not wanting to be excluded from marathon publicity, ultimately gave in. Like any reformer building a new movement, Lebow had different needs for different players. Some brought an array of skills that he desperately needed, some had to be lured into his enterprise, and some had to get out of the way.

The promoter always dealt skillfully with sponsors. Jan Laster, an Asics marketing representative, described Lebow as "a kind man who was interested in what you were doing. He never talked much about himself. I never heard Fred speak a bad word about anybody. Even if you tried to get him to speak badly, he never did. He didn't have a mean bone in his body."

He also displayed a closeness with others who shared his devotion to the mythic element of marathoning. "Fred was forever calling us, 'The Odd Couple,' " said Dr. Bill Burke, director of the City of Los

Angeles Marathon, referring to the friendship between the Transylvanian Jew and the African American. Running issues served as the focus for their lighthearted teasing: "We always wanted to race each other," said Burke, recalling that Lebow boasted, "I can beat you in a dash." When Burke challenged him back, "I want you to find a picture of an old Jewish guy beating an old black guy in a dash. . . . Fred laughed for an hour after that line. When we got together at other times, Fred always used the code word, 'I can get you a picture.' "

Dr. Bill Burke, who was one of the many intimates who kidded Lebow about his accent and asked for personal renditions, recalled drinking with the Transylvanian at a café in Rome during a world championship event. "Fred rarely drank," said Burke, "but this time he was drinking white wine, and I was drinking Jack Daniels. I was slouched over and teased Fred, 'Don't forget your accent.' " The promoter obliged, his words emerging more and more indistinctly.

By 1988, with nineteen marathons behind him, Lebow, aged fifty-six, considered his vision fulfilled. It was time to retire. Without any schooling in the art of mass marketing, this visionary had watched his race grow to 22,299 finishers. His budget had grown to $2.1 million, not including sponsor fees, from the mere $60,000 cost of the first five-borough marathon, in 1976, some of which had come out of Lebow's own pockets.

In 1998, for the first time, a two-level start took place on the Verrazano-Narrows Bridge. The global character of his show remained vivid, with runners hailing from ninety countries, including two thousand runners from France and four hundred from Japan. One of Lebow's biggest stars and personal friends, Norwegian runner Grete Waitz, had achieved her ninth New York City Marathon victory. Nearly $100 million was pumped into the city economy by this one day of celebration. And Lebow just could not see any new dreams for his party. "This has been very difficult," he said. "I've achieved world records. The number of people . . . We've got the lower level. The Road Runners Club is solid in every respect. What else can I do? How can I top all this?" Where would he find new challenges?

6

Wresting the Keys to the City

IT HAD BEEN THE SORT OF VICTORY to make race entrepreneur Fred Lebow proud. Mayor Ed Koch, with whom Lebow had feuded for years over the issue of under-the-table payments to runners, had agreed to let his marathon use a second level of the Verrazano-Narrows Bridge for its start in 1988, making it possible for 23,463 runners—the world's largest starting field at the time—to enter Lebow's parade. Koch joked, "If they fill up the second level, I'll build a third level."

Eighteen years had passed since Lebow had wrested the first keys he needed—to the New York Road Runners Club and New York's Central Park—to get his New York City Marathon off the ground. His means back then was a little white lie about millionaire runners willing to back his idea. His goal, back then, was a well-organized and aesthetically pleasing race in and around Central Park. His means, his goal, and the keys he needed to wrest were a lot more detailed now, but in a way, they were even simpler than they were back in 1970. "People don't understand how ridiculous Fred's vision must have seemed," said Frank Shorter, the American gold medal marathon Olympian, "closing down the streets in a city where even two cab drivers can't get along." But as the saying goes, "Success breeds success." And Lebow's show had indeed become a success.

The growth of Lebow's running dream did not happen in a vacuum, and politics and controversies abounded through the years. The first "political" arena he had to work in and with was the New York Road Runners Club. Early on, Lebow's Jewishness and drive were somewhat detrimental to this relationship. Conceptually, as Lebow took increasing control of the marathon he had cofounded in 1970 and the NYRRC he had been elected president of in 1972, his innovative mass-marketing style put him at odds with the club's prevailing elitist, nonpromotional marketing approach toward road running. Rod Mac-Nicholl, a commercial artist and marathoner who was to draw hundreds of cartoons for the race director, described Lebow's arrival on the New York running scene: "He came like a bombshell booming through with ideas. Most of the main New York runners were from Irish and German backgrounds, and this upstart comes along," his Jewishness causing the dominant ethnic groups to "fear" his suggestions. "They didn't want to be embarrassed by his bigger ideas, they didn't want to fail, and they didn't want to adjust." But eventually these runners, continued Mac-Nicholl, recognized that Lebow had "better ideas" as he transformed marathoning from an "amateur sport into a business."

Politically, there was no uncertainty about Lebow's governing approach. In his determination to implant his marathon vision, any means was justifiable. While projecting an image of lighthearted sportsmanship to his constituencies beyond the New York Road Runners Club town house—his sponsors, the media, the running public—his leadership style "in-house" was mercilessly pragmatic. He had never formally studied the evolution of social movements, but in his gut he sensed that cultural changes were not created by committees, but driven by "fanatics," a term he had no qualms applying to himself. "If I believe my bottom line is something that benefits the event, I can't stand it if people tell me what to do."

A dispute about the T-shirts for the first New York City Marathon in Central Park was an early indication of how Lebow would pursue his own strategies regardless of who disagreed with him. At the meeting to discuss which color T-shirts to order, a definite majority of club members said, "Let's get white ones," but Lebow said he preferred orange T-shirts. When the club members asserted, "Oh no, we'll have to get the white ones," it appeared as if Lebow agreed with the consensus, but following the meeting he went and ordered orange T-shirts anyway.

Realizing that knowledge is power, Lebow learned to reveal as little as possible about his promotional schemes while they were taking shape, a strategy that enabled him to avoid offending sensitivities and skirt demands to do things differently. "After knowing him for six years," said Dr. Edward E. D. Colt, a member of the club's executive committee, "I still don't know what he's up to and what he's not up to.

He's a mystery man." He applied this approach in dealing with the Board of Directors of his New York Road Runners Club. "Fred made his decision, and then he would tell the board about it," said board member Elizabeth Phillips. "If the board had a really negative reaction, he would make sure that either the event was so successful that he could prove the board wrong or he would put in controls so that the event would not be such a tragic mistake."

Lebow's behavior in connection with the contract signing for the purchase of a $1.4 million Eighty-ninth Street town house for the Road Runners Club in 1981 showed how his elusiveness also came into play when he became uncertain of a decision's success. According to Dick Traum, "Fred [simply] didn't show up at the signing. He felt he let things go too far. He was nervous the building would sink the club, that it would put it in bankruptcy." When Traum tried to lessen Lebow's anxieties with the argument that the race director with his many contacts could do fund-raising for the town house, Lebow replied, "I'm not good at raising money."

Lebow, as the definer of the marathon vision and reshaper of the world of running, did not brook challenges to his leadership. In a revealing comment, the race director expressed his philosophy of leadership to club treasurer Peter Roth. "I went to Fred saying that he must develop a more thorough chain of command," said Roth. According to Roth, Lebow replied, "There is no chain of command. I'm the papa bear. Everyone else [is a] baby bear. I play no favorites among the baby bears." In his 1984 book, however, Lebow did not argue for this autocratic concept, but casually dismissed the lack of democratic standards in his club's governance. Club elections? Things were "so wild and crazy" the first few years after the five-borough marathon began, he noted, the "club" (not Lebow!) simply "forgot" to hold elections. Besides, he argued, all his running projects were showing success in the absence of elections: membership was growing, the marathon was successful, merchandising was instituted, and a club magazine was launched. So why "be bothered with our own bureaucracy"? According to an October 20, 1981, *New York Times* article, " 'The way Fred controls the club is through chaos,' said one [club] member, who asked for anonymity. Critics also point to recent changes in the executive committee as another example of Lebow's attempt to consolidate power."

Regardless of Lebow's making light of the absence of democratic procedures, certain club members were highly opposed to his "illegality and immorality." In a telling letter of March 2, 1977, appearing in the New York club's newspaper, biologist Dr. Paul Milvy, took Lebow strongly to task and resigned from the club's executive committee, although he questioned, "[H]ow I am to resign from an imaginary institution that exists neither de jure nor de facto," a problem "I will leave for the philosophers to contemplate." Lebow, to be sure, was not oblivious to criticism of his exercising power unilaterally. "My big problem used to be delegating authority," he acknowledged in a 1984 interview. However, he did credit his second in command, Allan Steinfeld, with helping him share the load.

In 1978, a group of board members, seeking to clip Lebow's wings, wrote a set of bylaws designed to severely restrict his power—limiting the presidency to a one-year term, and requiring board approval for any expenditure greater than one thousand dollars. In a close vote, Lebow managed to maintain his power, but being the inveterate survivor that he was, he realized he needed to interact more with the board and keep them informed of his plans. Based on a change in the club's bylaws in 1982, Lebow was actually forced to hold regular board meetings.

Despite his autocratic style, Lebow did not only surround himself with yes men. If he respected someone's potential contribution, he was able to tolerate dissent. Such was the case with Peter Roth, whom Lebow asked to serve as club treasurer beginning in 1977. Though Lebow micromanaged most areas of his club, its financial records in the early years of his presidency were a total disaster. At first, Lebow and some of the other officers tried balancing the books on the kitchen table in the race director's apartment, but eventually, the Internal Revenue Service had been called in following written complaints from club members. As evidence of the problems, the auditing firm Ernst & Whitney noted in the club's financial statement for 1980, "Because of inadequacies in the club's accounting records for the previous year, it was not practical to extend our auditing procedures to enable us to express an opinion on results of operations." Lebow's continued disregard for financial accountability troubled his running club associates.

Details just didn't always concern Lebow. Showmanship, promotion, hype, and technique were his strengths. He did not even adhere to his own published race schedules, many times delaying the start so that he could hustle in late arrivals. Bill Noel, one of Lebow's race directors, estimated that out of some one hundred races annually sponsored by the club, only two—the marathon and the New Year's Eve Midnight Run—actually began on time. And did he worry about proprieties? "If Fred had an idea, he just went ahead with it," said Robert Laufer, the lawyer for the marathon. "He wasn't the sort of guy who needed to check things out with his lawyer."

"Sometimes, Fred acted independently in hiding deals we didn't know about," revealed Roth. "We didn't quibble much with the details, as long as we knew the boundaries," but Roth often had to oppose Lebow's freewheeling approach to finances. Reining in Lebow's grandiose promotional schemes was an ongoing challenge. "I never relented in fighting on issues when he was out of line." Early in the treasurer's tenure, Lebow's opposition to financial restraints surfaced when Roth presented his fiscal report. "I noted how we had lost money the previous year and how I was hoping to turn things around. . . . Fred got up while I was speaking, took the mike and said, 'I know we lost money last year, and if I have anything to say, we'll be losing money this year too.' " When in another report Roth questioned whether the club could afford paying its eight salaried employees, "Fred said, 'I don't know whether eight [employees] will be enough.'

"Fred and I were friendly enemies," Roth explained. "We both agreed with the premises of the club, and we knew we each needed to be there. . . . Fred asked me to stand up to him. He needed someone to break his impulsiveness. He knew he didn't dot all his 'i's, or cross his 't's. He didn't realize what he was asking. I fought him constantly. It got to a point where he would threaten me, trying to get me out of my job as treasurer."

Roth disclosed Lebow's bottom-line philosophy as the racing impresario had shared it with him: "Fred told me that what really counts in people is that they are successful. It didn't matter what you needed to get there. The mark of strength was results. . . . In the garment center," where everybody got paid off, according to what Lebow told Roth, " 'the mark of a successful person was one whose office at Christmas was loaded with gifts; then I know that the person has power.' People who were result oriented were the people Fred respected most."

And results were what Lebow was always after. Despite the recognition and fun that Lebow's party brought to New York City, the race director was continuously jockeying with city politicos over his races. He fought battles over his authority to pay elite runners, the participation of wheelchair athletes in his marathon, the usage of more levels of the Verrazano-Narrows Bridge at the marathon's start, and the role of police in controlling his course. Access to Central Park, the main site of his running club's races, was a hotbed of friction. Although Henry Stern, commissioner of parks and recreation during the administrations of Mayors Koch and Giuliani, agreed that the marathon and Lebow's other races were "mutually beneficial" to the city, he did consider Lebow an antagonist for continually escalating his demands. "Every week, he would come in with some other request," said Stern. "He wanted more signs, more flags, turning the park into a spectacle. If we allowed two-foot signs, he would now want six-foot signs. He tried to get a new race every time a new commercial sponsor came. Other groups also apply for events. Why should the Road Runners Club have a monopoly?" But even with all the aggravation the race director caused him, Stern did not find anything disingenuous about Lebow as the disseminator of the vision of an urban block party. "People devoted to a single cause are usually a little crazy," said Stern. "That's what you expect and you don't judge them by normal standards. I'd call him a combination of Joseph Papp [a theatrical innovator who made fine plays available to large and varied audiences through his New York Shakespeare Festival and Public Theater and who battled tirelessly against extreme conservatism and censorship] and Truman Capote. Papp," Stern explained, "in his single-minded promotion and development of an institution, and Capote in some of his odd behavior."

After moving beyond its Central Park beginnings, the closing of city streets during his show interfered with the nonrunning populace in the city, forcing Lebow to appear at times at community events to placate critics. Instead of considering these sessions "damage control," Lebow happily viewed them as additional forums from which he could publicize his running lifestyle.

A few weeks before the 1984 marathon, Lebow was asked by a Brooklyn church located at the nine-mile mark to reroute his race away from its Bedford Avenue entrance so as to not block the way of worshipers seeking to enter. Accompanied by Angel Nunez, head of Lebow's Urban Running Program, and other club officials, the race director, T-shirts in hand, journeyed to Brooklyn. Nunez was confident the clever Lebow could handle the complaint: "Fred always had the right answer to any question." When church officials tried to persuade Lebow to start holding the race on Mondays, based on the precedent that the venerable Boston Marathon takes place on that day of the week and that a Monday marathon would solve the problem of worshipers seeking access to Sunday services, Lebow simply replied, with conviction, "In Boston, it's a tradition for the marathon to run on Mondays. In New York it's a tradition to have it on Sundays."

Lebow truly believed that for one day a year he controlled the streets of New York City, but in reality, "ownership" was ultimately in the hands of the city's police, as shown by the time New York's Finest threw him off the course of his own marathon. As he entered Central Park, exhausted from all his screaming from the lead car to fire up the crowds, he confessed to bank sponsor Charlie McCabe, who accompanied him in the Mercedes, "Can't take this anymore." Still, just before the finish line, the tired race director jumped out of the car and sprinted to the posts, expecting to wave the winner in with his trademark Lebow windmill. Steinfeld was nearby, waiting to share Lebow's moment of glory, when, suddenly, cops appeared, wrestling both of them off the course. Struggling to free themselves, the two stammered who they were. "I don't care who you are," shouted one cop. "Our orders are to clear the course." Steinfeld eventually succeeded in getting the attention of a friendly lieutenant from the Central Park precinct, who ordered the two released, but the evidence was clear: although ostensibly there to help Lebow, when push came to shove, it was the police who were in charge.

New York City police were not only responsible for reining in the crowds, but also in charge of street closings, traffic patterns, the placement of barriers, the safety of runners, and the positioning of press vehicles. Captain Carl Jonasch, commander of the Central Park precinct between 1982 and 1985, before rising to police deputy inspector, spent the two days and nights preceding the marathon on nonstop duty and slept in the station house. The night before the race, and into the morning hours, Lebow's staff and the police drove up and down the course scouting "emergencies" like illegally parked cars, a contractor deciding to repair a sidewalk, a three-alarm fire, or any of numerous pitfalls that could ruin the party. Central Park, site of the marathon's last four miles, was more finely combed than any other part of the route: traces of potholes were filled in, fencing was checked and rechecked, and the finish line was exactingly laid out. On Marathon Sunday morning, a volunteer cordon of police and fire department runners at the starting line made sure the elite runners were not engulfed by the runners lined up behind them.

A *friendly* New York Police Department (NYPD) was critical to Lebow because the police were the entryway to the crowds. Excited crowds meant excited runners and a lively party for all. Could the crowds lining Lebow's stage be joyous if the NYPD was indifferent or glum? And how helpful would the police be in fixing the last-minute hitches Lebow always scoured from the lead car if they didn't care? In 1982, while heading down Madison Avenue, the race director's eyes settled on barriers positioned the wrong way, the runners inching up not far behind. "Move the barriers!" shouted Lebow. "They cut the race course by 25 yards!" Lieutenant Joe Cea from the Operations Unit, after transmitting Lebow's request to his inspector, shot back, "What's so important about 25 yards? Nobody will know the difference." But when Lebow, the runners closing in on him, screamed, "If a runner sets a record, it will be invalidated by the missing 25 yards!" it was an involved and caring Cea who immediately ordered the barriers shifted, because "then I understood why Fred was so excited."

In the marathon's early years, police—like parks commissioner Stern—had resented Lebow's nudging. "Each year, Fred escalated his demands to improve the race," said Cea. "He always had a different demand. . . . We felt the marathon was an intrusion on traffic." But Lebow cultivated them, tactically and tactfully, by giving T-shirts to the top commanders, inviting them to pre- and postmarathon parties, asking them to present awards at winner ceremonies, and reserving marathon places for last-minute police applicants. "We called Fred directly to get cops into the marathon," said Jonasch. "He would always save a few places for us." It became their party as well as Lebow's. And a day of glory for New York appealed to Deputy Chief Tom Ryan, commanding officer of the Traffic Division, who noted, "The biggest thrill in Fred's life was when he came off the Queensboro Bridge onto First Avenue."

Not so thrilling was when Fred was enmeshed in "political" controversies affecting his running vision. On occasion, his "keys" to the city were able to help him overcome his adversaries. In other areas, "city hall" was his biggest opponent.

Over the years, Lebow opposed charity races. Because they siphoned off road-racing monies, Lebow saw them as threatening his vision. For Lebow, his running club and the National Road Running Association were "every bit much a charity as the American Heart Association," noted *Road Race Management* on February 1, 1988. And, besides, argued the race director in 1988, charity races had proved to be failures, noting, "Most of the events which were run for charities have disappeared, like Chicago [America's Marathon]." Accordingly, he opposed charity races whether the fund-raising involved collecting monies from the entry fees or scheduling new races specially designated in a specific charity's behalf. What he feared was that the money needed for the club to continue to exist would no longer be there once the floodgate for making races into charity events was open.

Beyond the financial drain of charities staging their own races, Lebow also worried that the proliferation of individually sponsored events would weaken the clout of his own running club and its own program. It was because of this concern that in 1978 Lebow thwarted UNICEF's plans to put on a race in Central Park even though they already had a date set and an agent hired. Using his knowledge of bureaucracy, he created a series of three races—one of them on UNICEF's date—and enlisted Finnair to sponsor the series and fly the winner to the Finlandia Marathon. With these details worked out, he rushed to the Parks Department and filed his application. When UNICEF's representatives later arrived at the Parks Department, they were told the date was taken and had to abandon the proposition.

One controversy in which his "keys" to city hall in no way helped was the politically charged issue of wheelchair athletes. As much as he voiced an egalitarian theme in defining his marathon vision, he felt he had to draw the line regarding the participation of these particular athletes. He opposed wheelchair athletes in his show on two grounds. "First of all our marathon is a foot race, not a bicycle race or a roller skate race or a wheelchair race," he wrote. "My job is to develop the sport of foot racing like somebody else's job might be for sky diving or figure skating." Second, he was against wheelchair participation based on safety, concerned about the possibility that such competitors could crash into footracers, particularly on physical drops such as the descents on the Verrazano-Narrows and Queensboro Bridges.

Lebow recognized that his stance might seem selfish, but he claimed it was more selfish on the part of the wheelchair athletes to jeopardize the footracers. To try to appease the wheelchair athletes, and as a way of heading off the movement, Lebow persuaded Charles McCabe of marathon sponsor Manufacturers Hanover Bank to sponsor a national wheelchair marathon championship in New York City at a later date, under the supervision of his New York Road Runners Club. But the wheelchair athletes seeking mainstream competition felt only patronized by Lebow.

Significantly, Lebow favored participation of athletes with other types of disabilities, such as blindness or amputations. Interestingly, Dick Traum and his Achilles Track Club of disabled athletes supported Lebow in opposing wheelchair participation. Calling a wheelchair a "lethal instrument," Traum contrasted the speed of runners "going at about a speed of seven miles per hour" with a wheelchair that can reach speeds as fast as "thirty miles per hour going downhill on a place like the Fifty-ninth Street Bridge."

These arguments did not impress marathon star Bill Rodgers, who wrote, "If you want to talk about safety hazards in New York what about all the helicopters hovering over 11,128 runners at the start and stirring up dust all along the course? Or all the Subarus constantly zipping around the leading competitors? I think these were more of a safety hazard than one or two wheelchair athletes on the course." Rodgers cited the permission given wheelchair competitors to enter the Boston Marathon he was so involved with, but Lebow countered with the assertion that the New York race was different. Boston's race, the race director pointed out, drew only half as many runners as did the Big Apple's. Moreover, the New England course was not riddled with New York City's bridges and three hundred intersections.

The backdrop for the campaign to include wheelchair athletes was the 1977 issuance of recommendations by the President's Commission on Olympic Sports. "The differences in the problems of handicapped versus those of the able-bodied," the commission noted, "are differences only in degree and dissimilar only in the particulars of the individual situation. Essentially all are alike. Only the participants provide a contrast."

When Lebow persisted in barring wheelchair athletes, the New York State Division of Human Rights sued the New York Road Runners Club in appellate court, charging discriminatory practices. The court ruling, however, favored Lebow, holding that since his marathon was historically a footrace, the Road Runners Club was not discriminating against wheelchair applicants. Throughout the late 1970s and early 1980s, his opposition to mainstreaming these wheelchair athletes was actually upheld in various court decisions.

But, ultimately, the race director had to relent. Despite his legal victories, he finally permitted wheelchair athletes to compete because New York City mayor Ed Koch had threatened to withhold permission for staging the marathon. The survivalist in Lebow emerged. He did not press the legalities when he saw that politically he was thwarted. He dropped the tableau of the purity of the marathon vision and pragmatically backtracked so his party could go on.

Organizationally, he had fought so vigorously against wheelchair participation in distance-running competition that some runners, including Henley Gibble, who previously "thought running was a simple act," came to see the sport in more political terms. Gibble, who would later become executive director of the Road Runners Club of America, first met Lebow at RRCA's 1979 convention in New Orleans. "It was a very political convention," she recalled. "I didn't think running was that political. But Fred was articulate and vocal in trying to get us to establish guidelines to bar wheelchair athletes."

Given the hype Lebow introduced at his marathon party, the New York Road Runners Club president and race promoter-director saw sports governing bodies like the national RRCA as adherents of a stuffy status quo. But as a pragmatist, he knew the need for attentiveness to these governing organizations. "You can't buck governing bodies" was Lebow's assessment.

Stylistically, the contrasts between the showman race director trying to hype his festival and the bureaucratic bodies controlling the sport
were striking. On September 1, 1994, *New York Newsday* compared
Lebow with the U.S. governing body for track and field: "Fred is ideas,
action, responsiveness to changing tastes and needs. USA Track and
Field, at least in the view of your average road runner or race director, is
bureaucracy, stagnancy and a vision that sometimes doesn't seem to extend beyond a 400-meter oval. Fred is publicity, personality, the spectacle of the New York City Marathon. USATF is anonymity, red tape and
empty stadiums."

Lebow evaluated the role of national governing bodies (NGBs)
from a Machiavellian perspective. "They were useful when they passed
rules which supported Lebow's way of conducting business," reported
Road Race Management in October 1994. "However, NGBs were po-
tentially threatening because they represented an external source of
control over event selection (i.e., none of the Olympic Marathon trials
. . . ever wound up in New York), sanctions and athletes."

When it suited his needs, Lebow turned to national sports groups
to adopt his vision in order to strengthen his position, and it was for
such a purpose that he was so vocal at the 1979 Road Runners Club of
America convention where Gibble met him. Lebow, whose purist approach to marathoning caused him to oppose what he considered to be
the exploitation and commercialism of road running, including tie-ins
with charities and the participation of wheelchair athletes—two battles
his club was waging at the time in New York—sought to convince the
delegates of the two hundred RRCA chapters attending the convention
to adopt his positions. But, according to *Road Race Management* reporter Jim Ferstle, most delegates felt the role of the national body
should be mainly to provide information and assistance, rather than the
broad-based directives Lebow sought.

Politically, Lebow's embrace of New York did not always engender
support from others in the road-running movement who, according to
Ferstle, "feared that he wanted to be the guru of running . . . [and]
that he would walk over his mother's grave if he had to do it. . . . Moreover, delegates held a certain fear of New York City's 'Jewish corporate
world' as personified by Lebow."

The convention rejected not only Lebow's platform, but also his choice for president, Nina Kuscsik, winner of his marathon in 1972 and 1973. On the surface, Lebow lost because he lacked the delegate voting strength, but in a larger sense, disagreement with Lebow's position was a metaphor for opposition to the glitzy empire he was building in the Big Apple. Vince Chiapetta, cofounder with Lebow of the first Central Park New York City Marathon, in 1970, termed the convention politics as "coming down to mid-America versus ethnic New York." The defeat so strained relations between the running impresario and the RRCA, and caused such a major rift between Lebow's New York running club and its parent organization, that Lebow wrote in his book four years later, "[We] haven't had much relationship with them aside from the race insurance we get through them."

Money issues related to recruiting runners continually embroiled Lebow in controversy and drama, on more than one occasion threatening to wrest the keys to the city back away from the New York race director and his dream. In the late 1970s and early 1980s, while the popularity of running and marathoning was soaring, another then current sports trend—the decline of athletic amateurism—plagued Lebow's festival, and he was forced to confront the label of "commercialism" being applied to his sport. Should athletes get paid? How to differentiate between professional and amateur road running? How to maintain the fiction of his own "amateur" marathon party, which everyone knew served as a financial marketplace for star athletes? These were survival issues that Lebow faced as he fought to keep his festival on the cutting edge of sports glitz.

The sponsors, athletes, crowds—all knew the power of money in producing a world-class marathon. Lebow the deal maker certainly knew that without money, his show was dead. But publicly, he paid lip service to the myth of amateurism, knowing that the constituencies he must keep happy—city hall, sports governing bodies, and increasingly demanding athletes and their agents—were all parties to one big lie.

At first, Lebow denied making payments to star marathoners. But eventually he trapped himself in a boastful published admission of providing cash to runners. The cost of Lebow's uncharacteristic public hubris on this money issue was a much more expensive New York City Marathon production. Although it is difficult to trace the amounts and methods of payments, there is no question that Lebow paid under-the-table money in all his marathons, even though such payments violated the rules of sports federations. At some of his other races, a trusted aide showed up with cash. Patricia Owens, his coordinator of elite athletes—"I was the bad guy," she admitted—recalled coming to races with attaché cases full of money. The double standard regarding payments made to athletes was demonstrated in the RRCA handbook, in a chapter headed "Budgeting for a Big Race": "It is advisable to earmark some money for bringing in fine runners. They are valuable features in the promotion and publicizing of the race. However, they are costly; figures range from $500 to $2,000, plus transportation and per diem per runner."

Careful not to offend the NGBs, Lebow consistently denied making such payments. Even when the *New York Times* carried a front-page story on October 17, 1981, headlined "New York Marathon Offers Prize Money, Top Coaches Report" before the 1981 marathon, the race director was quoted on the front page as saying, "The New York Marathon is not giving any up-front money, and I personally know of no prize-money payments that will be paid." Why did Lebow make these denials when such payments were increasingly common knowledge? The *Times* understood where the pragmatic race director was coming from: "To protect the amateur eligibility of the 16,000 runners in the [1981] race, some of whom have to compete in the 1984 Olympic Games in Los Angeles, Mr. Lebow has no alternative but to adopt this public position." The race director adopted subterfuges to circumvent the amateur rule, like in 1979 when he purchased one hundred running-gear uniforms from Reebok, at a retail price in excess of one hundred dollars per uniform, to entice runners to compete.

Sponsors also cooperated in paying the allegedly amateur runners. In 1981, Adidas wrote a five thousand-dollar incentive bonus clause for the winner of the New York City Marathon. The shoe company also signed a secret contract with a top female runner to pay her a minimum salary of six thousand dollars a year.

Weighing in with its own proposal was The Athletic Congress (TAC). TAC wanted to hold guardianship over prize money in order to allow them to maintain control of the sport, heading off the rivalry from Lebow, who was advocating open competition among all runners. Top road runners, worried about their own future in the competition between Lebow and TAC, formed their own group, the Association of Road Running Athletes. The fear of losing control over the sport later prompted Lebow to throw in his lot with the NGBs. Lebow strenuously backed TAC, noting, "We were strongly working behind the scenes with TAC to come up with some form of above-board payments that might be channeled through the governing body." In 1980, the group rejected the guardianship proposal and turned to sponsors to launch a prize-money credit.

The following year, 1981 New York City Marathon winner Alberto Salazar attacked TAC as "hypocrites" and "thieves." Defiantly, Salazar acknowledged getting paid. "It definitely takes place in races. I do make my living off running." Why assume that runners, asked Salazar, are more corrupt or less capable than their counterparts in other professional sports? "Runners work just as hard as any pro football or pro basketball player," said Salazar, "and should be compensated in whatever manner a free, open system dictates."

Lebow attacked this Olympic amateur ideal, which proscribed payment, as an example of upper-class elitism. "The running boom has yet to reach the lower income segment of the population," wrote Lebow, "for whom it is ideal. The beauty of the sport is that unlike football, baseball or golf, one does not need formal equipment or a country club in order to be able to participate. And running emphasizes equality."

The prize-money debate climaxed in a crashing defeat for Lebow. In his book, *Inside the World of Big-Time Marathoning*, written with Richard Woodley and published shortly before the 1984 marathon, Lebow boasted that more than one million dollars had been paid under the table to star athletes in his marathons. "One million dollars!" he exclaimed. "It was a measure of what the marathon has been and what it has become."

But while Lebow's admission may have succeeded in showing his self-importance, it openly defied New York City mayor Ed Koch, who consistently opposed cash prizes. Koch, who joked that there were two things holy in New York City, the Talmud and the marathon, admired Lebow's party. "It was a tremendous asset to the City," commented Koch. "But in his commitment to amateur athletics—'Does the guy who shoots the cannon off get anything,' " asked the mayor, reflecting on a bygone era in referring to the marathon's start. Claiming that

Lebow never advised him that the marathon was paying under-the-table money, Koch denied awareness of that common practice. "If the New York City Marathon turns commercial," threatened Koch, "it will have to pay the expenses of the operation incurred by the City." Koch estimated those expenses to run about one million dollars. Furthermore, warned Koch, if the marathon refused to pay, "they can take it to Newark."

Commercialization of his marathon? A nonissue, asserted Lebow. "I understand Koch's thoughts about wanting the race to be for amateurs, like the Boston Marathon. But in our race, 99.5 percent of the athletes [of the estimated entering log of eighteen thousand at the time] have no chance of winning money. They are definite amateurs." Moreover, Lebow charged that the mayor gave his people's festival short shrift despite the positive way that it showcased the Big Apple. "The marathon brings more than $100 million to the City's economy," argued Lebow, "and it generates a lot of goodwill for the City, as shown by the millions of people who watch it along the course and the millions who watch it on national TV. People come away saying what a great city it is."

A year before the appearance of Lebow's book, the race director reported receiving a "private and disturbing" directive from the mayor, in which he once again "forbid us" to offer prize money. Lebow believed that Koch's decision resulted from the city's reported cost of five hundred thousand dollars for police and cleanup following a Diana Ross concert in Central Park. "So to avoid further protests about commercialism of city-supported events," wrote Lebow, "the Mayor was banning the marathon from giving open prize money. Not only that, the intermediary told me that I was not to say the Mayor banned it. Nor would there be any discussion; for the Mayor it was a closed issue."

Entering the fray, the *New York Times* editorialized on October 6, 1984, that "one of the world's worst-kept secrets" was the fact that Lebow was paying in order to attract big-name competitors. "The Mayor is charmingly Victorian in his view of amateurism," charged the *Times*. "Play-for-pay violated the principles from Britain's leisure class and it obviously still embarrasses both those who pay and those who receive. But most sports fans have long since understood that full-time athletes can't be expected to work for nothing. The best marathoners simply won't come to an event without financial incentives." Koch was on firmer ground, maintained the *Times,* in asking the marathon's sponsors "to pay something" for municipal costs. "In a city of shabby parks, collapsing bridges and dangerous subways, the private sponsors of public events should pay a fair share."

In the compromises between Lebow and the city, the race director agreed to turn over one dollar for each dollar paid out in prize money to the government. The city also continued to receive half of the one hundred thousand dollars ABC paid for television rights. "My own Victorian attitude should not be imposed on the City," confessed Koch. "I had to move with the times. If we wanted the marathon to attract the top runners, we had to do this."

In his "personal" life, Lebow had dropped his own quest for money once he decided to make running his life's mission. Before his full-time involvement with running, he said, he earned "in the middle five figures" as a garment-center knockoff artist. Since his living expenses at that time were very low (he paid only sixty-nine dollars a month for his apartment), he had managed to put away funds. Thus, even though he was elected president of the New York Road Runners Club in 1972, he didn't begin taking a salary until ten years later, in 1982. *People* magazine that year reported that because of his "monkish" devotion to running, Lebow spent only about three thousand dollars a year of his own money.

But Lebow rarely passed up opportunities to add to the coffers of his running club. *Road Race Management* in a March 1983 editorial strongly criticized the practice of Lebow's club requiring a three-dollar fee for eligibility for the year's lottery drawing. The running journal estimated that receipts from thirty-five to forty thousand runners would generate some one hundred thousand dollars for the club, a "morally questionable" practice for two reasons, argued *Road Race Management.* First, the expenses of the lottery should run far less than one hundred thousand dollars, and second, the New York Road Running Club already had at least one million dollars available to conduct the marathon. Why then did they institute this fee? asked the journal rhetorically. "To maximize its income," scolded *Road Race Management* in reply, advising marathoners "to howl" at the running club and sponsors or spend their money on other races unless this rip-off stopped.

In 1984, the year of his book's publication, Lebow declared an annual income of thirty thousand dollars. At the time of his death in 1994, Lebow's club paid him eighty thousand dollars a year. Worried that this figure seemed excessive given the race director's spare living style, club treasurer Peter Roth observed that this salary was "basically for Allan [Steinfeld]." What he meant was that it was necessary for Lebow to earn such an amount in order to justify paying a roughly similar sum to Steinfeld, the marathon's technical director. Steinfeld needed money more than Lebow because he lived more conventionally than his boss.

In view of his unadorned lifestyle, Lebow was surprised when critics questioned why he needed money. As a lifelong bachelor, he lacked the expenses of a husband or father. "If my travel is being paid for by the airlines or various sponsors or organizations," he said in 1980, "and if I'm continually invited for so many dinners I can't accept, where are my expenses? If I go out on a date, it's usually Dutch treat. If I want to spend money, I'd have a hard time." But why should his spending habits affect how much he and his position deserved to be paid?

Sponsors and media people admired Lebow's uninterest in accumulating money. He never personally received payment for product endorsements or for advising sponsors, though he could have easily sent out signals that he was looking for cash if he wanted to. This type of financial self-sacrifice no doubt contributed to his message being taken seriously. Chemical Bank's Charles McCabe contrasted Lebow's lack of materialism with that of many athletes he dealt with, whose main focus was "payday."

ABC sports commentator Larry Rawson queried Lebow about a trip to Moscow the race director made. "How much did they pay you?" asked Rawson. Lebow answered, "Ten thousand dollars," at which point Rawson commented, "I hope you put it away somewhere." When Lebow told him, " 'No. I gave it to the club' . . . I went into a bit of a tizzy," said Rawson, admonishing Lebow, "You've got to think of yourself." "Maybe next time," answered the race director.

Or maybe not! Based on his reputation of never carrying money, Lebow's companions always expected to pick up the bill. Following a taxi ride together, sponsor Jack Maguire of Vermont Pure Natural Spring Water said, "I knew I would pay, because Fred never had a place to put a wallet in his running clothes."

7

Squeezing Money from Sponsors

Like squeezing juice from a Big Apple, having the right handle helped eliminate any need for pressure.

MERCEDES-BENZ DEALERS and elite runners were celebrating at the 1989 postmarathon party at Manhattan's Gingerman Club when, suddenly, one of the automobile company's top officials remembered his plane was soon due to depart Kennedy Airport for the return trip to Germany. Even if he immediately jumped into a taxi, the prospect of the executive reaching the airport on time seemed nil. Turning to Mercedes' American production manager, Rolf Waldeis, the Mercedes VIP from Germany disclosed his plight. "Immediately, I told Fred the problem," said Waldeis. Undaunted by such conventional obstacles, Lebow darted toward the New York City police commissioner who obliged the race director by ordering a police escort to take the Mercedes official to the airport. In theory, this talent to maneuver a police entourage for a sponsor is not listed in the job description of a race director. But for Lebow, such off-the-course attention to a sponsor's predicament was part of what made them leave his pageants happy and come back again.

As he transformed the marathon from a race to a show, Lebow knew that attracting sponsors depended not only on selling an image or vision of the marathon, but also on providing personal services. Sometimes, these services were not at all related to the commercial aspects of the marathon, such as attending the funeral of a sponsor's mother, giving media and health advice, or arranging a date. Among sports promoters, Lebow stood out because of his obsession with meeting needs that went beyond the official race. As Jane Lazgin of New York City Marathon sponsor Perrier put it, "Fred did not shut down at the end of the event."

Thus, while sponsors put up hefty fees to market their image, there was the feeling that Lebow was not only an entrepreneur, but also a friend . . . that they were involved with him not merely in a sports marketing event, but in a populist demonstration of fitness and fun. With Fred, they did not feel like they were being squeezed for anything.

Tapping into corporate America's goal to reinvent its image before a live sports audience, Lebow changed the New York City Marathon from an elite footrace to an outdoor carnival open to the masses. Sponsors provided the dollars that would be used not only for prize money, but also for staging what was, in effect, a 26.2-mile festival. Their hope was that the runners, spectators, and television viewers would all remember that the show's enablers included a bank, a car dealer, a pasta manufacturer, an insurance company, a nonprescription pain reliever, and a garbage removal company, and that the recognition would affect their future patronage.

After the marathon culminated at the Central Park finish—with photos, medals, and roses, certifying that all those who completed the course, regardless of how slowly they lumbered along, were players in an elite theatrical production—it would be the race T-shirt bearing sponsors' names that would provide future proof these runners had performed in Lebow's urban block party.

In addition to grassroots marathoners wearing their John Hancock running caps and Chemical Bank T-shirts and drinking bottles of Vermont Pure Natural Spring Water and swallowing Advil ("official pain reliever of the New York City Marathon") tablets, sponsor exposure would be enhanced by the elite runners who were to become part of what the *New York Times* would call "a 26-mile dash for endorsements." The paper noted, for example, that in speaking at a prerace news conference at Tavern on the Green before the 1992 marathon, "no runner of any nationality" gave more value for corporate endorsements than did Kim Jones, the main American hopeful that year, writing that, while wearing the John Hancock signature on her white tennis sweater,

> Jones easily set a record when she mentioned the company's name at least a dozen times during the question and answer session. Afterward, when someone asked her about a scab near her left eye, Jones

deftly slipped in another plug, this time for her eyeglass sponsor. After explaining that she had been distracted by a barking dog and tripped over a rock during a recent training run, she added: "Luckily I was wearing my Oakleys or it could have been worse." Unfortunately, for her shoe sponsor, Jones was questioned further and had to admit it was her Nikes that stumbled over the rock.

When Lebow came on the scene, sports marketing for track events was in its infancy. Competitive running, whether for a marathon or for the more limited footraces, was not geared to the masses. But Lebow knew that for his party to grow, it needed financial support, and as a former businessman himself, he would have to provide the sponsoring financiers of his vision much more than a pro forma platform at his party if he wanted his show to be much more than a mere marathon. According to his staff public relations associate Laura Leale, "Fred knew the value of extending service. He understood it was important to do more things for a sponsor than just delivering a package. He gave added value." Some ten years later, sponsors were spending millions of dollars annually for his marathon, and *Forbes* magazine on October 24, 1983, cited him as being "more than any other man in the world" responsible for making running big business.

Lebow attracted corporate funding by changing the concept of the marathon. In its first six runnings, from 1970 to 1975, the nature of sponsorship of the New York City Marathon was limited because the event drew only a few hundred runners, making their way through Central Park, hoping to either place among the top ten finishers or at least compete for age-group medals. Runners of little athletic potential hardly considered competing in such an event, devoid of crowds and awards to validate their efforts. It wasn't until Lebow's event moved beyond Central Park and attracted a whole new type of attention that the new grassroots marathoner started participating, bringing in the upscale rather than the blue-collar runner who would provide the largesse for sponsor products and services.

As early as 1971, tying into the feminist agenda presented Lebow with prospects for further broadening his sponsorship base. The Amateur Athletic Union ban prohibiting women from officially running in distance races with men rankled Lebow; he strongly disagreed with its premise that a woman's body was too fragile for distance running. But what the race director needed to attract enough women to countermand the ban was "an angle."

The opportune moment arrived in 1971 when the public relations firm representing Johnson's Wax asked him to sponsor a marathon for women to promote a product called Crazy Legs, a shaving cream for women. "I said, 'Are you crazy?'" Lebow recalled in his autobiography. He was able to identify only two women in the state of New York who had ever run a marathon. But the company persisted, so, using the fashionable miniskirt as a basis, Lebow proposed putting on a shorter race—a six miler—and since the concept was so revolutionary, he hyped it by calling it a Crazy Legs Mini Marathon. Although the event would draw some seventy-five hundred runners in later years, attracting attention initially spurred Lebow to mine his bag of tricks. He handed out leaflets and taped flyers to light poles, his only goals being to attract a field of women runners and a bit of attention.

He eventually signed up seventy-eight women, but what stood out about the competition was its jovial quality. Six Playboy Bunnies recruited by Lebow hopped along in the race, and the sponsor required the runners to wear identical T-shirts. In their identical white T-shirts, bearing the name Crazy Legs shaving cream (with the runners' numbers listed below), the runners, wrote Tom Derderian, "looked more like a comic refugee regiment slowly plodding around the park in identical jerseys."

It was this breakthrough that had enormous implications for the running movement, leading to women's participation in Lebow's own marathon, to the sponsors' reach for this new market, and ultimately to a major cultural shift in the notion of female fitness. The gender rules were breached, responding to the new feminism.

The marathon course itself became an aid in recruiting sponsors. Winding through the city's colorful ethnic neighborhoods—with banners flapping, bands blaring, and the blue line Lebow painted along the course alerting the Big Apple that this show in sneakers was coming to town—the racecourse provided the exposure sponsors craved.

Lebow took advantage of the fact that at the same time he was seeking wider corporate sponsorship, the fitness movement was taking hold in America. On December 25, 1967, *U.S. News and World Report* had written that the "jogging regimen" was sweeping the country. Political protest had abated following the Vietnam War, and baby boomers refocused their energies on personal well-being. Marathoning, which together with hammer throwing had been dismissed as a nonspectator sport, became celebrated for its health virtues. Affluent runners, in possession of time and money for self-improvement, were alert to these benefits, and attracting them attracted sponsors. "It does improve the efficiency of the heart," reported a June 1977 *Fortune* magazine article on the running and marathoning pursuits of corporate officials. "Other executives and their wives claim even larger benefits: running has improved their sex lives, made them stop smoking, cured hangovers, jet lag, ulcers, constipation, alcoholism, depression, and insomnia and prevented the common cold."

Lebow's vision of "you have to bring the race to the people" meant constant worry about money in the early years. When he gave out ten-dollar wristwatches to the top finishers in Central Park in 1970, sponsorship was not an issue, because Lebow's drive to promote his race was limited. But even as he became more of a power broker and as a result his preoccupation with cash grew, he did not let the absence of money deter his New York Road Runners Club from putting on races. In 1978 the club held a ten thousand-meter "bagel" run in Central Park only a few days after they sponsored, without corporate support, another one of Lebow's initiatives . . . his "Run Up" the Empire State Building steps—all 1,575 of them! Bagels were served at the Central Park awards ceremony. "We can't afford lox," said the race director, "but tell the people we'll have cream cheese!"

Sponsors were not always as quick as Lebow to see the emergence of the running boom. Lebow tried to enlist General Motors as a sponsor of his marathon in the fall of 1972, for a mere two thousand dollars, following the surge of interest in marathoning after American Frank Shorter won the gold medal at that year's Summer Olympics. Noting the "big, classy building" the auto company had recently opened at Fifth Avenue and Central Park, he proposed that the marathon start and finish could take place in front of their structure, and that their new experimental pollution-free car could be put into service as the marathon's lead car. The auto company replied that it was sorry it lacked money for such an event . . . only to come back a decade later with a one hundred thousand-dollar commitment!

Although Lebow was clearly onto something major in promoting big-time marathoning in the early 1970s, he was limited by his inexperience in packaging a sports product for corporate consumption. Not having had any formal education beyond high school in Romania (other than some technical courses at New York's Fashion Institute of Technology), it was not surprising that initially he found it hard to attract corporate cash.

John Carroll, a sports marketer who represented Lebow in this period, was reluctant to have the fledgling race director accompany him to the corporate executive suite. "I didn't think I could bring him into meetings with his shorts on. I asked him if he owned a pair of pants." Carroll told potential sponsors that Lebow's office was "in a phone booth at Grand Central Station," but he stressed the value of being involved in a "major event in New York, the number one market in America. We would use Fred as a sales aid to authenticate the race and to authenticate plans. Fred didn't then know much about marketing. He was smart enough not to talk about things he didn't know."

What Lebow lacked in professionalism, however, he made up in chutzpah. The pressure of finding sponsors for his first five-borough marathon in 1976 grew especially sharp inasmuch as in the prior year's race in Central Park, no major sponsors surfaced once Olympic Airways dropped out. Where would he find the cash now that he had the political okay in hand for his inaugural citywide race?

George Spitz—the New York State's Social Service Department employee historians credit with conceiving the five-borough project—was deputized by Lebow to write to potential sponsors. After completing a run in Central Park in late summer 1976, the two of them, recalled Craig Jenkins, who headed Finnair's Sports, Student, and Athletic Travel Department, "just walked into" the airline's Manhattan office at Fifth Avenue and Forty-ninth Street in their hunt for sponsors. "Two crazy men jogged over," he recalled, "wearing old sweat suits with holes, looking like slobs, asking if we would be interested in getting involved. Could we work with them and bring the top European runners to their marathon?"

According to Jenkins, in addition to Finnair's proximity to Central

Park, Lebow had other motives for coming to them for sponsorship, including the airline's association with Finland's top long-distance runners, Finland's reputation for political neutrality (a magnet for Lebow's dreams of globalizing his party), and Finland's record of harboring Jews during World War II, which "these two Jewish guys must have known about." Despite the informality of Lebow's request, Jenkins recognized the benefits of sponsorship for the airline. After providing Lebow and Spitz with drinks, Jenkins took the pair to Ilkka Mitro, passenger sales manager. "I'm a runner myself," said Mitro, who remembered being "captivated" by Lebow's "energy and good mood." "Fred understood our position," Mitro explained, referring to the fact that Finnair did not rank in the major financial league as did the banks and auto companies Lebow would eventually recruit. Joining as a sponsor, Finnair brought over about a dozen Nordic runners. In later years, the airline would transport stars like Norway's Grete Waitz and set up packages for travelers planning to come to New York for the marathon. In response, during the early five-borough marathons, Lebow had set up a "Finnish line" where the race ended in Central Park, and printed the Finnair logo on T-shirts.

What was Lebow's strategy in attracting sponsors? Did his salesmanship match his vision? How did he see the relationship between the bottom line and putting on the best possible marathon? Was he willing to turn over parts of his festival to his corporate empowerers?

In setting his sponsorship objectives, Lebow operated from the assumption that he was not simply directing a road race, but also serving as the crowd's advocate. "You have to bring the marathon to the people," he said. Sponsors would surface more easily, he reasoned, once they took note of his pageant's fervid large crowds.

But certain members of the New York Road Runners Club criticized Lebow for his aggressive courting of sponsors. According to the *New York Times,* members would "periodically resign from the club to protest what they perceive to be an unhealthful corporate influence." A wary Lebow noted in 1978, with only two five-borough marathons behind him, "We are walking on a tightrope between the runners being used by the sponsors and what the sponsors would get out of it. There is a legitimate concern among runners over why corporations should use them to further their own concern."

Politically, Lebow's increasing ability in the late 1970s to attract sponsors strengthened his power within his running club. This bearded, heavily accented Jewish Romanian émigré delivered the cash that made club races possible. His Yiddish accent, which contributed to his self-marketing, often served as his bargaining device. In negotiations, he would deliberately throw the other party off guard by making himself appear less sophisticated and less articulate. Elizabeth Phillips, one of the directors of Lebow's club, surmised: "He came on like, 'I don't know English too well, I'm just a guy from Transylvania.' But Fred got exactly what he wanted. Sometimes he got them [sponsors] to pay more money then they originally intended."

It was hard to mount a candidacy against such a successful money machine. "He would be the one to meet the sponsors," said Dick Traum, a club board member and founder of the Achilles Track Club for disabled athletes, "and the others would respect his street smarts." But his salesmanship also spurred envy. According to Traum, critics of the race director complained, "Here I am, opening envelopes, and Fred is off to the Tavern on the Green. Who is Lebow—he doesn't even have a high school diploma."

Some of the elite runners also criticized the power that Lebow's skills in finding sponsors brought him over long-distance running. The night before the 1981 marathon, Lebow's longtime nemesis, Bill Rodgers, found himself in a bizarre predicament. Perrier and the New York investment firm of Rooney Pace had agreed to sponsor Rodgers, and in return he was supposed to wear their names on his running clothing. Although Rodgers did not go for the idea, the matter was settled, with *Perrier* to appear on the front of his shirt and the Rooney Pace logo on the back of his shorts. Rodgers rebelled, however, when the finished clothing delivered to his hotel also contained the logo on the front of his shorts. After more arguing with the sponsor, Rodgers came to a decision. He refused to wear the sponsors' names, and, moreover, he would not run the marathon. But Lebow, who had been counting on Rodgers to add glamour to his festival, did not learn of the track star's decision until hearing it on the radio the following day while riding in the marathon's lead car. Since male winner Alberto Salazar set a world record in that year's event, the race director did not bother to approach Rodgers to compete in the next year's race. The ill feelings between the two did not end there, and as evidence of what Lebow called Rodgers's inability to "resist being negative about me," the following September the runner attacked the race director's relations with sponsors: "Fred knows next to nothing about running. But because he's dealing with sponsors who know absolutely nothing about running, he has himself in a kind of guru position. They come to him, and do what he says. I've built the [New York City Marathon] as much as anyone, and Lebow . . . treats all of us in a very condescending way."

Although Lebow realized the marquee value of "name" runners, his populist persuasion caused him to not overrate the superstar element in obtaining sponsor financing. Lebow saw the appearance of quality athletes as a way of furthering two paramount goals: recruiting a larger field of grassroots runners and gaining greater publicity for his marathon show. He told *Road Race Management* in February 1982: "It gives the event an identity to have the slower runners with the top runners. It gives the press an angle. It gives the event a chance for national publicity. If Joe Blow wins the Baltimore Marathon, no one really cares."

Despite the promotional genius that would become more and more obvious as his show grew, Lebow refused to exaggerate in his quest for sponsors. "Don't promise your sponsor something you can't deliver," he warned. "I always underestimate the number of runners, and the quality of the field to the sponsor so that the sponsor is always pleased." Following his own advice at the Central Park New Year's Eve Midnight Run, which drew thousands of revelers in all sorts of colorful costumes, the race director was careful not to oversell the event to sponsor Moet champagne. "If I know I can get 4,000 runners," he said, "I will tell Moet to expect 3,000."

Lebow also refused to come back to sponsors for cost overruns. "Sponsors, once they have accepted a budget, don't want to go back to the till. We get bargained down. If you make a mistake in the marathon, it comes back 16,000 times," he said, referring to the number of runners in the 1982 competition.

In the conflict between the sponsors' goal of publicity and Lebow's goal of maintaining the hallmark title of his creation, the "New York City Marathon," the race director never wavered. However entrepreneurial he might have been, the integrity of his show's name was beyond purchase, and his marathon had two big noes: selling its name to a sponsor and putting the sponsor's name on the front of the T-shirts. "The name of the race is the strongest thing that you have. It is the trump card."

Lebow's conviction about not sullying the name of his creation was tested in 1978, when into his cubbyhole office at the West Side YMCA came a public relations executive representing a large company seeking sole sponsorship of the New York City Marathon. Without disclosing his client, the PR man asked Lebow to name his price. The promoter threw out a one million-dollar figure. When Lebow was told that the would-be sponsor was a beer company wanting to see its name on the title of the marathon, calling it the "——— New York City Marathon," he recoiled. To maintain the right image he wanted for his show, Lebow sought only "quality" sponsors. He proudly noted offers he had turned down from a food company that provided the wrong image and from a prominent clothing manufacturer that was too money oriented and flamboyant. According to Lebow, the spurned company was so determined to play a role in the marathon, it offered a six-figure award to the race winner whether or not it became a sponsor—an offer Lebow nixed.

Lebow stressed the need for flexibility when either sponsors or government officials asked for a change in the marathon's route. Race directors, he said, mistakenly "fall in love with their course."

Banner size represented another trapping where Lebow said he would yield to a sponsor. Since the first order of business for Lebow when he arrived at a race site was the erection of the finish banner, or marquee, this was no small concession. Yet the positioning of sponsor names on the marathon's finish banner, and disputes as to under which sponsor's name winners crossed the finish, always resulted in delicate jockeying. Lebow took flack from Chemical Bank, for instance, in 1981 when women's winner Allison Roe finished under the Perrier sign rather than that of the bank.

Hyping marathon mania to urban America was more than a labor of love. It was also a labor of details. Sponsors put up dollars for his fanciful designs, yet they measured performance not only on the quality of his shtick, but also on attention to mundane details. "If we are sponsoring a track and field event and there is no water at the water stations for the athletes, or not enough T-shirts to go around," said Barbara Paddock, vice president and director of sports marketing at Chemical Bank, one of Lebow's sponsors, her company "looks pretty bad. Sponsorship is not just sitting at your desk and writing a check."

When it came to the safety of his runners, however, Lebow refused to compromise. Thus, as much as both sponsors and Lebow wanted the largest possible audience for his festival, he opposed starting the marathon later in the day when, in fact, crowds might be greater. A strong midday sun, argued Lebow, would make completing the marathon course more onerous.

Jeff Darman, president of the Road Runners Club of America, noted in an April 17, 1978, interview in the *New York Times* that "sponsors have been known to dictate a race's site, distance and time of day, sometimes not in the interest of the runners' health." As an example, Darman cited the Boston Marathon that started at noon and continued through the warmest hours of the day. "I think it's asinine," he said. "No race should start at noon with the sun beating down, even in April. It's a tradition, I know. But it's still a crazy time to run a race."

Safety, sponsorship, and theatrics merged for Lebow when it came to carpeting four of the bridges along the marathon course. The need to cover the bridge gratings had become apparent after race officials viewed the bloodied feet of British runner Chris Stewart following the 1976 maiden five-borough marathon. The ritual of laying the carpeting a day before the marathon always involved Lebow, who often brought along top runners with him to the Queensboro Bridge ceremony. Originally, sponsor Dupont provided the carpeting, and in 1990 Hoechst Celanese took over the role. The sponsor boasted that the length of carpeting to be pounded by marathoners was "nearly twice the height of the two World Trade Center buildings combined." To make the carpet laying telegenic, Hoechst sponsored special programs—such as fashion shows in which Lebow sometimes modeled—at the bridge. "Every TV station showed up at the ceremony," noted Hoechst marketing communications manager Ellen Kate Sweeney. "Fred would do anything we wanted."

Whereas the course route was lined with New York City Marathon banners (which the Road Runners Club sometimes sold after the race to souvenir collectors), Lebow scrupulously limited sponsor product banners. In keeping his stage noncommercial, Lebow differed from many other marathon organizers who succumbed to the lure of sponsor cash. Lebow's "love of the sport" was what drew him to "protect the integrity of the event from over-commercialization," according to Bob Thompson, advertising consultant to marathon sponsor Mercedes-Benz. Lebow's position, he said, contrasted with that of other race directors who were mainly concerned with "maximizing revenue, not caring a whole lot about quality." Based on Lebow's commitment to the quality of long-distance running, Thompson believed that the race director understood Mercedes' opposition to a "cluttered environment" along the course. "We didn't want to see corporate sponsorship up and down the street. They belonged only at the start and at the finish."

Realizing that it was nearly impossible for a runner to overhydrate during a marathon, Lebow stressed the need to include a bottled water company among his sponsors. Through its sponsorship of the New York City Marathon in its early years, Perrier made big headway in the metropolitan-area market. "As a result of his European background, Fred knew about Perrier," noted Jack Maguire, head of its competitor, Vermont Pure Natural Spring Water. Not only did Perrier provide water for the marathon, but the company also publicized the party on award-winning posters displayed on New York City buses and subways. So it was with a bit of chagrin that the race director noticed that runners were not interested in mineral water when 1981 male winner Alberto Salazar refused to drink Perrier at the race's finish. "I have an existing contract with Perrier," an aggravated Lebow told Vermont Pure's Maguire, "but if they walk away, I'll give you first crack." Eventually, Perrier did withdraw, and Vermont Pure became the water sponsor.

To the public, the New York City Marathon may have appeared as a unified festival, but on occasion fights did break out among sponsors concerning the visibility of their logos. Seiko dropped its sponsorship as official timer of the marathon after claiming that ABC-TV found more and more ways to clip its signage out of the telecast. According to David Strauss, assistant to the president of Seiko, "ABC was becoming too powerful in telling us what we can and can't do." The cameras stationed in the television network's cherry pickers at the marathon finish, argued Strauss, failed to give the watch company's name on the marathon's finish banner enough "exposure." Prior to that, Seiko had complained to the race director that signs from other sponsors carried by car sponsor Hertz blocked the name of the Seiko clock situated atop Lebow's Hertz marathon pace car.

According to *Road Race Management* in July 1988, the Seiko dispute illustrated that "there is no such thing as a free lunch." ABC took the position, said the newsletter, that if a logo is going to be shown, then that company should put some of its dollars into the network's coffers in the form of advertising. Lebow went to ABC trying to bargain for more exposure for Seiko. "I was sorry to see Seiko go," he said, "but we don't control TV."

Sorry at having lost Seiko as a sponsor, Lebow approached Strauss some years later at a track meet at Madison Square Garden. "I'd like you back in," Lebow told Strauss. Sensing that he could capitalize on the race director's eagerness to reenlist his company, Strauss replied, "I would be happy to come back, if we could negotiate a lower fee." Seiko returned to the marathon, at a reduced rate, in the role of supporting sponsor rather than that of the major sponsor it had been in the past.

Product competition sometimes surfaced in spite of Lebow's having officially designated a sponsor. *Road Race Management* noted in November 1991 the signage sneaker rivalry in the 1991 marathon: "While Asics served as the official shoe of the race, Nike hung a banner at the high-visibility Adams Apple bar at First Avenue where the TV cameras often take dramatic wide shots of the runners and the large crowds just as the runners come off the Fifty-ninth Street Bridge. The banner [however] was not really noticeable on the TV camera shot."

As much as he sought to cultivate sponsors, Lebow refused to compromise when he felt the dignity of the sport was at stake. Thus, as much as Lebow considered the Marrakech, Morocco, marathon the most memorable one he ran, he was disturbed when, at the finish, trays of cigarettes were being passed out, and it turned out the cigarette company was a race sponsor. He told the race organizers he would never return until they dropped that sponsor, and eventually they agreed.

In a logo controversy of the mid-1980s, where, ironic ship money pitted athletes against the actual running even surprisingly, favored the primacy of the event. The confl when sponsors, sensing the worldwide appeal of track money into signing up athletes as well as into races. But what would happen, worried Lebow, if on television, the T-shirt of a sponsored race winner carried the name of a company that was a competitor of the actual marathon sponsor? In 1985, running star Ingrid Kristiansen, a member of the Mazda Track Club, came to the Chicago marathon wearing her Mazda jersey in a race that had Nissan as a sponsor. Earlier that year, after winning the Boston Marathon, she had posed with a T-shirt bearing Mazda in large letters across her chest while collecting her Mercedes prize. Lebow, who had reached a handshake agreement to pay Kristiansen an appearance fee of forty thousand dollars, said he would honor his commitment only if she ran without the Mazda logo. Ultimately, a Solomonic compromise was worked out, and Kristiansen reduced the size of the Mazda logo so it would be no larger than the little *B* in sponsor Beatrice Foods's logo on the runner bib numbers. Later that year, Lebow averted a similar conflict with his marathon sponsor Mercedes-Benz when Rob de Castella, another Mazda runner, who had won the Boston Marathon in the spring, agreed to wear a small-size Mazda logo. Critical of the greed that undermined the marathon ideal, Lebow angrily said, "The athletes have to have some responsibility. It's shortsighted to accept a few thousand dollars from Mazda when it threatens existing sponsors. [The athletes] have to think of the long range [good of the sport,] not just [their personal] short term gain."

Lebow was so persuaded of his marathon's marketing benefits that he actually once offered to *pay* a potential sponsor in order to prove his point. The New York-New Jersey Buick Dealers Association wanted to provide two lead cars—one for male runners and another for females— for the 1983 marathon. Lebow wanted seventy-five thousand dollars for the honor. After being told that the car dealers thought this figure was "outrageous," Lebow put forth a proposition: The dealers would not be required to put up any money; instead, he would give them ten thousand dollars. They would supply the lead vehicles and afterward hire an independent analyst to determine what such exposure was worth. Lebow predicted that the survey would show that Buick's participation was worth one million dollars. He wanted 10 percent of that amount. Eventually, Lebow settled with the car dealers for fifty thousand dollars, plus the use of a Buick for one year.

Although Lebow recruited different categories of sponsors to underwrite his marathon festival, two supporters in particular stood out: Charles McCabe, the banker, and the Rudin real estate family. In addition to money, they gave his marathon cachet, advised on finance, fought his battles with city hall, and smoothed the way for problems his vision wrought. A marquee at New York City's Brasserie Restaurant, at Fifty-third Street between Park and Lexington Avenues, a block from the Rudins' headquarters, testifies to their help: "At this table since 1976, Percy Sutton, Fred Lebow, Jack Rudin and Charles McCabe have been directing the New York City Marathon." Borough president Percy Sutton, listed first, had been instrumental in bringing Lebow and Rudin together, and in gaining the political entrée to launch the first five-borough marathon in 1976. The two New York City establishment figures, McCabe and Rudin, had a relationship with each other predating their connection with Lebow. Both were members of the Board of Trustees of New Rochelle's Iona College, and McCabe's father-in-law, Paul Wagner, ran a scouting camp to which Rudin, his father, Samuel, and brother Lewis belonged.

Appearing on the New York scene around the same time as Lebow, McCabe started Manufacturers Hanover's in-house sports event unit in 1975. Both of these farsighted men focused on the city's emerging baby boomer market—one by promoting his bank, the other his marathon. Their ties continued after "Manny Hanny" merged with Chemical Bank, with McCabe holding the title of executive vice president in charge of corporate marketing and communications. (Chemical later merged with Chase Bank.)

What attracted Lebow to McCabe, however, was not only the bank's money, but also McCabe's marketing genius. "Charlie was an intuitively skilled marketing person," noted John Carroll of Capital Sports, one of Lebow's sports marketing agents during the marathon's early years. "Charlie gave us his marketing objectives, and we would come back with our programs." Lebow spoke with McCabe at least once a week, keeping him abreast of various projects. "If you don't sponsor an event," Lebow sometimes needled McCabe, "then Citibank will." These threats, noted the banker, "were never said in a malicious way."

When Lebow sought sponsorship by McCabe's bank, the race director was too shrewd to ask directly for money, according to New York Road Runners Club board member Steve Wald. "Charlie we need something; could you be of help" was how Lebow innocuously framed his requests. "Fred saw Manny Hanny as a parent who would rescue us," said treasurer Peter Roth. "Somehow the policy bore fruit. We would get more and more money by being in jeopardy rather than by showing restraint."

What did the bank gain by sponsoring Lebow's races? McCabe put it succinctly: "If we can attract you when you're enjoying yourself, maybe we can get our message across." The bank knew it had a winner in Lebow's marathon when a photo of 1978 marathon winner Bill Rodgers, crossing the Central Park finish wearing the bank's name on his bib number, appeared on the cover of *Sports Illustrated*. "Our reaction was," said bank vice president Barbara Paddock, "this must be good—it's the sort of advertising you could never buy." McCabe received a more personal confirmation of the value of his bank's name on bib numbers when he went to his doctor for a checkup. "I got to my doctor's office and there on the wall is his number, framed . . . with our name on it."

In addition to sponsoring the marathon, the bank tapped into running's mass appeal by sponsoring the Corporate Challenge, a 3.5-mile race where runners represented their companies. Some 130,000 runners representing 6,000 companies took part, making it the largest such event in the United States. In New York City alone, more than 30,000 middle managers and upper-level executives competed. Such exposure to running pleased Lebow not only because of his advocacy of the running lifestyle, but also because, ultimately, this type of participation triggered more entrants for his marathon.

McCabe's bank supported the marathon in ways other than direct financial sponsorship. When the Road Runners Club bought its town house headquarters on Fifth Avenue and Eighty-ninth Street, adjacent to the running lanes of Central Park, Manufacturers Hanover put up the mortgage, even though the club budget showed a deficit. Before the event was moved to Tavern on the Green, the prerace pasta party took place at Chemical's Park Avenue headquarters. On race day, bank employees volunteered to staff the pressroom, and race results were posted at bank headquarters on the Monday morning following the

race. On behalf of the marathon, Chemical sponsored special luncheons and dinners. They also sponsored the Ambassadors Program that
encouraged those with physical disabilities to participate in the
marathon and other running events.

In the competitive New York City environment of sports sponsorship, Chemical carefully guarded its turf. *Crain's New York Business* reported on May 24, 1993, "All of the art connected with Chemical
sports productions that depicts the Manhattan skyline—from marathon
T-shirts to the Mets own logo—has one feature in common—the distinctive Citibank building is missing."

As an act of both flattery and gratitude, Lebow always invited Mc-
Cabe to ride with him in the marathon lead car. McCabe was in the car
during the 1979 incident when Lebow, seeing barricades set up the
wrong way on the Pulaski Bridge as thousands of runners approached,
wound up shouting obscenities at a noncooperative sergeant posted at
the site, who in turn took out handcuffs, threatening to arrest him. It
was McCabe, along with Lebow's chief ham operator, Steve Mendelsohn, who pulled Lebow back into the van and sped away. "I had to
mediate so they didn't throw him out of his own race," recalled Mc-
Cabe about the overwrought race director.

It wasn't Lebow's recruiting skills, but his vision, as sold by Sutton,
that brought realtor Jack Rudin and the Rudin family on board, drawn
to the marathon for two reasons: his father Samuel's experience as a
marathoner and a commitment to New York City's quality of life. The
original Rudin sponsorship began when Sutton approached Lewis
Rudin for twenty thousand dollars to cover the expenses of Lebow's
original five-borough run in 1976. Samuel, the founder of the real estate empire, had died earlier that year, and though Lewis noted that the
family "was not excited" about their father's running during his lifetime, it took "two seconds [for me]" to answer affirmatively. Family-
sponsored silver Samuel Rudin Trophies, designed by Tiffany &
Company, were awarded to the marathon winners by Samuel's widow,
May, and after her death, the couple's great-grandchildren took over
the honors.

Although among New York City's wealthiest realtors, the Rudin
brothers did not see their sponsorship as a type of charity donation.
"We didn't think it was a philanthropy," said Lewis, who occasionally

worked in his executive suite wearing a marathon windbreaker. "[Marathon Sunday is] a day sprinkled with goodness. . . . I rode around with the Mayor," he said in 1995, "and there were no boos, only cheering."

Unlike other sponsors who were important to Lebow mainly because of their cash, the Rudins were also important for the political access they gave him. If Lebow needed a detour around a construction site at Central Park South, for example, it made sense to have Lewis Rudin, president of the Association for a Better New York, on his side. Politically, they enhanced the race director's credibility. For example, pictures of the city hall press conference announcing the first five-borough marathon in 1976 show Mayor Abe Beame flanked by Lebow, Sutton, and Jack Rudin. Together with Lebow, Rudin attended various city hall meetings over the politically charged issues of appearance fees and under-the-table payments to marathon competitors in the early 1980s. Later, when Mayor Ed Koch asked Lebow for money to pay for services the city provided on Marathon Sunday, Lebow turned to Rudin for help.

Within the Road Runners Club, critics of Lebow were silenced because of his close ties with this powerful family. Other sponsors seeking entry into the New York marketing arena respected the Rudin imprint. When Judith Woodfin, corporate vice president of Hertz, was considering sponsorship, the fact that she lived in a Rudin-owned property whetted her interest in the marathon.

As Lebow became more experienced in producing his marathon show, he noted that corporate America had developed increasingly sophisticated notions of what it expected from long-distance running. Asked in 1982, "What are sponsors looking for?" he answered rather simplistically: "[T]he bottom line is publicity." Six years later, in a more sophisticated vein, he would tell *Road Race Management*, "When I meet with sponsors, I'm hearing language that I never used before. One just said to me, 'Can you tell me the objectives of the event' and 'Tell me the scenario for press expectations,' and, 'How are we going to capitalize. . . ?' This is all new to me. This is why I subscribe to the *Wall Street Journal* and *U.S. News and World Report*. I have to read these to know what sponsors want."

The *New York Times*, on April 17, 1978, had noted the role of the

New York City Marathon in "changing the image of long-distance running from one of personal struggle to a joyous one shared by an entire city." Corporations, continued the *Times,* "saw the upbeat middle-income college-educated market move onto the roads. What better way to sell an image than by identifying with a healthy amateur sport?"

A 1983 survey of Lebow's New York Road Runners Club found that of its twenty-two thousand members, nearly 90 percent were college graduates with a then impressive average income of forty thousand dollars. The buying potential of these new affluent runners was not lost on corporate sponsors. Supporting the notion that runners were a well-heeled group was a 1987 study by Mercedes-Benz, which sponsored marathons in New York, Boston, and Los Angeles. Their study found that 42 percent of family heads earning forty thousand dollars a year or more jogged regularly and that 47 percent of potential buyers showing up at Mercedes dealers were joggers.

Further supporting the surveys—and reflecting some newfound problems resulting from the massive influx of upscale runners one year—was a mob turnout at the running gear shop that New York's Bloomingdale's had recently opened when the department store was cosponsoring a race with Perrier, both sponsors being well known at the time for their upscale clientele. When a Road Runners Club staff member protested to a Bloomingdale sales clerk as runners deliberated between complimentary tank tops and T-shirts, asking, "Can't we get these people to move any faster," the clerk tersely shot back, "How can you possibly give the Bloomingdale customer a fashion decision to make and expect them to make it quickly?"

As the New York City Marathon grew into the million-dollar-plus range, Lebow was continually confronted by runners and agents demanding more money. Despite the steadfast support of McCabe and Rudin, and Lebow's unflagging pursuit of sponsors, the race director would have had a hard time raising the new level of cash needed without the entry of John Hancock Financial Services on the running scene. Instead of simply sponsoring a marathon in the traditional sense, David D'Alessandro, corporate president of John Hancock Mutual Life Insurance Company, took the concept a step further by signing up some two dozen of marathoning's biggest names as Hancock runners.

When he met Lebow in 1987, D'Alessandro had never yet seen the

Boston or New York City Marathon. "It gives me a headache to run," he said. Lebow had contacted the John Hancock executive when he heard rumors that D'Alessandro was considering title sponsorship of Lebow's fall arch rival, the Chicago marathon. Lebow appeared in the lobby of a Manhattan hotel in his customary sweatsuit after running there to save cab fare. Both being busy men, they struck a deal after a ten-minute conversation for a sponsorship fee of $400,000.

More important to Lebow was D'Alessandro's agreement to buy a third of the advertising time on the ABC-TV network telecast for $400,000 a year. This move appeased ABC, which had recently reduced the marathon's rights fee because of declining ratings and poor advertising sales. The network still complained that Lebow was producing a pedestrian field of runners. By paying Hancock-sponsored athletes, rather than treating them as "chattel," D'Alessandro maintained he was bringing marathoning into the twentieth century. Lebow, whom *Road Race Management* had voted the "most powerful man in road running" in 1988, felt that based on the millions D'Alessandro was contributing to marathons and marathoners, "[D'Alessandro had] beyond a shadow of a doubt" taken over that title.

Conceptually, however, the Hancock sponsor differed from the race director as to the desirability of promoting marathoning from a populist perspective. Perhaps because D'Alessandro did not even own a pair of running shoes, he did not appreciate Lebow's goal of focusing his race on the masses. "If we continue to have these spectacles in New York and the only real United States race is in Boston, eventually New York will be seen as a Sunday fun run," D'Alessandro chided Lebow in 1989. "It's in our interest to make sure this is truly a great athletic event as well as a New York happening."

"Be my guest," a chagrined Lebow replied, mindful that the ABC option expired the following year.

In 1994, after six years of providing the New York City Marathon with elite entrants at a cost of $500,000, Hancock backed off from bringing in its runners. D'Alessandro, citing ABC for having dropped its live coverage of the New York City Marathon after thirteen years of programming—a move Lebow desperately tried to forestall—added, "I'm not saying it's right or wrong, but you have to make a conscious effort to decide what you want to be." Lebow, proud of his race's grassroots orientation, made his decision by refusing to bow to D'Alessandro's argument that his marathon had deteriorated into one "for the serious but not professional runner."

Befitting the marathon enterprise, which by the end of Lebow's career would be leaving an impact of $100 million a year on New York City's economy, sponsorship was big business. Sponsors, divided into major and supporting categories, contributed $4.5 million in cash, not including product sponsorships of drinks, pills, cars, magazines, deodorants, caps, T-shirts, soaps, and the like. In the New York Road Runners Club's 116-page press book, in which major sponsors each received a page to describe themselves, the major sponsors—who by Lebow's final curtain in 1994 each paid up to $750,000—included Chemical (Chase) Bank, *Runner's World* magazine, the Rudin family, Mercedes-Benz, BFI Waste Services, Asics, and John Hancock.

Certain sponsorships brought "official" status to contributing companies, such as "the official marathon sandwich," "the official marathon mover," and "the official marathon pain reliever." Thus, Advil would boast that in addition to being the sponsor of the Advil Mini Marathon, "the most prestigious all-women's running event in the world," it had "once again been named the official pain reliever" of the New York City Marathon.

While Lebow was selling sponsorship of his marathon festival, he was also selling a presence in New York's retail and consumer market. Sponsors already well positioned in the city saw involvement in the marathon as consistent with business. Ronzoni's sponsorship of the marathon's prerace "carbo-loading" dinner fell into that category because New York represented 60 percent of Ronzoni's market. Similarly, most of sponsor Chemical Bank's customers were New Yorkers. And, according to corporate executive vice president Jim Quinn, Tiffany's, which provided 185 awards and trophies, including the handcrafted sterling silver Rudin trophies designed by master silversmiths, saw its sponsorship as a "natural association with a classic New York event." Since Tiffany's "flagship store" was based in New York, said Quinn, he wanted "to make sure there was a Tiffany touch in an event that brings positive attention to New York City." On Marathon Sunday, Tiffany's placed an ad celebrating the race on page 3 of the *New York Times*. Souvenir seekers were able to buy a Tiffany crystal paperweight, etched with the logo of the New York City Marathon, for less than $100, and the upscale jeweler showcased the Rudin trophy in its Fifth Avenue store following its policy of displaying the trophies of other sports events such as the Super Bowl and the U.S. Open Tennis Championship.

In addition to those sponsors already established in New York, other companies viewed linkage with Lebow's marathon as a way of penetrating the New York market. "We were a benign New York company looking for more support from young and old people," said Judith Woodfin, corporate vice president of Hertz, the company that provided lead vehicles and other cars for Lebow in the early 1980s.

When BFI Waste Services sought to enter the New York-area market, Phil Angell, assistant to the chairman, said the company told its PR agency to find an event that would give it "visibility and credibility." The New York City Marathon, according to Angell, lent itself to BFI's goal based on its reputation as "the premiere marathon in the world and one of the premiere institutions of New York City." "We were the first outside company trying to break into the trash market in New York City," Angell explained. "Fred was concerned that we were a respectable company and that we wouldn't embarrass the institution he created. We knew that Fred worked long and hard to build the marathon. Once he saw we were a billion dollar corporation, and who our chairman was . . ." Their chairman was William Ruckelhaus, twice administrator of the U.S. Environmental Protection Agency and former director of the FBI. The race director did become enthusiastic about BFI sponsorship.

As a young executive living on New York City's West Side in the 1970s, Jack Maguire never expected that some twenty years later he would supply Lebow with 130,000 twelve-ounce bottles of water for thirsty marathoners. After working himself up the ranks of the bottling industry, Maguire bought a sleepy New England company, changed its name to Vermont Pure Natural Spring Water, and approached his speculative venture with the same philosophy as Lebow: "First Fred had a dream, then he worried about money."

Sponsorship of the marathon, said Maguire, not only meant entering the New York market, but also increased the likelihood of his taking Vermont Pure into the public investment arena. Investment houses told Maguire, "You must have a solid foundation," such as being named the "official water" of the New York City Marathon. His marathon sponsorship did wonders for product recognition. Maguire saw sales rise from 500,000 bottles a year to 8 million. "Fred helped me grow my company," said the water company executive.

Lebow's loyalty to sponsors remained even if they formally withdrew from the marathon. In the years after Finnair ended its marathon sponsorship, Lebow made tickets at the finish line stands available to its company executives. Similarly, if Lebow needed a ticket for a trip to Europe, the airline would always be available.

Lebow's relations with sponsors were personal rather than corporate. With some long-standing sponsors, a handshake rather than a contract sealed the commitment. His sponsors developed into a network of friends who recognized they were involved with the central figure in the history of long-distance running. "With Fred you felt you were family," said Perrier's Jane Lazgin. She contrasted this personal tie with Lebow with other sports promoters, so anonymous in their style that "at times, I didn't even know their names."

Meetings between Lebow and his sponsors at the Road Runners Club office were vignettes of banter and improvisation. There was the race director seated in running cap and warm-up clothes, a small Romanian flag draped behind him, his office a patchwork of trophies, pictures, and packages sent by admirers. Opposite him were the sponsors in business attire with their marketing studies and printouts. Allan Steinfeld would be called in by Lebow to iron out specific business or race-course issues. From a nearby closet, the race director pulled out T-shirts as keepsakes for the sponsors as they took leave. Sponsor and publisher George A. Hirsch captured the scene:

> Meetings in Fred's office often took on a zany Laurel and Hardy style. People were constantly walking in and out to say something, and Fred would start flipping through the newspapers when he got bored. One time I brought Marc Cannon of Alamo Rent-a-Car to Fred's office to discuss a sponsorship idea. Among the numerous interruptions was a man on a ladder who fixed a ceiling light while talking with Fred. "It's like Grand Central Station in there," Marc said later. Still, he was charmed, and by the time we left, the Alamo Alumni Run had been created.

When Lebow greeted Seiko's David Strauss, he did not do so with a corporate handshake, but with a hug, the traditional European greeting of male friends. On his cluttered desk sat pictures of Mercedes' media consultant Bob Thompson's children; during their business meetings, Lebow asked about Thompson's wife, Alison, by name; and when Thompson's mother died, Lebow was among the first people Thompson phoned to reveal funeral plans, and both Lebow and Steinfeld attended.

Many of the sponsors, runners themselves, admired Lebow as the symbol of road running and global marathoning. Although Rolf Waldeis dealt with Lebow from 1988 to 1994, as Mercedes-Benz's production manager, he first met the race director in 1979 when they were both competing in a half marathon. "Fred knew the experience of a runner," said Waldeis. "He saw runners as professionals," a view Waldeis believed contributed to Lebow's understanding of the parameters of road race sponsorship.

Tiffany's Jim Quinn, a New York City Marathon finisher, said, "Fred was one of my heroes. Here's a guy who started with an idea some twenty-eight years ago and, just by force of his native personality, turned the idea into a world-class event."

Based on their friendship, Finnair's Ilkka Mitro was able to persuade Lebow to attend marathons in his home country on two occasions—Finlandia in 1978 and the Helsinki City Marathon in 1987—where Lebow helped to organize the finish line. "Fred was a citizen of the world," said Mitro. "He was a European, a New Yorker, a Jew."

When Vermont Pure's young Jack Maguire first met Lebow in the mid-1970s, he was drawn to running by the publicity of Frank Shorter and Bill Rodgers. "I was crazy enough to think I could land with those people," recalled Maguire. In order to be closer to Lebow, Maguire volunteered to stuff envelopes outside the race director's cubbyhole office at the West Side YMCA.

To sponsors, Lebow's dedication became a subject of hyperbole. "One might have laughed at him, because he had the force of a *meshugana* [a crazy man]," said Hertz's Judith Woodfin, "but I've never met anyone like him in his focus."

Lisa Sepulveda, vice president of Advil's ad agency, Edelman Public

Relations, considered Lebow's personal presence at their mini-marathon—their "flagship sponsoring event" that drew some seventy-five hundred women entrants—integral to the race's success.

Lebow performed all sorts of hands-on antics so sponsors would stay committed to his festival. At a running demonstration in 1993, during a Tavern on the Green press conference inaugurating BFI Waste Services' entry into the marathon, he showed how runners should dispose of used drinking cups along the racecourse. At other events sponsors asked him to appear at, Lebow bestowed his imprimatur by dressing in the sponsor's T-shirt.

The media-savvy Lebow turned to sponsors when he felt they could help his cause. In 1983 he was invited to a small private audience with Pope John Paul II at the Vatican together with *Runner's World*'s George Hirsch. After being presented by Lebow with a New York City Marathon T-shirt, the pope commented that it was a marvelous event known throughout the world. Lebow phoned Hoechst's Ellen Sweeney to ask her to inform the New York media about the meeting, then turned to Hirsch, who noted the "twinkle" in the race director's eye as he told him, "It should get good press tomorrow."

Lebow was a stickler about staffers and volunteers wearing the right sponsors' clothing at race events. Françoise Granville Levinsohn, who led runners in warm-up exercises at various events, remembered Lebow walking up to a friend of hers who was working with her to pull off the friend's cap because it did not have the right sponsor's name on it.

Some sponsors developed camaraderie with elite runners in addition to their close ties with Lebow. Grete Waitz, for instance, who often accompanied the race director to ceremonies dedicating the carpeting of the Queensboro Bridge, got in touch with carpet sponsor Hoechst's Ellen Sweeney for ideas about what to wear when she was asked to christen the Norwegian Cruise Line's SS *Seaward* in New York in 1988. Sweeney outfitted the Norwegian star in a Trevira Linensque suit by the designer Kasper, but when it came to finding shoes for Waitz and Hoechst was unable to provide any, she went shopping with Waitz at Bloomingdale's, buying her a pair for five hundred dollars.

Lebow used his running world connections to help sponsors set up publicity events and press conferences independent of the marathon. He helped Seiko's David Strauss "get a Norwegian thing going" at a

New York press conference in honor of the watch company's role at the Lillehammer Olympics and obliged Mercedes's Bob Thompson by autographing posters at a race the car dealer was sponsoring in New Orleans. He also traveled to Vermont to add stature to the 10K race sponsored by Vermont Pure.

To be sure, Lebow did not view these appearances and projects solely as opportunities to curry favor with sponsors. Seeing himself as a missionary for the running lifestyle, he welcomed such exposure for his own vision. As a missionary, he required a reputation for integrity in order to carry out his charge. After facing the race entrepreneur's sales skills, it would have been easy for sponsors to conclude that Lebow might have been inclined to cut corners for the sake of financing his party, yet an impression of honesty prevailed. "He could talk you into anything," said Perrier's Jane Lazgin, "but he did it with honesty."

Thus, in bringing his footrace to universal renown, appearing everywhere in freebie outfits given by sponsors, he transformed the notion of not only who should run in a marathon, but who should pay for it as well. He brought corporate America into the publicity-charged enterprise of marathoning.

So committed philosophically was the race director to the idea of corporate sponsorship that in a trip to Cuba in the late 1980s, accompanied by his technical director Allan Steinfeld, Lebow seemed to forget that the communism he had fled as a teenager had an aversion to private enterprise. According to Steinfeld, "[Lebow] didn't understand the Communist thing when we were in Cuba. We went to talk to Alberto Juantorena, the old Olympic champion, who was head of the sports federations. And Fred kept asking him, 'Who's your corporate sponsor? Who runs ads in your newspapers?' "

He had come a far cry from his first obscure Central Park marathon, devoid as it was of sponsor money—when from his own pocket, not corporate dollars, he had bought ten-dollar prize wristwatches, and heard complaints from runners that he forgot to bring a can opener for the soda. But even back then, Fred Lebow understood the need for shtick to make his dream a reality. And with corporate funds to add new shtick, he would be able to make it grow!

A young Fred Lebow participating in a traditional Jewish wedding. Courtesy of New York Road Runners.

Despite his painter's cap, Fred Lebow is out of uniform here, wearing a New York Road Runners Club T-shirt instead of one of his signature running suits. Courtesy of New York Road Runners.

Having survived a malignant brain tumor, Fred triumphantly runs the 1992 New York City Marathon accompanied by the members of his protective entourage. Courtesy of New York Road Runners.

Fred crosses the finish line in the 1992 New York City Marathon together with close friend, entourage member, and nine-time New York City Marathon winner Grete Waitz, their bib numbers reflecting their respective ages. Courtesy of New York Road Runners.

Closeup of Dominguez's statue of Lebow, showing the race director checking "his" runners' times as they approach the finish line in Central Park, where the statue originally stood. Courtesy of New York Road Runners.

Fred wore his signature painter's cap and running suit whether he was on the track or addressing his runners, his marathon sponsors, or the press. Rare were the times when he deviated from this basic outfit. Courtesy of New York Road Runners.

Here Fred is shown wearing the official New York City Marathon cap, standing in front of the New York Road Runners Club. Courtesy of New York Road Runners.

Another shot of Fred in his signature running outfit. Courtesy of New York Road Runners.

A rare shot of Fred Lebow in his office wearing ordinary business attire. Courtesy of New York Road Runners.

Founder of the New York City Marathon and instrumental in making distance running a sport for the everyman and everywoman, here is Fred Lebow hitting his stride! Courtesy of New York Road Runners.

New York City mayor Rudolph Giuliani and Fred Lebow's Bronx-born alter ego, technical director, and successor Allan Steinfeld accompany the frail race director. Lebow's contributions to the city were honored with the naming of East Eighty-ninth Street (around the corner from where his statue would later stand) "Fred Lebow Place." Courtesy of New York Road Runners.

8

Shtick

IT WAS TIME FOR FRED LEBOW TO PAY the bill for the feast at Tavern on the Green as it ended on the Saturday preceding 1988's Marathon Sunday. Walter C. Rauscher, Tavern's manager, asked the race director to pay for 9,000 brunches consumed by raucous marathoners who had snaked over to the restaurant from the United Nations in the International Breakfast Run. "You thief!" screamed Lebow. "There are only 7,000 runners here." Lebow had guaranteed 7,500 diners. "My people gave me the 9,000 number," insisted Rauscher, who recalled that "Fred then went crazy. He was screaming, chasing me around the tent, calling me every name in the book. . . . I said, 'Fred, how do you know better than I how many people are eating here?' Answered Lebow, 'I put out 10,000 T-shirts. There are 3,000 left. A runner will do anything for a T-shirt.' " Rauscher, being a runner himself, understood this logic. "We'll stick by your number Fred," he conceded.

For Lebow, the T-shirt was, from the beginning, the main fashion vehicle for showcasing his marathon and his other races. Not every runner, said Lebow, came away with a trophy. But all wanted this heroic garment added to their wardrobes identifying them as runners.

More than anything else in the athlete's wardrobe, the T-shirt epitomized the party spirit that animated the day. A jaunty fashion statement, a T-shirt revealed the wearer's direction. Some dressed in the marathon T-shirts given to each of them at the Marathon Expo. Others wore thicker, pricier Ts. With their comfortable quality, T-shirts came with scooped necks and V-necks and carried such messages as the runner's name, track club, city, profession, favorite song, hoped-for finishing time, pet political cause, a blurb about their love life, or a humorous connection to Lebow's show. What message to display on the T-shirt was a weighty decision for runners because their T-shirts truly made a statement. Not only did they tell something about the runner, but they also helped make a connection with the crowds.

According to sociologist Jeffrey Nash, psychologically the practice of awarding T-shirts to all finishers "symbolized the individual conquest of failure." But to Lebow, with his customer-based strategy, the T-shirt certified the runner's role in his party. It showed the world that the wearer epitomized clean living and fitness.

Lebow did not begin the T-shirt fad, but he was clever enough, from his garment-center exposure to human vanities, to see its promotional value. Not only did he supply his runners with this piece of apparel, he also gave T-shirts to presidents, and even to a pope. His Upper East Side apartment held little in the way of conventional clothing, but the closets were stuffed with no less than 1,000 T-shirts.

T-shirts figured in the race director's strategy in recruiting volunteers for the marathon. "People asked me all the time," said Lebow, "how we get over 7,000 volunteers for the marathon (not to mention the 6,000 [other helpers] along the course, and volunteers for [all] 100 [of our] events. I answer: 'Never underestimate the power of a T-shirt.' "

Like a Santa Claus figure, Lebow would schlep a big box of T-shirts to the annual premarathon warm-up meeting of New York City agency heads to finalize race details. These meetings took place at police headquarters at One Police Plaza. Lebow well knew that the successful execution of his marathon depended on the goodwill of the police and other city bureaucrats. When the meetings were over, Lebow and his staff brought the T-shirts to the center of the room. "They were like lions going after raw meat," said Bill Noel, Lebow's deputy. "These big civil servants and ranking police officers were just grabbing T-shirts."

When the star runners came to town a few days before the marathon, T-shirts were also used by Lebow to make headway. Ellen Finn, Lebow's elite-athlete coordinator in the late 1980s, gave marathon T-shirts to hotel chambermaids for supplying the invited runners with such amenities as extra bars of soap, garbage cans, or king-sized beds. Appreciation in the form of a marathon T-shirt would be shown to the 150 bus drivers who transported the runners from the steps of the New York Public Library to the Fort Wadsworth staging area early Sunday morning. The T-shirt became so connected with the marathon that when Lebow tried to give mementos other than T-shirts, the response was flat: shorts, hats, socks, headbands, shoelaces—none of them ever made the same type of hit.

The desire for the right-sized T-shirt was so strong that Lebow himself was once hounded by an angry runner in a Central Park race in which they were both competing. Lebow was trying to break forty-six minutes in the 10K meet, and a mile into the race, a runner shouted, "Hey, I ordered a large T-shirt and I got a medium." Lebow apologized, and the runner continued, "It's the second time it's happened." Once more Lebow apologized, looked at his watch, and found he was two seconds behind schedule. "The guy started complaining about the T-shirt again. I didn't say anything, and tried to speed up, but he stayed with me for the rest of the way, just keeping at it." An aggravated Lebow missed breaking forty-six minutes by three seconds, but the angry runner was still not finished. Getting in his last dig, he nudged Lebow in the race chutes and told him, "You know, you're one stuck-up guy!"

Sponsors also eagerly sought Lebow's marathon T-shirts as promotion vehicles. From 1988 and 1994, Rolf Waldeis, Mercedes-Benz's production manager, carefully rationed out New York City Marathon T-shirts among its twenty-five New York-area dealerships and its national sales force.

T-shirts were not, by a long shot, the only promotional tool used by Lebow. Once his vision caught on and marathons sprang up in Los Angeles, Berlin, London, and Moscow, and in Asia, Africa, and South America, Lebow's constant challenge was to add a new dose of magic to his creation to set it apart from would-be competitors. He relished coming up with innovations designed to make his urban theater more exciting—innovations such as personalized T-shirts, more extravagant race parties, tighter competition among elite runners, new international trappings, prettier medals, growing number of bands along the course, greater numbers of celebrity runners, and more passionate, burning, and excitable crowds.

In searching for new ways to plug his marathon show, Lebow voraciously studied newspapers. Newspapers served a more important role for Lebow than simply reporting yesterday's races and games. For a showman who thrived on not playing by the book and in improvising glitzier challenges, it was critical that he be aware of the latest social trends and the types of stories the media featured. Eating breakfast alone in his office, he scoured the papers daily for an hour. If anyone joined him for the meal, he would ignore the visitor. "That was his private time," insisted his assistant Allan Steinfeld. To escape distraction, Lebow would even retreat to his private office bathroom on occasion. Wherever he was, he first turned to the sports pages, pleased to see his name in print, and then examined the papers with an eye for promotional strategies. "He looked for products to give out at races and scrutinized logos," observed girlfriend Paula Fahey. If he found a story or ad especially informative, he tore it out for future reference. Intrigued by creative marketing strategies in print, he told Fahey how taken he was with the subtlety of a gay magazine ad that avoided directly mentioning a gay market for its product.

Promotion was basic to Lebow's marathon strategy. It helped that the times were so favorable—when Lebow arrived on the New York scene, the running boom was in its infancy and social movements marked by "to be equal" themes were in vogue. Whether in terms of gender or race, notions of limitations or exclusions were being abandoned. But it was with his promotional skill that Lebow fused both of these incipient movements: the running boom that was part of the greater fitness movement and the wider social revolutions of the 1960s and 1970s. Marathoning manifested the spirit of fulfillment and opportunity in the new pop culture.

To help him attract people to his marathon and the running way of life on a large scale, he developed a relationship and rapport with the media and created shtick and news connections as handles for them to grab onto to keep the excitement of his show in the news. His campaigns used billboard displays, city hall ceremonies, and press conferences, but mainly they featured Lebow in his signature running outfit doing his shtick. He missionized to all population groups, but he most highly targeted the yuppies with their lifestyle of fitness, hedonism, and personal secular achievement.

Though no official religious breakdown of his marathon exists, given the high educational and professional level of New York City Marathon runners, it is fair to assume that a sizable number of the athletes, at least from the New York metropolitan area, were Jewish. Perhaps it was Lebow's background that enabled him to show awareness of his Jewish constituency in special ways, like the time when, in his desire to add new attractions to his show, he offered one thousand dollars to any Hasidic Jew running in side curls and tzitzit (religious fringes) who completed the race. Although nobody took him up on his offer, Lebow did make his point, and the offer got a little of the much-sought-after press coverage.

Lebow's shtick came in *all* variations. Possibly the most absurd, yet quite practical, was "the world's largest urinal" that was first put into service in 1979 when Lebow, trying to reduce the number of Port-O-Sans, asked engineer Logan Hurst to design a large trough to accommodate the marathoners. Using plastic piping, Hurst designed a 288-foot monster that always wound up getting great media play. Between marathons, the urinal was stored in a Jersey City warehouse. "It's seasoned like a good frying pan," said Vic Navarra, in charge of the Fort Wadsworth start.

When interviewed by a running publication about "advice" for other race directors, Lebow focused on the shtick necessary to add excitement to his party. "Just this week we are changing our club's race entry forms to announce the 'race party' instead of the 'awards ceremony.' . . . We realized all of a sudden that only one percent of runners in a race are getting awards so why should the rest of them go to the awards ceremony? Now, we will focus the post-race attention on a party for everyone."

But the postevent party was not the only party of his show. In fact, a large percentage of Lebow's shtick was geared toward making his marathon one big series of parties, one after another, beginning with the Marathon Expo where the runners received their official T-shirts, and a whole lot more. It wasn't with music and dance, but through the camaraderie and benign sense of heroism it fostered that the crowded Expo lifted the spirits of Lebow's marathon runners. On exhibit at the Expo were such items as running gear, power drinks, nonprescription painkillers, and a race video where a scene of the marathoner triumphantly crossing the finish could be dubbed in. Concurrently with the Expo, Lebow ran clinics on the psychology, health, training, and business aspects of his marathon dream.

The day before the event each year, thousands of competitors, carrying flags from nearly all member states of the United Nations, ran from the headquarters of the international organization to the Tavern on the Green where a buffet breakfast awaited. The picture of this colorfully moving column was certain to alert the Big Apple to the imminence of Lebow's show.

That night, a complimentary pasta party would be held at Tavern on the Green for the thousands of frolicking runners. This bash proved the old carbohydrate adage that "more is more." In 1988, a group of six thousand marathoners consumed ten thousand pounds of hot and cold Ronzoni pastas, ten thousand Bellcicco bread rolls, five hundred cases of Miller Lite beer, and three hundred cases of Perrier. They topped it off with ten thousand sweet but healthy Crystal Light Frozen Juice Bars for dessert. In his New Age marathon, what happened in Tavern on the Green's dining room was no less critical to Lebow than the design of his five-borough racecourse. When seventeen thousand runners were frolicking at the premarathon carbo-loading party in 1989, Lebow neither schmoozed nor traded quips. Rather, the impresario was on a mission, inspecting the jammed area, making sure that food and drinks were constantly replenished for the next day's marathoners. "I would follow him around," Tom Monetti, the restaurant's managing director, said. "I knew he would find something. He'd find a place setting getting low, or that we ran out of yogurt cups."

The Marathon Sunday party began early in the morning, with one hundred or more buses transporting the runners to Fort Wadsworth from their gathering place beneath the watchful eyes of the stone lions that guarded the steps of the New York Public Library. When they arrived at the staging area, they were greeted by huge tents where they could stretch, grease themselves, join exercise classes, listen to well wishes from politicians, and tank up on a variety of hot and cold beverages as curtain time drew closer.

Lebow's parties continued at the foot of the balloon-swept Verrazano-Narrows Bridge with the runners falling into formation to the "tunes" of the first music of the marathon, including the droning of the helicopters and the chutes of water sprayed by boats in the harbor, all reaching a crescendo with the cannon shot that would launch that year's edition of the New York City Marathon extravaganza and the excitement of more than twenty-five thousand runners heading out over the bridge.

Party decorations lined the course for the runners and viewers alike: marathon banners hung on lampposts, countless homemade signs were held aloft by fans, intermittent water and sports drink stands were manned by volunteers in yellow raincoats, and Lebow's traditional blue line told runners and viewers alike where the party was heading.

To help keep the runners' in the party mood, and help dispel any sense of runners' pain, some fifty bands—ranging from rock to jazz, from Dixie to Japanese and reggae—lined the course, providing rhythmic inspiration during the 26.2-mile party. A 1995 issue of *Runner's World* noted how the members of Avant Garbage—a "Zen guitar-drum duo"—saw the chemistry between the music and the marathoners: "We send out energy, the runners send it back," observed guitarist Phil Sudo.

Those spectators who preferred to get a taste of Lebow's carnival gastronomically rather than athletically could party at the sumptuous $125-per-diner "Start-to-Finish" banquet and open bar—feasting on such delicacies as Scotch smoked salmon, penne with shrimp and basil, miniature cheese ravioli primavera, and raspberry charlotte russe, in an enclosed and heated tent adjacent to the finish line at Tavern on the Green—while they earnestly commiserated, via fifteen color television monitors, with the sweaty-faced marathoners they could see pounding their way through the Big Apple.

The marathon party ended, officially, as the marathoners crossed the Central Park finish, many of them waved in by Lebow himself, and received medals and refreshments. Women finishers were also awarded with roses, a prize idea the race director had picked up in Vienna.

Following a press reception for the winners, the postmarathon "awards ceremony" that blossomed into the "race party" as Lebow's expertise grew was held with much fanfare at the Imperial Ballroom of the Sheraton Hotel. Underscoring the solemnity of honoring the winners of Lebow's extravaganza, Tracy Sundlun, executive director of the Metropolitan Athletic Congress, presided in black tie. A musical background accompanied the presentation of awards, and a video replay of the marathon's highlights was shown. "It was the premiere, most formal, most staged" running awards ceremony in the United States, said Sundlun. "In this festive, high level atmosphere, Fred tried to show off the event." But for the majority of marathoners, the closing party took place at the postrace disco at Roseland, where, according to *Running News* magazine in 1988, marathoners of all ages and dancing styles were able to "work out the lactic acid building up in their muscles to the beat of Mindy and the Cyclone Rangers from 9 P.M. till the wee hours. The single-level format of the dance floor and lounges made for easy viewing of ABC's video coverage of the day's race."

In addition to creating his own media attractions, Lebow tied into politics and news-making events to provide him with additional outlets to promote his message. A careful follower of what was happening in the news, he moved to exploit developments by connecting them with the running lifestyle. With his ability to find "the silver lining," Lebow was quick to seize news events as promotional opportunities; political labels were unimportant to the race director, and politicians were there as a means to generate publicity. Like many visionaries, Lebow disseminated his message with an unflagging optimism that spread: a New York City transit strike was a chance for people to put on their running shoes and get out on the streets—he even set up a water station on the Brooklyn Bridge—and the infamous Central Park-jogger rape was a catalyst for a safety patrol by his running club and the establishment of community programs in the park.

When Democratic presidential candidate Senator Gary Hart of Colorado sought to give a zing to his core boomer constituency before the 1984 New York State primary elections, his campaign staff wanted to make use of Olympian Frank Shorter's endorsement of his fellow Coloradan. But they were uncertain how to best use the star runner's backing to gain support among New York voters. Bill Michaels, race director of Denver's Mile High Marathon, suggested that Hart and Shorter run together in New York, the obvious locale being Central Park, and since Central Park was New York Marathon turf, Hart's staff asked Lebow for help. "When Fred saw a chance to publicize running," reported Michaels, "he went after it," and candidate Hart, Fred Lebow, Frank Shorter, and *Runner's World* publisher George Hirsch went for a run together, in Central Park, in front of a crowd of several hundred onlookers. Hart, who according to Michaels "never ran more than 100 yards in his life," dropped out of the race early on, yet the scheme worked. According to Michaels, photos of the "icons of running," Lebow and Shorter, accompanied by Hart, made the political pages in a big way. "It looked in the press like there were thousands of people present," he said. The coverage probably helped Lebow as much as, if not more than, it helped the politician.

Lebow also promoted marathon mania by giving his party an aura of exclusivity. Each year tens of thousands of applications were turned away because of lack of space, so why not publicize the great lengths runners went to in order to have their applications accepted? The stories of desperados seeking admission to Lebow's party ranged from the ordinary to the outrageous. Claims of lost mail, the need to run the marathon in order to maintain one's sanity, or errant secretaries who bungled their bosses' applications were regular fare. Marathon officials reported turning down bribes running in the thousands of dollars, and Lebow personally reported rejecting applicants who used sexual games. One year, a tall, blonde thirtyish woman came down from Massachusetts to appeal to the race director. Running in the marathon, she said, would prove to herself and to her ex that she was worth something. She wanted to spend time with Lebow in New York, but when he asked directly whether it was his company or gaining admission to the marathon that was her goal, she confessed that her priority was, indeed, a ticket to the five-borough race. In spite of potential problems from women such as this, adding women to his party gave Lebow a lot of timely promotional material in addition to fitting in with his dream of total inclusivity. It is said that the first women's Olympic marathon, in 1984, took place largely as a result of the impetus the sport received from his shows.

After the 1971 Central Park marathon, where Beth Bonner and Nina Kuscsik became the first women in the United States to break three hours, a media-attracting controversy arose, to Lebow's benefit. Angered by the participation of the two women, the AAU, which at the time served as the national regulating body of track and field, called them illegal entrants. In a spirit of grace, however, they ruled that the following year women would be allowed to compete, but that they would be required to start ten minutes earlier than the men. All of

Lebow's few hundred entrants that year, men and women alike, signed a petition, circulated at the starting line, demanding a common start.

In 1972, this controversy gave Lebow's young creation another promotional boost when the six women registered to run became outraged and staged a sit-in at that year's starting line. They wouldn't, and didn't, begin the race until the men's starting gun went off, and they subsequently sued the AAU for promoting discrimination in a public place, a violation of the landmark 1964 Civil Rights Act. By the following year, women were competing on an equal footing with men.

When the promoter instituted the tradition of giving each woman to finish the New York City Marathon—all seven thousand of them—a rose, "Some people complain[ed] that I'm sexist," quipped Lebow, "[but] I don't care. Seven thousand women love it." And speaking of roses. . . ! "Running into romance" was another way Lebow hyped his marathon party. By hooking up with Lebow's races and social events, a couple took the first strides to intimacy. "More romances are made on running courses," Lebow claimed, "than in singles bars," and his club's magazine, *New York Running News,* also committed to love on the racecourse, noted in November 1987, "In this most personal of sports, even small gestures can become intimate; a smile at the starting line, a nod of encouragement in the middle of a race, or a glance at someone sporting a sharp running outfit."

Tales of runners finding spouses began appearing in *Running News,* which, in one such report, told how running had paved the road to romance for Allan Steinfeld (Lebow's right-hand man and eventual successor) and Alice Schneider (director of data processing at the racing club). Picturing them formally slicing their wedding cake, the magazine noted, "So when they married on May 17, not only was a romance celebrated and confirmed, but two NYRRC logistical operations were brought under one roof."

The fun setting of the New York City Marathon inspired romance in and of itself. Two marathoners married at the nine-mile mark in front of the Brooklyn Academy of Music. Elena and Brian arrived in New York from Atlanta, Georgia, to compete, reported *New York Running News* in February-March 1996. The couple dined at the Rainbow Room. Elena said: "Much to my surprise, Brian got down on his knee and proposed. . . . The enthusiasm of the runners, volunteers, and spectators practically carried us through the entire race. . . . The weekend will be fresh in our minds for the rest of our lives. Thanks for the memory, New York!"

The "personals" column of Lebow's magazine was designed to find a match for the fantasies of a high-energy, accomplished yuppie mate. Running prowess alone was insufficient to whet the appetite of this upscale reader. The October-November 1988 issue, for instance, carried this personal notice from those running strong in their romantic races: "You found her . . . Blonde, bright, beautiful, SJF, 31, 5"6', thin, athletic, great shape, successful, sweet, and sincere; has the best life can offer to share with you: tall, handsome, fit, accomplished, very successful, sincere male."

As the years progressed, with problems such as non-English-speaking marathon winners and the rise of other competitive sports, Lebow needed to work harder to keep his sport in front of the nation, and the world. Never at a loss for creative ways to use money to promote his party, some of his schemes smacked of hucksterism, like in 1992 when he offered a bonus of one million dollars to any male breaking 2 hours in his marathon, or any woman finishing in 2:15 or less. True, the offer drew publicity, but *Runner's World* columnist Joe Henderson accused Lebow in January 1993 of "cheapening the sport" by setting such impossible goals. A 2-hour men's record would have required clipping the existing record by nearly 7 minutes, a 5.5 percent drop. When Lebow announced his bonus, the men's world record of 2:06:50 had just dropped 22 seconds from the previous record, which had been set by Belayneh Densimo at Rotterdam in 1988. In the intervening years, no one had come within 45 seconds of Densimo's record. And for a woman to run 2:15, she would have to surpass the world's record by more than 6 minutes, or 4.3 percent. Ingrid Kristiansen had set the women's record of 2:21:06, and no female competitor had come within two and one-half minutes of Kristiansen's mark.

Given the physical impossibilities of realizing Lebow's offer, why did the impresario announce such a seemingly outlandish proposal? According to Lebow, it was to put running in the same high-paying league as other big-time sports. "Most runners haven't been exposed to big money," he argued. "In light of what Michael Jordan and others make, this is peanuts. Runners have to be motivated. They have to have a dream."

Despite the motivational power of money, argued critics of Lebow, the speed of the human body cannot be accelerated beyond a certain point. Lebow's reference to Jordan, wrote Joe Henderson, begged a comparison: "Would Jordan be told 'Here's your chance to win a million dollars per game, but you must score 150 points to earn it?' Of course not. Jordan is paid, and paid extremely well, to do the improbable, not the impossible."

Beyond this frivolous standard set by Lebow, his proposal was also at variance with a basic theme of his marathon show. On many occasions, the race director stressed that he wanted to produce a competitive race, rather than a speed race. Head-to-head competition was Lebow's formula for exciting the crowds, satisfying the sponsors and drawing the media. *Runner's World's* Henderson argued that the marathoners who deserved to be honored were those who competed at their best. Lebow's plan, claimed Henderson, "detracts from competition and instead contributes to runners' growing emphasis on times and records. It paints a race—and the top runners—into a no-win corner, where anything less than a record time is considered a failure."

How much was the marathon—with all its shtick, its glitz, its theater, its world fame, and the attention it would bring to its founder, promoter, and director—a narcissistic experience for Fred Lebow? How much a show he produced? How much truly an attempt to promote the running lifestyle? True, his activities as president of the New York Road Runners Club and as race director of the New York City Marathon were a road to prominence for Lebow, but for what reason did he want to be on this road? According to club treasurer Peter Roth, it was so he could work toward his goal. "He saw the presidency of the club as a place where he could make a mark. Having a purpose for him, was more important than money."

As marathon mania grew, and this peripatetic Jewish refugee emerged as the single most identifiable attraction in the fun Sunday he created, the *New York Daily News* was unable to separate the race director from his creation: "Trying to imagine this marathon without Lebow is as futile as trying to run it without training. It takes no effort at all to see him now in his race-day perch, in the back of the pace car,

barking out orders in his Eastern European rasp." If it ended there, it
might seem as though Lebow had built his show for his personal glory
. . . for the feeling of being in control . . . or for the adrenalin rush of
having succeeded in creating such a huge and successful event. But, as
the article continued, "his face [was] a study in worry. If it was your
child, wouldn't you worry?" Wouldn't you care, as a parent, in a mostly,
if not totally, selfless way?

A zealot in promoting his marathon, he continually rejected trivial
distractions such as money, clothing, and home furnishings. He had
neither time nor patience for such meaningless bric-a-brac. The one
worldly indulgence he continued to permit himself was the company of
gorgeous women. "Fred always noticed an attractive woman," said
John Hughes, race director of the Disney Marathon. "He liked to hug
and be hugged." His colorful persona was attributable to the belief that
an individual could serve as a metaphor for a movement. Thus, in his
own eyes, "promoting Lebow" amounted to the same end as promoting the marathon. Whether Lebow was the object of attention or the
marathon institutionally was the object, it meant the same thing to the
race director. The question of Lebow's self-promotion must, therefore,
be seen from the perspective of how he was trying to buoy his
marathon. Don't worry folks, went his message; we're all on the streets
together, supplying entertainment via the medium of running. His
show's stars were Everyman and Everywoman, spurred on by their
dreams of going the distance, and Lebow saw to it that enough shtick
was on hand so that these magical performers—his grassroots, "ordinary," and commonplace runners along with the elite and star runners—would not be dragged down before they reached the Central
Park finish. "Think of him as an artist," advised Dick Traum. "But instead of working with clay, he worked with a concept." Within that concept stood the role of the race director as both hustler and charmer. As
Lebow confided to his club's treasurer, Peter Roth, "The strength of
the marathon has to be the strength of my notoriety."

9

Manipulating the Media

AS A NEOPHYTE RACE PROMOTER in 1970, Fred Lebow knew the importance of publicity, but, try as he might, he had no luck getting any until he "accidentally" learned the benefit of a personal visit with the press and the hype of a well-known name to get their attention . . . just in time to save his first marathon.

It didn't take him long to start courting the media in selling his party. According to *Runner's World* publisher George A. Hirsch, Lebow stroked the press "with a mix of finesse and gamesmanship. He knew the press needed real stories and good quotes, and he gave them what they wanted."

Nina Kuscsik remembered how Lebow, always looking for something to hype, prodded her as the date of his first marathon-producing endeavor, the 1970 Central Park marathon, approached. "Before the first New York City Marathon," she recalls, "Fred Lebow, the organizer, called me daily to see how my training was going and to urge me to predict a possible sub three-hour marathon. That time would set a world's record and the predictions would help publicize the race." (Kuscsik ended up getting the flu, "probably from all the stress he put on me," and spent that first Marathon Sunday in bed.)

Regardless of the absurdity of some of Lebow's shtick, there was always an awareness of the need for play in the media, plus the confidence that his vision would prevail. As spokesman for his vision, Lebow's persona—his gaunt figure, deep-set eyes, and signature running cap and warm-up outfit—added a measure of offbeat celebrity to his invitation to cross his party's finish line. "He was very identifiable," noted Jim Ferstle, a writer for *Road Race Management*. "He was a distinct character who stayed in your mind. He was a great caricature. People tried to mimic his accent. He gave people something to latch on to."

Rather than treat the media as outsiders doing a job, the impresario shrewdly involved them in his plans. He wanted journalists to feel that they had a stake in his festival's success. Whether it was a marathon-entry lottery at city hall or the welcoming of disabled Achilles Track Club athletes at the finish line, Lebow staged events for their media value. He manipulated the media's goal for a scoop. When interviewed, Lebow often prefaced his answer with his standard line for winning a reporter's confidence: "I've never told anyone this before." With this seeming confidentiality, "he was letting you know, not terribly subtlety," wrote *New York Daily News*'s Wayne Coffey on November 2, 1994, "that you had your scoop and you had darn well better put it in the paper." Lebow was especially close with media figures he considered useful in promotional schemes. "I had a direct-dial button to Fred's office, and we talked virtually every day in person or on the phone," reported Hirsch. "We talked about various things, but usually it was about running—the politics, the gossip, the athletes, the events, and the business of our sport."

Lebow maintained relationships with television meteorologists Storm Field and Mr. G, who were not only media representatives, but veteran marathoners as well. In addition to potential promotional pitches now and again, they provided the race director with weather updates as his marathon approached each year.

Television proved vital in drawing more attention to his sport. A large TV audience was an end in itself for Lebow. It would expose viewers beyond the streets of New York City to his marathon vision. He was so eager to obtain television coverage that he said, "I don't give a damn whether ABC paid us $5,000 or even if we had to pay ABC $5,000—I just wanted to get us on the network."

Despite Lebow's enthusiasm, broadcasts of his marathon failed to attract big television audiences. In its thirteen years on ABC, the race drew only 3 to 4 percent of viewers, in comparison with 45 percent for the Super Bowl and 22 percent for a popular prime-time program. How were these low viewing numbers explainable amid the American running craze? As David Downs, ABC-TV vice president for sports marketing, explained, "Participating in sports doesn't equal TV viewing. People who are fit aren't sedentary, watching TV."

The race promoter cultivated ties with ABC officials that went beyond the actual marathon telecast. Many media figures shared an ongoing relationship with Lebow because they themselves were committed runners. "I would bump into him while running in the park," said Downs. "We did not have a cold business relationship, because Fred understood our needs; it was far easier to deal with him than with other sports figures." "The marathon was not a money maker for us," Downs admitted. But ABC continued carrying the marathon, downplaying commercial considerations. "We did it because of the unique technical challenges, and the pride it engendered in our staff. It was the hardest sports event to broadcast. It was beyond belief what we had to do to cover it." Their coverage consisted of hundreds of people who operated two dozen cameras, five motorcycles, and five helicopters. Microwave technology was used for pictures that had to be transmitted from the motorcycles to the helicopters and the two television studios.

But getting his show on TV to promote it as an event was not the race director's only goal. He wanted the coverage to reflect the strivings of his grassroots runner. Curt Gowdy, Jr., coordinating national producer for *ABC Wide World of Sports,* said:

> Fred wanted to make sure that over the course of years the race became a celebration day in the lives of thousands of runners. . . . [He] stressed that the race went beyond the elite runners. He wanted to tell the stories of the back of the pack runners, the everyday people who enjoyed competing and finishing. It was important for the marathon to have important runners, but he was very interested in how we would tell the other side, the non-elite runners.

So ABC sent four or five reporters to run alongside the back-of-the-pack runners, "everyday people who enjoyed competing and finishing. We told the story of the seventy-five-year-old runner, or the airline pilot who went the distance. Fred wanted to make sure that in his marathon, all [the] men and women who wanted to participate could do so."

In its coverage, ABC's production crew also concentrated on the human aspects that made Lebow's production a special New York City event. Cameramen filmed offbeat street scenes. For New York City, the joyous spirit of Lebow's race brought an infinite capacity for celebration. "People came out to show joy, excitement, and exaltation. A lot of people were there to share the joy of watching their friends, their mom or dad, grandfather or grandmother," said Gowdy. More than ten thousand foreign runners, and the slightly smaller contingent of Americans hailing from outside of the New York area, pumped some one hundred million dollars into the city's economy. City employees involved in putting on the marathon benefited from its morale-boosting hype. The police took pride in closing the streets. Firefighters decorated station houses along the route. Sanitation workers and emergency medical personnel were caught up in the excitement of Lebow's invasion. "We tried to give viewers a sense of the place," Gowdy concluded. "We used creative vignettes about one of the world's great cities." So much did ABC focus on personal vignettes that, in 1990, the *Road Race Management* sports newsletter criticized the network for missing crucial breaks in the marathon: "ABC tended to drift away from the event, and mix in soft features about New York neighborhoods, rather than concentrate on the developing action in the streets."

Although the gaunt race director loved the drama of the athletes competing simply to finish number one, he did recognize the boost a new running record would give to his marathon vision because of the story it would provide the media as well as the renewed athletic validation it would provide his show. He became ecstatic when one was actually broken, even though he knew the ecstasy would quickly dim upon realizing that the coming year's race would not likely have the same sensation and he would, once again, need to work hard to give the media stories to keep his show in the news.

Lebow reached a true high in 1981—and gave the press a great story—when Alberto Salazar and Allison Roe both set world records at his marathon. Jumping from his director's Jeep at the Central Park finish, before the vehicle had even braked, Lebow threw aside the bullhorn with which he had been shouting his commands along the route, raced through the crowd, and embraced Salazar for the world record he had just set. After clearing room so Salazar could walk off his cramps, he watched Roe on a television monitor and proclaimed proudly, "Yes! She knows she can do it, and she's only got 200 yards. . . . She's got it, got it," and then threw his arms around the New Zealander, as soon as she crossed the line, for the women's record *she* had just set. But soon the TV interviewers took control of the winners, and Lebow was almost completely alone for the first time since before the break of dawn when, along the lines of a military operation, he had begun putting the last touches on his show at the Fort Wadsworth staging area. He was functioning on just one hour's sleep for the two prior days, and according to the *New York Times* on October 26, 1981, "[He had] heard his name called on the street corners in Bay Ridge and Harlem, just as Patton must have heard his name as his army raced through Italy." But rather than being in ecstasy about the tumultuous festival he had created, Lebow's letdown was saddening. When asked by a *Times* reporter about the shattered records, Lebow answered softly, "This is more than I ever imagined. *One* record I thought was possible . . . but I did not imagine. Now there is nothing left to dream. And for a few seconds," added the *Times*, "he turned his face to the vacant wall of a television van, and he seemed close to tears."

Lebow subscribed to the philosophy that the end justified the means. Hyping the show sometimes meant exaggerating, or simply changing the facts. Understatement or dispassionate descriptions were not the ways to showcase his festival. "From time to time," observed *Runner's World* publisher George A. Hirsch, "a good story might require him to alter the facts." Thus, when an entry to the marathon became a hot ticket, the impresario, in apparent pain, told Hirsch, "Just today I had to turn down requests from Koch and Cuomo." By capping admissions to the race, Lebow felt he added glamour to his party.

What was the nature of Lebow's lies? How did this tactic benefit him? Tracy Sundlun, executive director of the Metropolitan Athletic Congress, dismissed Lebow's reworking of the facts as being neither sinister nor selfish. "He didn't want to hurt anyone. He was out to do what was best for the sport, which also happened to be his life. He didn't say things, just to help Fred." Illustrating the lack of harm in Lebow's exaggerations, according to Sundlun, was the race director's habit of rejecting marathon applicants, even though there might have actually been spaces available. "He wanted his event to look exclusive," said Sundlun.

So important was media coverage to Lebow that when Stu Mittleman was about to set a record in an absurd one thousand-mile distance race, he congratulated Stu's mother, saying, "Well, Mom, you finally have a world champion," and in nearly the same breath turned to the ultramarathoner's handler and demanded, "Make sure he gets off the track now so he finishes when the TV crews are here in the morning."

10

Shrewdly Assembling His International Entourage of Runners

He was able to bring together a field of elite and "ordinary" runners.

FRED LEBOW'S WHOLE PUR-POSE in wresting the keys to the city, squeezing money from sponsors, creating his shtick, and manipulating the media was always to help him share his excitement for running with others. His goal was to convince everyone—Everyman and Everywoman—to put themselves to the test and join him at his marathon festival.

The racing impresario understood early on that he would need to recruit the world's best runners even though the marathon he was creating was designed as a "people's" footrace. Only the presence of world-class runners, he had learned, would enable his party to register an athletic impact and attract media recognition and sponsor money. Excited crowds lining the streets to see top runners perform would confirm—for the media and sponsors, as well as for the runners, and especially the "grassroots" runners—the force of Lebow's show.

For his first New York City Marathon, in 1970, Lebow's future prowess as a recruiter of runners didn't come into play. That marathon's world-class draws, Olympian Ted Corbitt and nationally known distance runner Vince Chiapetta, had entered the race because of their own involvement with the birth of the budding event.

Racing veteran Nina Kuscsik was the first female elite runner Lebow recruited. Signed up for his first Central Park marathon, in 1970, illness kept her from running in his show until 1971. By then,

Beth Bonner had also come on the scene. Lebow had cleverly recruited Bonner through her coach, Dave Romansky, who was, like Lebow, a women's distance-running advocate, and that very year, Bonner went on to become the first women's winner of the New York City Marathon, setting a new women's record time. This was all at a time when many believed long-distance running could prove physically harmful to women; women joked that it could even cause their reproductive organs to fall out! But Lebow saw women as capable runners, and as a constituency just ripe for his party. Including them also fitted right in with his desire to make his show inclusive and egalitarian.

The drive for there to be women runners in Lebow's festival reflected the social forces of feminism, yet certain athletes—committed to the sport rather than to the women's lib movement—resisted pressure for their participation to be seen as mainly an egalitarian statement. Bonner was one of the women who resented any tie-in between her running and the incipient feminist movement. "I didn't want my sport to be used as a tool," she said. "I just wanted to run. I wasn't there to prove that a woman could run 26 miles. I was there to win the race. . . . I came from an athletic realm where we were viewed as athletes," she continued. "I really resented road runners who used women's lib." So when feminists wanted her to join a Central Park photo session after her victory, "I conveniently never got there." Bonner admitted, "I wasn't going to have my picture taken with people who weren't good runners, but primarily a women's lib front." Excusing herself from the photos, she told them, "I have to get a drink of water. I have to go to the bathroom."

How did Lebow draw big-name runners once his show had caught on? For one, he capitalized on the two-dimensional lure of New York City: First, the professional exposure was unmatched and, as Lebow said, "Running in New York means you might get less money, but you may benefit from the additional coverage in the media." Success in New York City for top runners meant international exposure, and job offers by sponsors and the media. And second, the excitement of competing in Lebow's show was second to none, as Grete Waitz would observe: "The crowds in New York are so supportive that I sometimes feel more a New Yorker than a Norwegian. [The New York crowds] treat everyone like a winner . . . the last finisher as much as the [actual] winner." Lebow played his hand superbly in drawing these athletes to the city.

For star runners, participating in Lebow's party represented a professional sine qua non. A career in distance running was simply incomplete without competing in New York's five-borough spectacle at least once. "Fred created this theater . . . this stage," said running commentator Jim Ferstle. "You had to be here if you wanted to make a mark. Your career wasn't complete until you came here and proved yourself."

So the New York City stage was one lure, but it was not enough, especially once the 1980s arrived. By that time the marathon mania Lebow pioneered had emerged globally, and in this movement of big-time marathoning he had spawned, several other cities and countries provided their own drama-filled arenas. Still, when competing with other marathons for top athletes, the appeal of New York City was Lebow's bottom-line recruitment strategy. He knew full well in 1983, for instance, that he could not match the $135,000 in prize money offered by the rival Chicago marathon, yet he defiantly declared, "Chicago is throwing all kinds of money to buy top runners, but they cannot buy the vitality of New York. New York is magic."

The issue of prize money was another area that showed how much Lebow had become a victim of his own success, for two main reasons: First, although grassroots runners everywhere were happy simply to finish the race, the presence of world-class runners became more and more necessary to give the marathon credibility, and, ultimately, both sponsors and crowds would balk if Lebow let his show become identified with the five-hour finisher alone. Second, as the race directors of growing numbers of marathons competed with Lebow for the limited number of elite athletes, and as the athletes' agents started bargaining for more and more appearance money, and soon big money, became a necessary tool for recruiting top runners to the urban street theater Lebow promoted.

Lebow, however, did not rely on outbidding other race directors alone to clinch his deals with elite athletes. So how did he craft his deals? Chutzpah, not cash, served as his primary recruitment device. "He didn't want to pay more, but to make it look like more," said Tracy Sundlun, executive director of the Metropolitan Athletic Congress. Recruiting top runners often meant tricky negotiations. He didn't reject proposals outright . . . he stalled. Survival skills taught him that putting some distance between himself and the other side was not necessarily detrimental. "My usual philosophy . . . Listen, stall, gain time to re-assess." And he used another of his survival skills, flexibility, to govern his payment arrangements, engineering all sorts of payment schemes, including prize money, appearance money, combinations of prize money and appearance money, performance bonuses, American runner bonuses, hot-weather bonuses, million-dollar bonuses. . . .

Bill Rodgers and Frank Shorter had given the first five-borough marathon, in 1976, its athletic credibility. In addition, the two young, educated white runners had provided a role model for Lebow's emerging boomer constituency, such identifiable figures making it easier for Lebow to draw this new generation of competitors.

In those first marathons, Lebow signed up top runners for prize money rather than appearance money. Naturally, this emphasis on prize money did not sit well with the athletes. Rodgers, winner of Lebow's first four five-borough marathons, was insulted by the scheme. "What does he think, that I'll run it in half-speed if I get my expenses going in?" Despite his four victories in Lebow's marathon, Rodgers probably gave the race director more trouble than any other athlete. In arguing over payments, he called Lebow "cheap" and his marathon "snobby." He was especially upset because Lebow never once predicted him as a marathon winner. But in spite of all the trouble he gave him, and even though he believed the white-gloved runner had seen his best days, Lebow still wanted Rodgers to compete in 1981. Since it was not simply a race, but a show that Lebow was promoting, Rodgers's value was that he brought glamour and publicity.

So how did Lebow convince Rodgers to run in the marathon that year while refusing to pay his fee? He did stress the value of "running New York," but his negotiating style was much more subtle than that. Certain that Rodgers needed him more than he needed Rodgers, he simply adopted his "do nothing" negotiating maneuver. He just let time go by. As the marathon drew closer, Lebow hoped Rodgers would give in, while press speculation about Rodgers's plans only helped the race promoter's cause. Anytime the press cited the feud, the marathon got free publicity.

The two eventually met at the Bank One Marathon in Columbus, Ohio. Lebow had flown there to compete, but also to see where Rodgers stood. Rodgers still wanted to run in New York, so Lebow worked out a deal getting Rodgers personal sponsors, a deal that cost the promoter nothing.

There were times, however, when neither the lure of the city nor its race director's tactics worked. And since Lebow's main focus was on his innovative shtick for his marathon party, he generally invested conservatively in payments to runners. But when he wanted a certain runner to enhance his show, appearance money was somehow produced, as in 1983 when he offered world record holder Alberto Salazar twenty thousand dollars just to appear, another twenty-five thousand dollars if he came in first, and twenty-five thousand dollars more if he set another world record. With his biggest payments going to established athletes rather than long shots, though, he sometimes lost out on major opportunities.

In an October 18, 1985, article about problems Lebow's race was having at the time, "New York Marathon: Is It Almost Out of the Running?" *New York Newsday* referred to Lebow's refusal to gamble on less well-known runners, saying, "Ironically, Lebow was a victim of his willingness to pay promotional appearance money only to defending champions, assuming everyone else would come for media exposure." Women's world record holder Ingrid Kristiansen, whom Lebow desperately wanted to run in 1985, had acknowledged that she "never considered New York's offer because she was insulted at not having been recruited [by Lebow] until *after* she set a world record."

And in 1987, Lebow's repeated response to calls received from Priscilla Welch's husband, Dave—even after Welch won the London Marathon with an impressive time of 2:26:51, accentuated by the fact that she was already forty-two years old—was to refuse to pay appearance money, offering airfare and hotel accommodations only. Welch appeared at the marathon anyway, and she got even with Lebow when, after winning it, she turned down his requests to do press interviews. "I'm not going to do any job for you," she told Lebow, and announced, "I came down hard on that." Being rooted in the youth-oriented boomer culture, Lebow might have incorrectly downplayed such a "master" runner's promotional value. Welch further hurt the race director and his show by declaring that she was actually turned off by the glitter of Lebow's party, claiming that, in victory, "you get pushed and shoved every which way. You've got to behave yourself, but be a bit of a showman. All that razzmatazz, you can keep it."

Despite such disappointments, the continued success of his show well beyond these 1985 and 1987 incidents indicates that it was considerably more often than not that Lebow's skills, and the draw of his venue, would enable him to recruit the runners he needed to keep his marathon athletically, theatrically, and promotionally alive. And the peace agreement he reached with Mayor Koch about the issue of paying runners came none too early, because it was money constraints, more than his failure to anticipate some of the long shots' potential, that had indeed prevented Lebow from attracting the best runners to New York. Neither of the two world record holders at the time—Carlos Lopes of Portugal, with a running time of 2:7:11, nor Ingrid Kristiansen, with the best women's time of 2:21:06—entered Lebow's 1985 marathon.

Seeking to bring the world records—established at the 1981 New York City Marathon by Alberto Salazar and Allison Roe—back to his city, Lebow offered $50,000 for a new world record and $10,000 for a new course record. But it was a futile move. Lebow's nemesis, as always, was Chicago's "America's Marathon," directed by Bob Bright. Maintaining the primacy of the New York City Marathon over such other major events was one of Lebow's chief goals in the marathon boom years of the mid-1980s. The focus of his competition with Chicago was elite runners, the bearers of prestige to their races; the marathons were usually scheduled only a week apart, so since it was virtually impossible for even the elite athletes to run in both, they were forced to choose whether to run in New York or Chicago. *New York Newsday* had claimed that a year earlier, Lebow's marathon had turned into a "debacle" because of the unseasonably high temperatures and the loss of top talent to Chicago. As the article pointed out, "[Although Lebow argued that] all he needed was the city and its two million spectators, no amount of New York's majesty could prevent ABC's ratings from slipping 25 percent."

But in the bidding wars between the two marathons, Lebow was unable to match the cash put forth by Chicago's sponsor, Beatrice Foods. The prize and bonus structures for the two marathons were similar, but Lebow could not match Chicago's appearance fees. Although

Lebow gave Grete Waitz, his perennial winner, $25,000 to run, Bright paid each of at least four top athletes—Rob de Castella, Steve Jones, Rosa Mota, and Ingrid Kristiansen—that same amount. "Imagine what a field I could assemble," lamented Lebow, "if I had his unlimited budget."

In 1985, Chicago paid $370,000 in appearance money, not including the $150,000 Joan Benoit Samuelson received as part of her endorsement contract with Beatrice Foods. Lebow, by contrast, could come up with only $70,000 in appearance fees, but he figured he could at least deny Chicago the publicity edge. When Bill Rodgers's agent asked $25,000 for Rodgers to run in New York, Lebow knew there was no way he could match Chicago's bid; however, for Rodgers to be of value to Bright, the Chicago race director needed time to publicize him as an entrant. "They couldn't publicly claim him until they were sure I wasn't going to get him," reasoned Lebow. "And if they couldn't claim him, they couldn't promote him," so he kept Rodgers and his agent dangling. By the time Bright was able to announce that Rodgers was running, it was so late in the game the papers gave it only a small blurb.

Associates of Lebow insisted that the rivalry between the two race directors smacked of good-natured hype—"like two wrestlers in the ring," said elite-athlete coordinator Patricia Owens—orchestrated to draw attention to each of their marathons. But the print record gives one reason to conclude otherwise, as the invective was indeed sharp. Bright claimed, for instance, that although Lebow operated under handicaps from New York's city hall regarding prize money, "there was a lot of deception involved." Moreover, about Lebow's legendary talents, Bright opined, "If [Lebow] didn't have New York, he'd be lost. The only reason he's still in the game is his stage. Lebow is the second generation of what he invented, but he stopped reading his own book."

And although never directly referring to Lebow as a "Jew," it was Bob Bright who, in one attack against his competitor, made a "garment-district" reference that left little doubt as to what he had in mind: "The reason Fred can't compete isn't money, it's because he doesn't know how. If he has a decent race this year, it's only by accident, because he was able to build his field with people who were afraid of our competition in Chicago. I put my cards on the table. He's still approaching it with a Seventh Avenue mentality, a garment-district mentality: Get it for as cheap as possible." (On the other side of the "ring," during his fierce 1984 bidding war with Bright, Lebow didn't directly refer to his Jewishness, either, when he answered a question of who would be running in his marathon; however, when he said his runners would be "[world-class runner] Rod Dixon, [record-setter] Grete Waitz, and Charlie Rosenthal from Brooklyn," linking the two marathon stars with an obscure runner to underscore the everyman status of his athletes, it was obvious that he *had* chosen an overtly Jewish name to make his point.)

Joining the attack against Lebow from Chicago was 1983 marathon record holder Rob de Castella. "New York is tending toward mediocrity. . . . It's lacking the runners with something extra, the charisma, the sparkle. New York is more for the masses. Someone who wants to run just one marathon may prefer it because of the tradition, but people who want a fast time are choosing Chicago." In reply, Lebow made three arguments for the superiority of his creation over Chicago: First, citing his marathon's democratic character, he noted, "We have 5,000 runners from 74 countries and 10,000 from the other 49 states. It's a people race. We don't want to lose sight of what we're about. We're more than speed. . . . Their priority was just the top. Our priority is the 18,000 runners, and it shows." Second, noting the exuberance of New York and insisting that the big bucks of Chicago could never match the excitement of his five-borough festival, he claimed, "I don't mind losing Joan [Benoit Samuelson] as long as we don't lose the Verrazano Bridge or First Avenue." And third, citing his marathon's mystique, he bragged, "The New York marathon has a mystique. The World Series is the World Series even if [such low-profile teams as] Kansas City or Toronto plays in it. We are the World Series."

Despite the two men's high-profile competition, though, Lebow ran in the Chicago marathon during most of the 1980s, mainly because running it each year enabled him to be so tired when his New York City Marathon came around that he was less envious of the pack of runners that would follow his lead car. But even when he was in Chicago as a runner, the rivalry between the two directors sometimes surfaced. Once, when Lebow picked up his running number at the America's Marathon headquarters, he found three apples—ostensibly referring to New York City's nickname, "the Big Apple"—on the bib designated for the front of his shirt, but on the back his "number" showed up as three apple cores!

As Lebow transformed the New York City Marathon into Big Apple Day and realized he was offering fun and excitement totally independent of the field of elite athletes, he changed his opinion regarding payments to athletes—a practice he himself had pioneered. He reached the conclusion that these payments no longer enhanced the marathon's glory: "Last year's appearance money totaled $200,000," he wrote in December 1988 in *New York Running News*, "and as far as I am concerned we did not get our money's worth. . . . In short, it is hard for some runners to put 100% effort into the event when their pockets are already lined."

Lebow's opposition to such payments strengthened when he became convinced about the enthusiasm his party was attracting in the streets. Once crowds put their seal of approval on his party, the survivalist in Lebow showed the flexibility to adopt new tactics. Crowds, rather than star runners, became the watchword of success as the marathon moved from athletic event to show, and for the crowds, the crown jewels were not the stars, but the assortment of tens of thousands of runners in an atmosphere of glitzy theater. What mattered most to his redrawn vision was the hoopla of the block party, not the stars that came to play. So as his marathon vision evolved, his focus switched to shtick to excite the crowds and away from a spare *Chariots of Fire* competition. The $50,000 he spent on marathon banners in 1984 drew the rationale: "That's the money we saved by not bidding for Olympic champion Carlos Lopes."

Previously, running times had been used to determine "elite-runner" categories. Prize money had its own set of rules, depending on such things as breaking records, age, and American citizenship. On all these fronts, Lebow was competing with other race directors and agents for the stars, who, because of the rigors of running a marathon, selectively chose their races. The race director said, as he announced his 1987 decision to forgo appearance fees, "New York doesn't buy stars, New York creates them."

When asked, in 1988, "Do American race directors fail to think big," he replied, "Yes." But when further asked if this failure was based on an inability to attract elite athletes or to raise enough funds to pay them, he answered no. The failure was in "[not] making a race into a show," and as evidence of his changed perspective from the original spare five-borough 1976 race, he observed that "the days of bringing in elite athletes such as Bill Rodgers to build the field are over." Particularly nettlesome, charged Lebow, was the way these elite athletes took advantage of appearance money. "What I saw this year was Americans who have run 2:16 or 2:19 asking for appearance fees. I had one who ran 2:10 several years ago ask me to bring in his whole family. Many who are asking for fees shouldn't even have their travel paid. We do so much for the runners anyway, with appearance money, prize money, per diems, travel, all that."

Using the barometer of crowd size as the yardstick of his party's success, in 1990 the race director even began talking about eliminating prize money. By then, sponsors such as John Hancock and some of the auto and sneaker companies were bringing their own paid athletes to the marathons, reducing the pressure on Lebow to come up with exorbitant fees.

In a revealing winter 1990 interview with *FootNotes,* Lebow dismissed the reputations of star marathon performers as being the draws for either crowd or television audiences, claiming the hoopla of the marathon party was what now sparked spectators. "The crowds were not affected by who was running," said Lebow about that year's marathon. "They didn't know who Juma Ikangaa [a Tanzanian, number-four men's winner] or Douglas Wakihuri [a Kenyan, number-one men's winner] were. . . . [Still,] we had great crowds [and] our television ratings were the highest we'd had in 21 years. I don't think they came out to watch Wanda Panfil [a Pole, number-one women's winner]." Taken aback by Lebow's train of thought, *FootNotes* noted, "You're the man who brought big money to the marathon and now you're the man who's going to take it away," to which Lebow replied, "Yeah, exactly," and "I wondered what would happen. . . . [O]ur ratings on television will not be affected by not having Ikangaa and Wakihuri."

But what about finishing times? Unimportant, argued the race director. "What's the difference if the winning time's 2:12 or 2:13. Would the crowds know about it?" "You don't think ABC will care if they don't have some big names there?" inquired *FootNotes,* with Lebow answering, "They *will* care, they *should* care, but the crowds on First Avenue weren't there to watch Wakihuri and Ikangaa."

Taking a final swipe at every type of payment for runners, and falling back on the "masses" as his main constituency, Lebow asked:

> So what is the bottom line? We spent half a million dollars on appearance money and prize money this year, and the effort, we have to hire people to handle it, it costs a lot of money, and to put up with some of the agents who are totally irrational . . . we don't need it. I've had some bad press in this, too. I've talked to Ken Martin [an American, number-two men's winner in 1989], offering $7,500. He wanted $20,000. I mean, I'm very fond of him, but is he worth a half-million dollars? Would we be better off putting the money into the masses of runners? Would it be a better race?

In spite of whatever competitions and controversies were going on "back home," Lebow, fully convinced that his marathon needed to be a global event, tenaciously pursued his goal of recruiting new performers to introduce to his show from countries that had never previously competed in the United States. New athletes enhanced the world-class character of his marathon, and items about the "first" runners from a remote nation were certain to draw media play.

Foreign travel was integral to Lebow's global agenda. While overseas, he advised on setting up marathons, ran in them himself—particularly if they were staged in exotic places!—and scouted races to get ideas for his own festival. Bill Rodgers commented that he saw Lebow at Fukuoka in 1977, "taking notes on how the Japanese run the marathon there and riding the press bus to observe the logistics of the race and how it is policed." But figuring out how to convince Poland's Communist athletic federation that it should allow its runners to come to New York, for example, remained Lebow's focus. In that particular instance, luck, bolstered by Lebow's shrewd perception, showed him the way. During a winter walk with an official there, when Lebow was shown where he could buy a sweater on the black market, he realized the Pole wanted to buy something for himself, but didn't have the money to do so. When his host admitted he couldn't afford anything, Lebow offered to buy him what he wanted. From then on Polish runners were among the pack in the New York City Marathon.

Not always so lucky with his perception or his money, the race promoter once gave a $500 bribe (the suggested amount had been $1,000) to an official in East Germany. He later found out the "official" was merely a clerk. That "swindle" was not the only problem Lebow had in Germany. In all his running, including sixty-nine marathons in more than thirty countries, Lebow's only direct reference to his own Jewishness was in the context of the 1983 Berlin Marathon, his fifty-fifth race overall. Here, the pain of the Holocaust association spurred him on to demonstrate his running prowess. Blaming the Germans for ruining his childhood, he had the attitude that he would show them: "When at last I saw the finish banner and clock right in the middle of Berlin, I saw I had a chance to break 3:40. . . . I finished in 3:39:02. . . . And then I threw up."

Lebow's Jewishness had also surfaced while he was in Moscow to run in its 1982 marathon. Even though he was trying to score a political breakthrough as a bonus of his trip—to get the okay for future Soviet participation in his own five-borough race in the United States—he couldn't resist personally identifying with the plight of Soviet Jewry. Despite the precariousness of such a visit, he went with companion Dody Burkey to Moscow's main synagogue, where worshipers recognizing him conversed with him in Yiddish. The synagogue, just a few blocks from the Kremlin, was closely watched by government informers at the time, making it dangerous for Jews to speak with foreigners, but still, said Burkey, "He went out of a sense of duty." Burkey, who was originally seated seven rows from the front, reported that he was taken to the third row and carefully watched by government agents to further isolate Lebow during the service. "I had this feeling that something was going on during the service when one of the men in front of [Lebow] passed a note." The message contained a New York phone number. Lebow knew that such a simple intervention might have made him a persona non grata, damaging his dream to add more international character to his marathon through new Soviet participation. Still, he accepted the note and phoned the messenger's relative on his return to New York.

Whether it was from his visit to the synagogue, failed negotiations, or a physical problem that presented itself while he ran in the Moscow Marathon, the running recruiter had to leave the country before he had reached his goal. Dick Hochschild, who along with Burkey had accompanied the race producer-promoter-recruiter-runner, remembered Lebow accidentally smashing into overhanging tree leaves while running in Gorky Park. "The next day," said Hochschild, "his face puffed out looking like somebody had slugged him from both sides."

When he left to go to Athens for the European Championships the following month, Lebow was still unsure of Russia's participation at his own 1982 marathon. But "luck" was once again on his side. While in Athens he met a "gorgeous" Greek woman who served as the marathon's official interpreter. When he learned she spoke fluent Russian, he grabbed her arm, brought her to the head of the Russian delegation, and urged her to impress upon the Russians the importance of their participation in New York. The Russian official loved her, and was also tremendously taken with a film of the 1981 marathon Lebow had brought along. Russia was now in! Replying to a query in *FootNotes*'s winter 1990 issue about the marathon's future, Lebow proudly noted, "We had runners from Mongolia here this year, from Estonia. They paid their own way. We had thirty Russians here this year, paying their own way to come to the New York marathon."

New York's ethnic universe provided welcome touches of home for Lebow's foreign runners. Along the marathon route, cheers in one's native language represented sweet sounds of encouragement. The *New York Times*'s Roger Starr described how, on November 7, 1988, cheers from Brooklyn's melting pot spurred on seven of the first ten women finishers, hailing from six foreign countries:

> Members of the Norwegian Christian Home & Health Center based in Bay Ridge cheered Grete Waitz, the fastest woman. Tovel Lorentzen from Denmark heard cheering echoes from home that emanated from the Danish Seamen's Church on Willow Place as she turned into Lafayette Avenue. Laura Engli, the second fastest woman and Garziella Strulli, who came in seventh, explained in the interview that they liked New York because spectators cheered them in Italian.
>
> A Hungarian bookshop along the route was perhaps a source of

applause for Karolina Szabo, who finished fourth. On Fourth Avenue, many fans of German ancestry rooted for Kristin Pressler, fifth. As for sixth place Russian finisher, Alevina Chasova, [Starr hoped that in the absence of a historic Russian community in West Brooklyn], the Poles of Greenpoint overlooked centuries of blood to cheer for her.

In addition to its athletic and promotional benefits, politically, Lebow saw a large foreign running contingent—it would grow to nearly twelve thousand of some twenty-eight thousand entrants at its height—as a shield from would-be problems with city hall because, as Tracy Sundlun of the Metropolitan Athletic Congress noted, "Foreign athletes spent more time in New York City than other American runners. This meant greater value for the city. The question Fred asked himself, was 'At what point do I have enough foreign runners to keep the city politician happy?' "

Ironically, this globalization of marathoning proved to be a mixed blessing for Lebow. On the one hand, Lebow was proud that at his own race the international flavor stood out, with runners from more than one hundred nations, their flags prominently displayed, necessitating interpreters and multilingual announcements and signs. On the other, as marathoning became more popular, non-American and Third World athletes increasingly became race winners and set course records. Lebow recognized that, in addition to hurting him personally, his own sense of nationalism as an American being affected, the rise of non-English-speaking running champions, unable to connect with his American television audience, presented marketing problems. For Lebow's purposes, a running star could not simply be a winner who took the money and disappeared; he saw his ABC-TV ratings decline in the late 1980s as a result of that trend, and fewer viewers meant less willingness on the part of corporate sponsors to pay for his party. Mercedes, for example, from whose pace car Lebow had led the marathoners for more than a decade, dropped their sponsorship in 1995 to concentrate, instead, on the more traditional, upscale American sport of golf. Still, to keep his party athletically at the top level of marathoning, Lebow was forced to keep his race stocked with the world's best running talent.

Among all the stars Lebow recruited to his party—including males and females, Americans and foreigners, elite and grassroots runners alike—none stood out more than Grete Waitz, a Norwegian school-teacher who would go on to win the marathon nine times. Millions on the sideline simply referred to her as "Grete," yet her first victory had been a long shot . . . her number, 1173, not even listed among the pre-race entries in 1978. Scurrying around the course at the end of the race, seeking to learn the identity of the women's winner that year, the only information Lebow could get was that it was "some blond girl."

It was Grete's husband, Jack, who originally persuaded her to ac-cept Lebow's invitation to come to the marathon, as a one-time chance to visit the United States. Although she had distinguished herself in Eu-ropean track events, she had never before run a marathon. Aware of her inexperience, Lebow assumed she had at least put in heavy mileage in preparation for her New York race, but when he asked her, at a pre-marathon reception at Tavern on the Green, what the longest distance she had run was, "Twenty kilometers" was what she answered. With twelve and a half miles as her longest distance, Lebow doubted she would even finish the race. Most runners train with at least a few twenty-mile runs before competing in a marathon.

At the starting line, twenty-five-year-old Waitz was overwhelmed as she watched Lebow, "hopping up and down, bellowing into his mega-phone . . . bark[ing] endless orders at a sea of runners." She remem-bered that, looking for more women runners to hype his show, he had called her in Oslo and argued, "It doesn't matter that you're a short dis-tance champion. I want more women to enter, and you'll be a drawing card. I want this to be a race for everybody."

Not knowing the difference between kilometers and miles, when Waitz came off the Queensboro Bridge, she assumed the number ten referred to kilometers. "I thought I was close to the finish, in three or four miles. I wanted this to end. Each time I saw trees, I thought it was Central Park." Aching all over, and beleaguered by the pushy crowds at the finish line, Waitz screamed at husband Jack, "*Aldri!*" (the Norwe-gian word for *Never!*) Even though she had set a world record, she blurted to Jack, "I'll never, *never* do this again!"

Worried that she had not arranged for a substitute to cover her classes on Monday, Waitz explained, "I had to get back to Norway. I wanted to go home, that's all I wanted." Always on the lookout for media-appealing homespun athletes, Lebow saw in Waitz a new star. He liked her shy, gracious style, minimizing the awesome feat she had accomplished in setting her record. So in response to her hesitant request, Lebow gladly gave Waitz twenty dollars for the cab ride to the airport.

But being showcased by Lebow, in addition to her other running goals, took a big psychological toll on Waitz. "I know I have to get first place all the time, and then if I do, people ask why I didn't set a record," she remarked in 1984. "I'm not a running machine, you can't switch me on and off. It's getting harder and harder every year. It's mentally tougher to be motivated and up all the time, and without motivation you can't go out there and compete. That's my problem. I don't know how long I can keep it up."

Lebow was as sensitive to his runners' needs as he was to his sponsors', so as important as it was to hype his show, he understood the value of keeping it low key once his already tense athletes arrived in New York. In 1980, before the first of his three marathon victories, Alberto Salazar was alarmingly intense. "Fred took me to lunch at the Russian Tea Room and we talked about kids or something else, instead of 'What are your splits going to be on Sunday,' " Salazar recalled. "He was the one guy who could make me relax."

In recruiting the world's top athletes, Lebow drew on all his extensive talents—from cutting deals to reaching out to runners on a personal basis, from cultivating his mystique as the maven of marathoning to capitalizing on his New York City stage. He even used his skills in finding dates for lonely male runners, helping to boosting his runners' social lives and, sometimes, as a result, engendering their trust.

Before he ever met Lebow, English runner Chris Stewart called the race director when he arrived in New York in 1973. His fellow runner Kathrine Switzer had recommended Lebow as the man who could fix up Stewart with a date for the evening. Always willing to cut a deal, Lebow told Stewart he could recommend a woman, providing the Englishman ran a race in New York. Stewart agreed, ran the race, and set a course record. A few weeks later, Stewart again called Lebow inquiring about his "escort services." This time, Lebow asked Stewart to compete in a 15K race in exchange for the woman's phone number. The distance was longer than Stewart's normal range, and at first the runner balked, but the lonely Stewart soon called Lebow back saying he would run, but only if the race director provided another attractive friend. At race time it was, again, a happy Stewart who ran, and again he set a new record.

Sometime afterward, Stewart called on another quest for a woman, but this time Lebow had a 20K race scheduled for the next day. The race director-escort provider's terms really upset the Englishman, so Lebow placated Stewart further, setting him up with a gorgeous model from the garment district. But the next morning, with the race ready to start, Stewart was nowhere in sight. Lebow delayed the race, waiting for Stewart to surface, and when he finally appeared, emerging from a taxi, he was wearing a blazer and looking glassy-eyed. After changing his clothes quickly, Stewart miraculously won again, establishing another course record. Lebow's purpose in making such bargains was rarely selfish. Through his "negotiations" with Stewart, he had shown the runner, as he must have known from other similar experiences with world-class "short-distance" runners, that distance running, and marathon running, was, indeed within his capabilities.

The fact that Lebow himself was a runner and marathoner provided access to other runners and fellow race directors beyond what was normally available to sports promoters. He schmoozed with these athletes in their vernacular, and raced with them in America and abroad—although at a distance, given his mediocre speed! They knew that the running lifestyle and the culture of the track were the main elements of Lebow's life, so they thought of him in more positive terms than they did the run-of-the-mill sports promoter.

Lebow kept in regular touch with his party's main stars. "He visited me in Oslo many times," said Grete Waitz, "and sometimes for no particular reason. Every time I went to New York, I went to the club to see him. He would call me in Norway just to ask how I was doing or how [my husband] Jack was doing."

The personal ties that Lebow established also caused Alberto Salazar to think of the race director "as part of my family." He told about the time Lebow was "yelling and twirling his arms," cheering for the three-time winner of the New York City Marathon at a 5K race in the Meadowlands where Lebow was a spectator rather than a race director. And he remarked that Lebow was "one of the few people who kept in touch with me during the 10 years that I was not racing."

Despite his special attention to his runners, which certainly did not hurt his recruiting capabilities, not always did Lebow, given to absent-mindedness, remember the names of the star performers coming to his show. "Sometimes he was [so] bad at names," noted Patricia Owens, Lebow's elite-runner coordinator in the early 1980s, "I would [have to] whisper . . . the names of some runners." Trying to cover up for him, Owens would apologetically blame Lebow's thick accent, telling the runners, "He doesn't speak so well," though admitting later, "He always remembered the names of women runners, even though he might forget the men's names."

There was one woman "runner" Lebow would probably have liked to, but was very unlikely to, forget. Although always seeking to add runners to his party, and making such a huge effort to attract *Every*man and *Every*woman to marathoning, this was one "runner" he regretted having at his festival. Her name was Rosie Ruiz, and she showed up at the 1979 marathon finish line with a time of 2:56:29, ranking her 663rd among finishers, and 24th among women. The only problem was that Rosie had ridden the subway to the finish. No one would have known of her cheating had she not been designated the women's winner at the following spring's Boston Marathon with a time of 2:31:56, the third-fastest marathon ever run by a woman. When two Harvard students testified that they saw her jump into the race less than a mile from the finish, and no road runners remembered seeing her along the course, suspicions about the declared winner were aroused, and eventually, the embarrassed Boston officials canceled her victory. By the time the New York City Marathon finally disqualified her, Lebow considered these incidents no laughing matter: "I did feel sorry for her when she initially cheated," he said. "But when she perpetuated it, I no longer felt sorry, I felt angry." But not everyone responded in the same way. Those not directly involved took the incidents with a sense of humor. Rosie, having put one over on the running establishment, became a household word. In the spring of 1980, a "Rosie Ruiz Marathon," in which competitors jumped into the 10K race 26.2 meters from the finish and still received T-shirts, was organized in Moline, Illinois.

That not being the type of "gimmick" he would latch onto—not even for any of the hundred smaller races his club held in addition to his five-borough festival—Lebow chose to enliven all his races with star runners. Carey Pinkowski, director of the Chicago marathon, recalled picking up the phone at the track office at Villanova University, where he was a student in March of the year the "Rosie Ruiz Marathon" was held, to find Lebow on the line. The New York race director was seeking competitors for a 10K (6.2-mile) Central Park race sponsored by Bloomingdale's. "Fred said he would pay for our gas," remembered Pinkowski. "When we got there on Friday, he was standing counting applications. He was already a celebrity, but he seemed relaxed with a good sense of humor. I was only twenty-one. When we reached Central Park, Fred said, 'Just remember, the last part of the marathon is here.' He was always recruiting."

And always most important to Fred Lebow of all were the "grassroots" and "commonplace" runners he was recruiting not only to his marathon, but to running as a whole. His "ordinary" runners were drawn more by a dream than by athletic prowess. They had been turned on to the idea of running, so often directly or indirectly by the work Lebow had done, and continued to do, to hype the running lifestyle. In their first taste of running, the prospect of going a marathon's distance seemed too preposterous to even fantasize. For most, the goal of testing one's limits across a terrain more than 26 miles long had been an evolving process. But as they ventured into the marathon fray, the race itself became a defining event. Performed before enthusiastic crowds, family, friends, and coworkers, their journey of self-discovery seemed less fearsome because Lebow had redesigned it into a day of celebration, and each year thousands more people became willing to make the attempt.

Who were Lebow's "grassroots" marathoners? Young, single boomers were especially drawn to the social exposure of Lebow's festivities. At a 10K event in Central Park in 1978, the race director observed, "It was almost like a runner's fashion show. Some of the women entered for social reasons, not athletic, because they thought it was a great chance to meet clean, handsome, single men." Always seeking to put a fun spin on running for these young boomers, sometimes, during these Central Park races, Lebow would crack through a megaphone that the sport boosted one's sex life. Some competitors, reported the *New York Times* on November 7, 1978, "were so unfamiliar with the ways of racing that they pinned numbers on the backs of their jerseys instead of on the front. Others thought 10,000 meters was closer to three miles than 6.2 miles."

Jewish runners were comfortable kibitzing with Lebow in an ethnic style. One Sunday, Morris Sopher from the Bronx, a veteran of fifteen New York City Marathons, jokingly suggested to Lebow, "Maybe we should recite the Rabbi's Kaddish"—the Jewish prayer of affirmation, said daily during prayers and after Torah study—when he saw a baptism taking place in the sanctuary of the Church of the Heavenly Rest, which stood across the street from the New York Road Runners Club's headquarters and served as a place to change for Central Park races. And when New York City Marathon applications were distributed in Central Park on Saturday, which is the Jewish Sabbath, Arlene Trebach—a Riverdale, New York, realtor—berated Lebow, scolding, "Why on *Shabbas* do I have to come down here for an application?"

Many of Lebow's "ordinary runners" were ordinary, perhaps, in running talent, but *extra*ordinary in their unsung heroics. For librarian Mrs. Betty Morgenroth, a Westchester County, New York, mother of three teenagers, "It was the appeal of doing something that would take a certain amount of dedication and challenge" that spurred her to sign up for the 1985 marathon. "I thought it was a good idea for my kids to see that after a certain age you can still pursue a goal," she said. "After a certain age, the years become badges of honor." She was uncertain as to whether her marathon application would be approved, so "when the envelope arrived, it was like receiving your acceptance to college. My husband said it was like what we went through when our daughter was applying to college. It was a fat envelope, and I knew I was in."

When Mary Rodriguez registered for a Saturday exercise class at Lebow's running club, she "couldn't even run a city block. It was embarrassing. That first week, the exercise teacher said to me, 'Don't give up. You can't expect to undo 35 years of inactivity in one week.' " So by the time she waited in line with thousands of other runners at the Marathon Expo preceding the 1983 race, this sixty-one-year-old mother of four children and seven grandchildren viewed herself in a different light. She had already run 185 races, including 10 marathons.

Phil Converse, one of twenty-five runners from Memphis, Tennessee, competing in the 1983 marathon, found his motivation in the gym. "Things like this begin when you're sitting around the locker room after a 10K [six-mile] race, and somebody says, 'What we ought to do is run a marathon.' The next question is 'Which one,' and the obvious answer is New York. It is THE happening among events that you don't have to have a qualifying time to get into."

Marathon qualifying times were a world away for Emily Altschul, who was unable to complete even the 1.6-mile loop around Central Park without stopping during her high school physical education classes. At that time, she considered marathoners people who "must have some kind of mental disorder," and as an adult she was convinced she had "virtually nothing in common" with Lebow's marathoners. But she cheered in Central Park as they streamed by, and, strangely, found herself crying as the midpack runners struggled past, though she was not sure where the tears came from. In 1991, when she finally made it around the Central Park Reservoir, she jokingly likened herself to a marathon runner. Her distances increased until, as a twenty-six year old, she was emboldened to send in her application for the 1995 marathon, secretly praying for rejection. But sure enough, she was accepted. Boarding the bus under the darkened sky in front of the Forty-second Street New York Public Library, she "silently contemplated my fears and doubts" of the realities of the 26.2-mile course ahead. Crossing the Verrazano-Narrows Bridge, entering Brooklyn, "the cheering crowds brought back the feeling that I have had as a weeping bystander. But this time I was the runner and they were cheering for me." First Avenue was a dream for the maiden marathoner, who said, "As far as I was concerned, I was [world-renowned record breaker] Grete Waitz." The end was the toughest part of the race, she recalled, not because of a fatigued body, "but the agony of realizing that perhaps the most rewarding and fulfilling experience of my life was about to end. I crossed the finish line with tears of joy and sadness."

Forty-three-year-old Dan Alberti shared certain sports interests, such as horseback riding, bicycling, bowling, and karate, with fellow marathoners, but he was blind. Rather than being led on a leash like other blind marathoners, Alberti preferred a side-by-side, shoulder-to-shoulder running strategy with him and his marathon partner holding onto a piece of yarn about fifteen inches in length. Though he occasionally tripped, he was not discouraged. Taking part in a marathon, he said, meant more than simply covering 26.2 miles. "It's the preparation, and the camaraderie. It's the carbo-loading parties that take place beforehand. It's a fantastic social experience."

Going through a painful divorce, George Davis, a vice president of the Wall Street brokerage firm Bear Sterns, was disheartened. He was losing weight, could not concentrate, and felt as though his skin was just hanging on his body. "I needed a discipline," said Davis, "and I also needed a way to get rid of the aggression I was feeling," and training for the New York City Marathon seemed like a solution to his problems. "It got me into shape and cleaned my head. I would run and use the time to think of ways to kill my wife, of ways to kidnap my child. But then I would think of ways of working things out."

Schemes of another sort racked author Erich Segal's imagination as he ran in Lebow's pageant. "Imagine the childhood fantasy fulfilled," said Segal, "running *practically* naked through the streets of your native city."

All of these special people—*all* his runners—were important to Fred Lebow. It wasn't his party's fanfare but rather his people who were the race director's primary concern. His vision always focused on his marathon as a *people's* race. In 1982, for instance, Lebow realized there was a need for a special prayer service for Jewish runners arriving early at the Fort Wadsworth staging area because observant Jews—who do not recite their morning prayers before the break of dawn, but do not begin the day's "business" before praying the morning service—require a minyan (a quorum of at least ten men) for some parts of that service. "When Fred saw me *davening* [praying] on the lawn with my *Talis* [prayer shawl] and *Tefillin* [phylacteries], he did a double take," said Rabbi Jim Michaels of their first 1982 encounter. So the following year, Lebow made room in a medical tent for those Jewish runners interested in praying with a minyan, and announcements in New York's *Jewish Week* newspaper and at Manhattan's Lincoln Square Synagogue alerted Jewish marathoners to the service. With Lebow's permission, announcements about the service were broadcast at the staging area that morning in several languages. Peter Berkowsky, cofounder of this Marathon Minyan, as the service was to be called, brought a box of prayer books, and posted American and Israeli flags outside the tent to attract Jewish runners. The sight of marathoners standing around in prayer shawls and tefillin invariably drew crowds. Marathoners developed the traditions of shouting aloud the blessing, thanking God, "Who gives strength to the weary," and passing around a *pushke* (charity box) during the service. In 1985, two young Lubavitcher Hasidim appeared at Fort Wadsworth with the aim of encouraging and instructing nonobservant Jewish runners regarding putting on tefillin—an admittedly strange sight at a race staging area.

As the only marathon in the world with a prerace minyan, the New York City Marathon was unique, but although he was the one who provided the means, Lebow himself didn't stay to pray with the minyan for many years. However, he did stop by every year to make announcements, to wish the runners *mazel tov* (loosely translated, "good luck") on their journey, and on unusually warm Marathon Sundays to caution the runners to fill up on water or to drop out if they were unprepared for distance running in the heat. (The Marathon Minyan subsequently spurred the organization of a Catholic mass that drew some one thousand worshipers.)

Avoiding scheduling conflicts from the very beginning was another one of the ways Lebow accommodated his Jewish constituency. To be sure, on the Jewish holy days of Rosh Hashanah and Yom Kippur, the New York City Road Runners Club did not sponsor any events. But a special problem emerged regarding the date of the 1986 marathon. Prior to that year, the marathon had always been set for the last Sunday in October. In 1986, however, the Jewish holiday of Simchas Torah (the Rejoicing of the Law) fell on that Sunday, which would prevent observant Jews from participating in the marathon. Peter Berkowsky launched a lobbying campaign in mid-1985 to convince Lebow to put off the 1986 marathon to November. In deference to Jewish runners, and to avoid any future conflicts, the date was permanently moved to November, the month where the marathon now stands, even though Lebow worried that this colder autumn month might bring new hardships to the runners. He told the *Bergen (N.J.) Record* on November 13, 1985, "We received many letters from the Jewish community and from the Governor's and Mayor's offices. Now the main concern is, instead of having dehydration problems, we'll have problems with hypothermia if we have a cold day." Perhaps not coincidentally, that first

November marathon, in 1986, was the first time the minyan was able to read a portion of the Torah scroll, which is not generally taken out on Sundays. That particular Marathon Sunday fell on a *Rosh Hodesh* (new month, according to the Hebrew calendar), which has some of the added holiness of a holiday or Sabbath, but none of the restrictions that would prohibit Jews from running.

In addition to taking care of his runners' special needs, Lebow was *very* careful about their safety. When a "prop" like his conversation piece, the two hundred-foot "world's largest urinal," held publicity value, all the better. But water stops, first aid stations, psychologists to counsel needy runners at the parade's start and end, and Mylar blankets to warm them at the finish—these were priorities the visionary never minimized. "If I . . . wanted three water stations," Lebow's assistant Bill Noel said, "Fred insisted on four."

Even as important as media coverage was to the race promoter, when the security of his runners came into conflict with the media, the publicity considerations proved secondary. The two interests literally collided one year when Lebow was notified that fumes from the press bus were suffocating the runners. Since a ham operator was assigned to every marathon vehicle, with chief operator Steve Mendelsohn riding with Lebow, Lebow tried to get word to the operator assigned to the press bus, only to learn he had been thrown off to make room for an extra reporter. Lebow then tried to tell the motorcycle cop who had first notified him of the problem what to do, but with all the noise from the crowd, the radios, and the motorcycle, his screams and attempts at sign language were unsuccessful. When he tried to contact the bus himself, quickly writing a poster saying, "Joe Stay Away From The Runners," it was too late. The bus was gone and the motorcycle cop was telling him it had been thrown off the course. This was good for the runners, and Lebow was pleased about that, but he lamented the loss of media coverage. He never questioned why he didn't just tell the cop to leave things alone, or why he didn't try to move the runners over. His only question was, "Who the hell threw the damn ham off the press bus?"!

As diligent as he was in taking care of his runners, Lebow's ultimate nightmare struck in 1984 when, for the first time, a runner died in his pageant. With the temperature rising to seventy-nine degrees, and the humidity at 98 percent that October Sunday, Jacques Bussereau, a forty-year-old Frenchman, collapsed after running 14.5 miles and died an hour later. As a result of that day's heat, no water was left at some stations by the time Bussereau arrived. "I went home and could not sleep," said Lebow, exhausted after weeks of fine-tuning his show.

> So around 3 o'clock, I did the best thing I know to do: I went for a run on the Fifth Avenue side of the park—in the street, naturally. I saw two other people running at that hour. Then I went home and went to sleep. . . . It was the same way when Jim Fixx died. I was in a hotel in Chicago, and I ran up the stairs to the 20th floor and put on my sneakers and went for a run along Lake Shore Drive, even though I had already had my run for the day.

Trying to soften the tragedy with a light spin, Lebow added, "The time will come for all of us. I can only say, if we have a chance to choose the way we leave the world, what a way to go." But humor and running therapy were not enough to help a broken Lebow recover. Bill Michaels, race director of Denver's Mile High Marathon, saw him at a press conference at the New York Road Runner Club headquarters the Monday following the race. "Fred was distraught," said Michaels. "He was not just putting on an act. He really felt awful. The press conference was over. Everybody was leaving. Fred was staring ahead. He looked over the banister and dropping his shoulders on the banister, it looked like he was crying. . . . It was eating him inside. This event was his life. It blew his mind, the thought that 'someone under me died for lack of water.' "

Lebow's devotion and concern for his runners was evident in so many ways. One year, two days after Marathon Sunday, Lebow received a phone call informing him that someone was still out on the course. The report said it was a Vietnam veteran, with no legs, who was "running" on his hands. "I immediately [personally] went out and looked for him, but couldn't find him anywhere," Lebow reported. "Finally I did find him, in the Bronx, about 17 miles into the race. [It took him four days to finish, but] I came out every day to see how he was doing . . . [and] I put him up in a hotel at night. It was really remarkable."

This runner's dedication to the goal Lebow had envisioned and "sold" was a true example of "the heroics of" the world's *extra*ordinary citizens. And these were the runners Lebow most wanted to recruit to his vision—to his dream of letting everyone experience the feeling running gave him!

11

Amassing a Crew to Help

ALTHOUGH LEBOW WORE THE MANTLE of showman, the New York City Marathon's structure would have collapsed lacking the genius of Allan Steinfeld, the race director's technical director and alter ego. Runners and close friends, they both understood the terms of their relationship. "I always deferred to Fred," said Steinfeld. "I ran the organization internally. Fred was the showman." And Lebow readily admitted his dependence on Steinfeld: "Without him I'd be lost. Allan makes me look good."

Lebow saw his own mission as adding glitz and hype to his party, whereas Steinfeld's role was to fill in technical details for the race director. "Allan, I want you to arrange for three hundred runners a minute to cross the finish line" was the type of assignment Lebow threw at Steinfeld.

Steinfeld's 1987 wedding was one of the few occasions when the two failed to act in concert. By then, shoes were no longer part of Lebow's attire. His outfits consisted of sneakers as basics, plus running clothing for daily attire and an occasional sports jacket or tuxedo for more official functions. But for the wedding of Allan Steinfeld and the running club's head of computer services, Alice Schneider, the race director relented: "He told me that for this occasion he would wear shoes," said Steinfeld. "You and Alice are very special to me." The ceremony was set for 2:00 P.M. at Rockefeller Center, and to accommodate the wedding party, marathon applications were distributed in Central Park earlier that morning, rather than in the afternoon as in past years. After the applications were distributed, Lebow returned to his apartment to dress for Steinfeld's wedding, and it was his shoes that did him in when the Salute to Israel Parade closed down Fifth Avenue and tied up traffic through Manhattan's East Side. Steinfeld had arranged for his mentor to hold up the *chupah* (bridal canopy), but when a struggling Lebow, mired in his unfamiliar shoes, still had not appeared by 2:30, the ceremony had to start in his absence. Eventually, the shaken race director appeared, toasting "L'Chaim!" to the new couple. Steinfeld acknowledged that "Fred couldn't find a cab. With his sneakers, he could have run there in twenty minutes. This way it took an hour."

Beneath the surface, a professional staff and army of volunteers made Lebow's party operational. Volunteer ranks included ham radio operators, massage therapists, marshals, finish line-chute pushers, Expo bag stuffers, bandit catchers (assigned to spot interlopers who ran the marathon without registering), psychologists, water suppliers—in all, thirteen thousand volunteers, nearly half the number of runners at the marathon's height (twenty-eight thousand), were there to help Lebow showcase his festival.

The runners competed for the obvious reasons of fun, fitness, self-esteem, and prestige, but what drew the volunteers to what were often colorless, demanding assignments? Many of these volunteer positions involved training sessions and a week's worth of volunteering.

The T-shirt was the purveyor of status at the time. As much as the runners, volunteers wanted to send the message that they were in on the marathon mystique. For large categories of volunteers such as ham operators, T-shirts were specifically designed to demonstrate their participation. Volunteers higher up in the hierarchy received other clothing perks, such as sneakers, caps, pants, and jackets, from marathon sponsors. A free night's lodging at a midtown hotel where the top runners were staying spelled real recognition for the volunteer elite. Steve Mendelsohn, chief ham operator, once threatened Lebow that his four hundred-member crew would not show up at the race unless some of these hotel rooms were made available for them.

Beyond the T-shirts, and other clothing perks, another motivation was the marathon challenge itself. Here was an event on which they worked that made the front pages of all the sports sections. And just as Lebow's parties served as social meeting places for runners, they also provided social outlets for volunteers scouting other singles. Lebow's fun atmosphere made it simply easier to land a date!

From Lebow's perspective, volunteers were not just there to assist.

Since, according to the race promoter, human society consisted of runners and nonrunners, in his mind volunteers were runners in the making. Their transformation to this "higher" status was a goal Lebow worked on, and his presence at the races spurred the volunteers on. He epitomized the running values the volunteers came to races to promote. "It meant a lot to people, especially to the volunteers, that Fred was out there," said Anna Noel-Mayberry, who organized the pre-marathon Saturday-night carbo-loading party. "They would see him at the finish line cheering on the runners, shaking hands."

Bill Conway took a week off from his presidency of New York's multimillion-dollar Gotham Construction Company to direct the marathon marshals. His nineteen hundred marshals were responsible for crowd control along the course route and at other pre- and postrace festivities. Conway's marshals were prepared for Lebow's efforts to put his imprint on their assignments. "We used two-way radios," said Conway. "We didn't mention his name, because we didn't want him to know we were talking about him. We knew that when he came along, he'd be sure to change something." So when Lebow surfaced, the marshals radioed one another, " 'the conductor is coming.' That was Fred's code name," said Conway. "If he was going to change something, we would say, 'the conductor is raising his baton.' If the change affected other people, we would say, 'the band is playing.' "

Sharon Applebee directed the Marathon Expo's packet party, where some five hundred volunteers, mainly senior citizens, stuffed sponsor freebies into bags that the marathoners picked up. Lebow came in during the packet party, said Applebee, and insisted that the volunteers take marathon caps as souvenirs. "We need the caps for the runners," Applebee told Lebow. "Invariably, he'd come in several times during the day, take a packet and put a hat on his head," apparently having given his away.

On Marathon Sunday, some one thousand volunteers made sure that nearly thirty thousand exuberant runners crossed the Verrazano-Narrows Bridge once the blast of the howitzer went off. In the chill of the night preceding the marathon, these volunteers examined one hundred thousand square feet of tenting for cleanliness; tested the public-address system; checked the fencing, electricity, and water; and, as a special gesture to Lebow's theatrics, hoisted thousands of balloons into a multicolored arch above the starting line. As marathoners began arriving before dawn, volunteers served breakfast—coffee, energy bars, doughnuts, muffins, Gatorade, yogurt, hot chocolate. Other volunteers gave massages and directed exercise warm-ups. Some one hundred psychologists, psychiatrists, and social workers counseled nervous runners. As the runners sped into Brooklyn, some six hundred Boy Scouts and Cub Scouts scooped up marathon paraphernalia ranging from coffee cups to Vaseline jars. Thousands of warm-up suits discarded by runners at the start were collected and donated to charity. At the Marathon Expo, the race's medical director, Dr. Andres Rodriguez, handled marathon-related health queries of all kinds. One male contestant asked, "Is it bad to have sex before a marathon?" and Dr. Rodriguez shot back, "Bad for you or for her?"

Despite all the preparation and the marathon's party spirit, some of the runners were unable to make it unaided to the finish. Even if they completed the course, their weakened bodies often fell from exhaustion. Lebow's medical volunteers were numerous enough to staff some of New York City's premiere medical centers. Fifteen hundred sports medicine specialists were on hand to treat ankle and foot injuries, shin splints, muscular and quadricep stress, and other injuries. First-aid stations stacked with Vaseline, rubbing creams, stethoscopes, and tongue depressants were stationed at mile intervals.

The most-sought-after volunteer assignment was on the finish line. These volunteers were as close as possible to the runners in their moment of triumph. Nearby stood Lebow, waving in runners with his windmill hand motion, shouting congratulations. Seated in the stands were the mayor and other celebrities. Background music of "New York, New York" or "Chariots of Fire" hyped tired runners to put forth one final explosion of energy.

In the marathon's final stretch in Central Park, 450 marshals controlled the crowds. At the finish line itself, 100 volunteers clicked and counted as runners crossed. Volunteers wielding "swing ropes" directed runners to one of three finish lines. On the other side of the lines, other volunteers directed runners into eighteen chutes. Another 125 chute pushers kept exhausted runners moving along. At its most crowded time—the four-hour mark—six runners every second, or 360 runners a minute, were crossing the finish line.

Seventy-five volunteers stood ready to tear the identifying bar codes from the runners' bibs. Sixty others handed out roses and medals. Sixty volunteers—the blanket crew—clothed the exhausted runners in Mylar blankets of polypropylene, vacuum coated with aluminum. And beyond the finish line, 150 people worked the family reunion area, and another 250 handled food and baggage, one of the least-popular jobs. Despite the lack of glamour in that last assignment, Marybeth Sullivan found it highly gratifying. After spending seven hours deep in the belly of one of the forty buses in Central Park that held runners' clothing and cash, she reported, "Some of these runners are so exhausted they can't lift their arms to reach the overhead racks. Others are so stiff and cramped they are unable to bend over to pull a bag stuffed underneath a seat. I was thanked in about a dozen languages Sunday afternoon."

In building his marathon party, it was not enough for Lebow to conceptualize a vision and scheme to implement it. His leadership was highly personal—from supervising the distribution of marathon applications in Central Park to cleaning up garbage at the Staten Island start, from leading the pack from his pace car to exhorting the crowds and waving in tired or injured runners at the finish line, from enlisting sponsors and cutting deals with star athletes to enticing the press and soothing politicos. For Lebow, it was a highly focused pursuit.

Some of the race director's crew "unofficially" assisted him in personal ways in order to help him stay focused, or simply to help out. His absentmindedness and forgetfulness being at variance with his native pragmatism, Lebow's more devoted staffers and volunteers shielded him. Sometimes, after a run in the park on a Sunday afternoon, he would buzz Sandy Sislowitz to come down with her spare set of keys and open his club's doors. Sislowitz was a social worker who lived across the street from Lebow's club's town house, and the race director had once again forgotten to take his keys with him.

Volunteers and associates who assumed housekeeping and social responsibilities made life easier for Lebow. An office secretary washed his laundry. Neighbor Sandy Sislowitz and Muriel Frohman from Riverdale, the Bronx, sent "business-related" gifts and carried out errands for the promoter. In romance as well, Lebow's helpers wanted him covered—so much so that for one of her birthdays, girlfriend Paula Fahey in Minnesota received *three* gifts, each bearing the race director's name.

"When he was out there," said Achilles Track Club founder Dick Traum, the race director concentrated on one salient goal: 'What could I do for the club? How could I help road running?' He developed relationships. He talked with his constituency at races. If he saw someone, he asked himself, 'How can he become a sponsor? Maybe he could contribute money.' If Parks Commissioner Henry Stern came out to a race with his dog, Fred would go over and talk with him."

Since he was always running instead of taking taxis, it was not unusual for him to encounter players from the executive side of his marathon production in streets along the way. "In the mornings, I would frequently see him running slowly to his office," said Lebow's agent, Barry Frank of International Management Group, regarding their spontaneous Park Avenue encounters. "My father was in the *shmatte* [clothing] business," said Frank. "We met on the street and used Yiddish expressions. I felt a great deal of affection for him, both of us being Jewish, and not many Jews being in the sports area."

Inasmuch as there were few Jews among the top marathoners, nor many who were highly involved in sports organizationally in Lebow's era, it is enlightening to ask what drew so many of them to relative prominence in both the New York City Marathon and the New York Road Runners Club. In addition to agent Barry Frank, his Jewish affiliates included his technical assistant and successor, Allan Steinfeld; real estate developers Jack and Lewis Rudin; Democratic Party activist and marathon promoter George Spitz; New York Road Runner Club workhorses Joe Kleinerman and Kurt Steiner; NYRRC treasurer, secretary, and board member Peter Roth, Gary Meltzer, and Steve Wald, respectively; Achilles Track Club founder Dick Traum; ham operator Steve Mendelsohn; finish-line coordinator David Katz; marathon attorney Robert Laufer; and a number of other NYRRC board members. Although among the factors might have been the relatively high Jewish population in the New York metropolitan area, it was more likely their cultural affinity for trendiness—whose earmarks marathoning began to take on beginning with the Lebow years—and their ability to relate to the style and mind-set of fellow Jew Fred Lebow that attracted and held their interest.

Certainly, Lebow's ability to relate back to these support-staff members and volunteers played some part in keeping them involved. In staff interaction, for example, signs of the nation's most visible race director's Jewishness regularly appeared. He used Yiddish expressions in conversations with Steinfeld, and public relations associate Laura Leale said she learned Yiddish terms such as *meshugana* (crazy), *treife* (nonkosher), and *shiksa* (non-Jewish woman) from Lebow. Beyond the ranks of the staff of the New York Road Runners Club, he also bantered with Jews whom he felt were aware of their heritage. Television meteorologist and marathoner Mr. G. recalled that "[Lebow] was shocked when I answered 'Yitzchak' " to his question, "What's your Hebrew name?"

When Lebow was on the road, fellow Jews occasionally invited him to religious events. When he and Joe Kleinerman once found themselves in Boston for the Boston Marathon on Passover eve, NYRRC board member Steve Wald invited the pair to a Passover Seder with his family in that city. "They were both so touched by the Seder they had tears in their eyes," recalled Wald. And when Democratic Party activist George Spitz, the man who conceived of the 1976 five-borough marathon, decided to become bar mitzvah in 1986, at age sixty-three, a half century after the traditional age of thirteen, Lebow was overjoyed. "Fred was so happy that I was returning to my roots," noted the bar mitzvah "boy." Accompanied by *Runner's World* publisher George A. Hirsch, Lebow attended Spitz's weekday service and reception at Congregation Orach Chaim, an Orthodox synagogue on Lexington Avenue, sitting in his running cap rather than a yarmulke during the ceremony, and presenting Spitz with a bar mitzvah gift that came from marathon associate sponsor Tiffany & Company.

Passover was the most joyous Jewish holiday for Lebow, and unless he was out of town, he celebrated it in a unique way, with his running-world associates, at what they tongue in cheek called the "Orphans' Seder." The term *orphan* referred to the single status of most of the guests, in contrast with the family celebrations traditionally marking Passover. The Seder was held at the Eighty-ninth Street apartment of Road Running Club volunteer Sandy Sislowitz, which Lebow's colleagues facetiously called, "Fred's Jewish home across the street." Some fifteen to twenty "orphans" attended. Most of the group, according to Phil Greenwald, a Road Runners Club volunteer, consisted of "people fairly lapsed in religious observance," and not all of the participants were Jewish. Lebow came dressed in his standard running outfit, and the men wore skullcaps known as yarmulkes on their heads. In the clubby atmosphere, Allan Steinfeld served as "rabbi" and directed the reading of the Haggadah that described the Jewish Exodus from Egypt, with excerpts from the Haggadah being recited aloud by both Jews and non-Jews. They read key passages in both Hebrew and English, with "the Four Questions," traditionally read aloud by the youngest member present, recited by Victoria Phillips of the Road Runners Club marketing department. When his turn came, Lebow recited the prayers in the Hebrew he had learned at the cheder in Arad.

The first part of the Haggadah reading lasted about an hour, following which Sislowitz served a dinner of traditional kosher holiday dishes: gefilte fish and horseradish, chicken soup, chicken, Israeli matzo, and kosher wine. Following dinner, the orphans spent another hour on the second section of the Haggadah. At the end of the Seder, based on the final verse in the Haggadah—"Next Year in Jerusalem"—Steinfeld led the orphans in a relaxed examination of the year past, citing such events as the dismantling of the Berlin Wall in his review. "Fred would be very pensive while Allan was talking," noted Phillips. Lebow, insisting that the entire ritual be run along traditional lines, one year jumped out of his seat, warning, "You can't do that! You're not Jewish," when Sislowitz's friend Jim Ellson, a New York City fireman, rose to open the apartment door for the entry of the invisible Elijah the Prophet.

Chanukah marked another festival that Lebow observed with his road-running Jewish family. In 1988, Phillips started inviting the Jewish staff of the club into Lebow's office to light the menorah on the first night of Chanukah. "I brought the Chanukah candles," she said, the menorah was placed on Lebow's crowded desk, and the group stayed until the candles went out.

It was not only with his Jewish associates that Lebow related so well. Despite his relentlessness and drive, he was often playful with staff members, especially women. Susan Hoffner, one of the first two paid members of Lebow's club, was the object of his mischievous sense of humor. "At first he'd beat me in the Central Park races and then I got better and beat him regularly. One year in the Mike Hannon 20-miler, I thought he was way in back of me. But instead of racing, he waited in the bushes for me to come by, and then jumped out behind me!"

What was perhaps most binding to associates, as with most relationships, was Lebow's willingness and desire to confide in them, and
bounce ideas off them. In 1988, when after the success of that year's
running the race director was thinking of retiring, New York newspapers wrote about his possibly running for mayor, and taking charge of
his old nemesis, the Chicago marathon, loomed as another option. But
it was with NYRRC board member and friend Steve Wald that Lebow
talked about a career as a Broadway producer. Unfortunately, brain cancer struck within the year, and whether the showman would have transferred his legendary status to any of these other areas remains
unknown.

The Race to the Finish

12

The Race Against Cancer

BULLHORN IN HAND, a drawn Fred Lebow sat passively in the backseat of his white Mercedes lead car on Marathon Sunday 1990. The fifty-eight-year-old race director was neither shouting orders, erecting barriers, nor lining up banners as in years past at his festival. Sapped of his strength by an inoperable brain tumor diagnosed nine months earlier, Lebow put a transforming somber spin on the party spirit of the twenty-first edition of his race.

More important than the race itself, Lebow was simply glad to be alive. Thankful he was well enough to at least be driven to the finish line, the gaunt impresario allowed his race to be associated with a charity for the first time ever after years of vetoing such tie-ins because they would diminish his marathon's purist and party character. In his weariness, Lebow also agreed to let the theme that year be "Fred, This Run's for You." Although he enjoyed the spotlight, he had always felt it immodest to have his name figure so prominently in the party he created. As is common with cancer patients, wanting to still disbelieve their diagnoses, Lebow—who had always been the unflinching realist—was in denial: "I don't think I have cancer. I think the doctors are talking about some other Fred who has cancer."

At least a year before Lebow was diagnosed, he had declared that his street theater lacked the excitement it had generated in the past, and, clearly thinking of other challenges, he announced he would retire if Grete Waitz won his race a tenth time. The curtain could then fall on a performance never to be surpassed. He confessed to *Runner's World* that his excitement had ebbed, but that the roar of the crowd still thrilled him as he exited the Queensboro Bridge in the Mercedes lead car, heading for First Avenue:

I was thinking about that last year, at the halfway point to be exact. The race was not as exciting as the days when Alberto Salazar was going for a world record. I realized, though, that I expected too much; you can't have a world record all the time. Also, I realized, you don't have to keep the same level of excitement for twenty years. When I came off the Queensboro Bridge and heard the crowds scream, I thought, "What's wrong with me?" and I got rejuvenated.

As though being punished for his waning devotion to the marathon, his running time had slackened about the same time. But he did not connect the slower speed with oncoming illness: "I was abroad at a marathon," he said, and "I usually run an eight or nine minute pace. All of a sudden, I was doing a twelve-minute pace. It was hard to run. I thought, 'OK, no big deal.' Then I went to Belgrade and I was jogging. I was slow. I figured it was all the traveling. I came back to New York and went jogging in Central Park. Same thing. I didn't pay much attention to it."

At the New York Road Runners Club town house, subtle signs of deterioration appeared. His walk slowed, his ability to focus declined, he was more forgetful. All these changes were out of step with the persona of the promoter who knew every angle.

Girlfriend Paula Fahey became suspicious when the race director phoned her in Minnesota declaring, "I love you." Lebow, in his years of womanizing, made it a point of honor to withhold such spoken intimacies.

At the Empire State Building Run Up in early 1990, Lebow's public relations associate Laura Leale noticed, "[He] became very clingy, he wouldn't let me get away from him." The race director, in tuxedo and race cap, rose to speak at the annual New York Road Runner Club Awards Banquet on February 10, but his words came out so garbled that most in the audience suspected he was in trouble. He confused the names of close associates, prompting Leale to whisper corrections in his ear. A few days following the banquet, Lebow was brought to 1974 marathon winner Dr. Norbert Sander. In order not to alarm him, running club associates gave the race director's pained left knee as the reason for the visit.

A worried Dr. Sander referred Lebow to Dr. Seymour Gendelman, a neurologist at Mount Sinai Medical Center. Never losing sight of his identity as race promoter, Lebow felt pride that Dr. Gendelman, and several of the other doctors treating him, were members of the New York Road Runners Club. Having runners as physicians also gave him peace of mind. Not only did they understand him better than nonrunners, but they also supported his need to keep exercising during even the bleakest days of his illness.

After giving Lebow several tests, including an MRI, and taking a biopsy in the left frontal lobe of the skull, Dr. Gendelman reported the bad news to the race director: he had a tumor in his brain the size of a tennis ball. Known as lymphoma, it was a type of cancer that normally developed in other parts of the body, such as the chest or stomach, and rarely appeared in the brain. Unless the tumor shrank dramatically, Dr. Gendelman informed Lebow, he faced death within three to six months.

At first oblivious to the diagnosis, Lebow's response was defiance. He thought: "What do they mean six months to live?" He was still able to move his arms and legs. There was nothing wrong with him. But at 2:00 A.M. that night, family and friends having gone home, the race director, still awake, asked himself the question that haunts every cancer patient. "Oh God, why? Why me?" He thought about his sins. Over the years he had neglected Talmudic studies and the Orthodox Jewish lifestyle. He remembered the Hebrew prayer book his mother had given him with its embossed metal cover . . . and the loving inscription on the flyleaf in Yiddish: "My dear son . . . I hope you read your morning prayers every day." In the darkness of the hospital room, Lebow wanted to confess his sins. He thought about smuggling diamonds as a boy in Europe, and about the women he had loved. His only real sin, he concluded, was in not being married. But then he remembered the "episode of the chick," an episode from when he was six years old, in pre-World War II Romania.

Walking on a road with friends in the Jewish section of town, Fishl had been passed by a farmer who was being followed by a mother hen trailed by a dozen chicks. Young Fishl Lebowitz wanted one of those yellow fuzzy chicks as a pet, so he scooped up the last toddler and ran quickly down the road to the security of his house, thinking he was safe. But later that night, he overheard the neighbor, who had traced the chick to the Lebowitz home from the cap Fishl had inadvertently dropped on the street, reporting the missing chick to his father. Fishl's parents gave back the chick and never punished him. He never found out the fate of the chick. Now in the hospital, he felt so ashamed that he cried. And that was what had bothered him for more than fifty years. It was the only bad deed he could remember, and he was crying for the first time since the incident. Then he thought: "So this was my secret worry all these years." Such introspection—unusual for Lebow, a man who never looked back—lasted about two hours. It felt like the longest night of his life. Finally, he concluded that he had nothing to feel sorry about. He woke at seven the next morning ready to do battle with his cancer.

A "minor sin" about which Lebow's illness stirred repentance was fibbing about his age. Upon meeting new women, or in filling out applications for marathon races, Lebow routinely sliced five years off his birth date. Thus, in initial press reports about Lebow's hospitalization, he was referred to as fifty-two years of age, although he was actually fifty-seven, and references cited his date of birth as 1937, although it was really 1932. This information, disseminated by the press office of his running club, had the purpose of making the race director seem younger. But coming to terms with this deception, Lebow, still in the hospital, told alter ego Allan Steinfeld, "I may die soon. If I do, let my tombstone have my right age."

Rather than philosophically accepting the fate of his illness, Lebow remained certain of his recovery. "If willingness and desire count," he said, "I'll make it." Basic to overcoming the disease was his stress on motion and exercise. Physical fitness was critical. He made sure not to stagnate. Though sick in bed, unable to do almost anything, a patient can still wiggle his fingers and toes, he declared. Over the months in and out of hospitals, he refused to let himself be ruled by disease. He fought with exercise. So encouraged, from the tenth-floor room at Mount Sinai Hospital, the race director proudly watched his club's Central Park races. He knew he was not forgotten when runners waved as they passed the hospital.

And always the improviser, Lebow adapted the hospital setting to his new condition. In one of his hallway jaunts he discovered that his room was near a circular rooftop terrace. The terrace was only about fifty feet long and thirty feet wide, but it was big enough to serve as a makeshift track. He calculated that sixty-seven times around the terrace equaled one mile, so why not walk laps around this improvised race-course? Ignoring the chilly March wind, the running promoter trudged through his walking regimen without telling Dr. Gendelman. Eventually, he was able to increase his circular distance on that obscure hospital rooftop to two miles. When he finally revealed his secret exercise routine, Dr. Gendelman, instead of being critical, praised Lebow's will to recover.

Still in the survivor role, Lebow continued this fitness program after his brain biopsy at Mount Sinai. Undeterred by weakness, he got out of bed the day following the biopsy and walked twelve steps in the hospital hallway. Each day, his distance increased. At first he walked five minutes, then ten minutes. He figured out that eleven laps around the corridors equaled a mile. "Just like the [Madison Square] Garden track," he joked, and when Eamonn Coghlan, holder of the world record for the fastest indoor mile, joined Lebow in his eleven-laps-to-the mile route during a visit, the race director declared, "You won the Millrose miles by running eleven laps," to which Coghlan quipped, "Yes, this feels like eleven laps to the mile."

Proud of his womanizing reputation, Lebow had never shown any desire to become a father, but in a moving reference to his fatherlessness, Lebow asked about Coghlan's four children, saying, "You have so much to live for. I envy you. I have no kids," and Coghlan replied, "Fred, you have all the runners."

In April 1990, Lebow transferred to Memorial Sloan-Kettering Cancer Center for radiation and chemotherapy treatments. Once more he improvised a running track. He meticulously counted hallway tiles, forging a two hundred-yard circuit. This time, in addition to walking his own laps, he recruited other patients to join him. Lap walking with Lebow became a new recreational program at the world-class cancer treatment facility. He had managed to transform hospital corridors and rooftops from antiseptic medical passageways into running and speed-walking courses. The showman's skills in fighting pain in hospital corridors eventually led to a Road Runners Club-sponsored program for cancer patients.

Based on these two hospital stays, the impresario concluded, "Hospitals need to have more of an emphasis on keeping people active. They need to have workout rooms, and they need to get the patients into those rooms and make them take care of themselves."

Athletes, sponsors, and volunteers alike were all greatly affected by Lebow's illness, greatly admiring his courage and wherewithal as they lamented the loss to road running his disease brought on. The running philosopher Dr. George Sheehan observed:

> When it comes to running, it's the race itself that builds up enthusiasm, the recruiting of new runners and the future of the sport. So it's the race director who's the most important member of the running community, and Fred Lebow is head and shoulders over every other race director in the world. He's the most imaginative, resourceful and most demanding. I always said Fred would be a millionaire if he wanted to do anything else.

"I equate Fred with the Road Runners club and with running," said Lisa Sepulveda of Edelman Public Relations. "His being at the start and at the finish [of our client, Advil's, minimarathon] brought so much charisma to the race," she said. "Once, Fred came straight from a chemo session at the hospital to start the race."

Having never viewed Lebow only as an instrument for promoting their corporate goals, marathon sponsors were deeply affected when the race director was diagnosed with cancer. During his battle with the disease, they saw his suffering as much more than that of a stricken business associate. From sponsors who poured money into his show, genuine grief went beyond the perfunctory get-well cards or hospital visits.

The poignancy of one sponsor's concern was shown in the summer of 1990, only a few months after Lebow was released from his first hospitalization. Jack Maguire invited Lebow to join him in a publicity event at the reservoir at Central Park and Ninetieth Street, only a few blocks from the race director's town house Road Runners Club headquarters. There, under the warm sun, Maguire and his staff gave out bottled water to passersby, simulating a race-day scene. "Fred looked like a skeleton, very fragile," remembered Maguire. "We were supposed to walk back to Fred's office. But he was too weak to walk that short distance. He would never say how sick he was. My hero was breaking down in front of my eyes. We both cried together. We walked back hand in hand." Maguire also recalled a conversation he'd had with his friend, in which Lebow, toward the end of his life, emphasized his vision of the marathon as a people's race: "He didn't talk about the presidents and the famous people he met, but about the people whose lives he changed, about how running was good for the little guy, someone, for example, who was thinking of committing suicide, but who went on to enjoy life after he started running."

In a literary show of concern, Tiffany's Jim Quinn turned to American colonial history to compliment Lebow on his courage in fighting cancer. At a premarathon luncheon at Chemical Bank's headquarters, Quinn cited a letter Abigail Adams had written to her husband, John Quincy Adams: "It is not in the still calm of life or in the response of pacific station, that great challenges are formed. Great necessities call our great virtues." Unable to stand such eloquence, Lebow replied: "Stop it. It sounds like my funeral!"

A lighter, though no less affectionate, example of the closeness between Lebow and his sponsors was a "conversation" he had with Hoechst's Ellen Sweeney. As Sweeney told it, "He [always] yelled at me to quit smoking. . . . Fred thought I had a sick sense of humor, so when I visited him at Mount Sinai Hospital, he said jokingly in a rasping voice, 'Stop smoking.' 'Fred,' I said, 'you're the one with cancer.' "

To his New York running circle, Lebow's hospitalization signaled a time to take stock of his accomplishments. The first day after chemo treatments, his personal doctor, Norb Sander; early marathon winner Nina Kuscsik, who worked as a patient representative at Mount Sinai; and Bob Glover, director of classes at Lebow's club, all visited. "We laughed over old marathon stories," recalled Kuscsik, who also brought the inveterate newspaper reader the main New York and national dailies. She was struck by the humanizing effect of his illness and talked about how Lebow's tendency to fade out, or lose interest in his conversations, seemed to have changed: "In the hospital, he developed a long attention span."

Feelings of helplessness and loss of control, emotions common to many cancer patients, did not plague Lebow. He capitalized on two strength-giving mechanisms: the confidence of the Holocaust survivor and the drive of the professional athlete. According to *Whatever It*

Takes: Athletes Against Cancer, Robert Brody's study of athletes recovering from cancer, Lebow fought his illness with the same mental attitudes as elite athletes: aggressiveness, determination, and emotional control. "We both knew he had a disease," said longtime friend Brian Crawford, "but we never talked about it. We never really discussed it, because he said, 'I'm going to get better,' and he felt he had nothing to discuss."

Lebow was not unworried about his disease. After an initial four weeks at Mount Sinai, he returned home, resuming a limited scale of running. While running one day, he suddenly felt a pain just below the right knee. Returning to the hospital, Lebow was told the bad news by a vascular surgeon: he had developed a blood clot, very possibly related to his brain tumor.

Following surgery for the clot, the race director, still abreast of current events, compared his condition with that of Republican National Party chairman Lee Atwater. The politician had been diagnosed with cancer and eventually died from a blood clot. What worried Lebow was that Atwater, who died at age forty, was a six-mile-a-day runner. "Panic invaded me for the first time since my troubles began," said Lebow. "I made a connection and felt an eerie identification with Lee Atwater."

In Lebow's strategy to fight cancer through running, exercise became both a statement of gratitude and a mode of defiance. Returning home after removal of the blood clot, a tired Lebow took up walking in Central Park. Starting with a one-mile trail, he was up to walking two miles by the third day. After three weeks of walking, he inserted ten- to fifteen-yard jogs into his running regimen, amazed that although he, who had completed sixty-eight marathons, was jogging, every walker in the park could pass him by! Rather than lamenting that he had lost the power to run 7.5-minute miles and had to walk around the reservoir loop, an unconquerable Lebow declared, "I actually got more satisfaction out of my twenty to thirty-minute miles than when I was running fast."

As a result of a thirty-one-day cycle of radiation at Memorial Sloan-Kettering Cancer Center that spring, Lebow's weight dropped from 144 to 124 pounds. By his own description, he had "very little meat on my bones," yet he continued his slow loops around the park, sitting down and resting for a minute or two between miles.

Radiation and chemo had altered his facial features. He ran in the park with a hood over his head so he wouldn't be recognized. He had no hair, no beard, and no reason to call attention to his illness. But some old friends, recognizing him anyway, used humor to encourage him in his outings. Nina Kuscsik teased, "Fred, you'll trip, you're going so slowly," and "Fred, you're going more slowly now than when you were walking." Sandy Sislowitz, the social worker and volunteer who lived across the street from his club, joked, "Fred, you're so skinny, watch out that your pants don't fall off."

Lebow felt he recaptured his old zip when he returned to stair climbing. For years, he had either run or walked up the ten flights of his East Seventies apartment house. Once, he had covered the distance in thirty-nine seconds, but in the early stage of his illness, he had resorted to taking the elevator, afraid that if he climbed up, "I might collapse between floors and nobody would find me."

Lebow the showman had improvised at so many turns in his life that he determined not to be bowed by his new trouble. He searched for the reserves to live in pain. Now his chutzpah had to be applied to rolling back the disease instead of promoting his party. Striking him at the same time as the aging process, the pain of the disease forced him to come to terms with his physical limits.

He was conscious of every minute pain and discomfort, from constipation to side stitch while running. Developing a new relationship to that pain, he gave up fighting it. No longer would he fight to push himself beyond pain while running a race. If he were hurting, he would walk until the finish. He observed how experienced runners wisely respected the changing needs of their bodies.

Lebow's cancer not only transformed his running agenda, but also changed him as a man, recasting his priorities. The single-mindedness he used to develop his marathon party was replaced with a new appreciation of the balanced life. He developed an empathy and awareness of human fallibility, traits far different from the mind-set of the pragmatic showman who had created the fun marathon. He became willing to delegate, though in the past he had been convinced he could do a better job than anybody else in supervising such marathon details as the placement of balloons and banners. "I think I began to care more about people, to be more patient," admitted Lebow. "I got a call in the hospital from a friend I hadn't spoken to in years; a couple from my building I didn't speak to sent a basket of fruit. Why should people carry grudges?"

He developed a reflectiveness that he had all but abandoned in the entrepreneurial years when he had operated on gut instincts to make the deal. His new agenda went beyond running. "I used to think only about improving my own running or other people's running and I never realized the other stuff. Now I realize I can also improve their lifestyles."

Each morning, he awoke thanking God he was still alive. Thanking God did not mean a return to the Orthodoxy of his youth. "I wouldn't say I'm more religious, but I am more traditional." His religious rededication did see him taking his Jewishness more seriously. "When you're in the hospital for eight weeks, you have lots of time to read and think," he said. Though he remembered hating Hebrew school, Lebow's illness made him "a little more humble" and "much closer inside spiritually." He said that respect for religion and tradition "calmed me and made me aware of the need for compassion toward others. I realize that I am not a man here by myself, but that I exist within a world community of other people." It brought a stronger commitment to Jewish peoplehood. "[Beforehand, when] Jewish people would call to invite me to banquets and functions," he usually said no, but "Now I usually say yes. . . . I feel more of a kinship now to other Jews." Spiritually, Lebow asserted that he was "definitely a stronger Jew than I was 10, 20 years ago." He believed in God, went to temple more often, and "read more Jewish books."

Lebow's greater seriousness about his Jewishness was apparent to those close to him in so many ways. He asked Allan Steinfeld to succeed him as head of the New York Road Runners Club, while he retained directorship of the marathon, so he could devote time to Jewish charities and cancer patients in recovery, and to travel to Israel. (Steinfeld declined the offer, arguing that Lebow always had the necessary "freedom" to pursue his interests.) Warm-up exercise leader Françoise Granville Levinsohn realized that "in his last years, he missed religion" when Lebow commented to her, "something like this is what I need," as they passed Temple Emanuel while running together in Central Park. Girlfriend Heather Dominic noted his more Jewish frame of reference following dinner at an East Side Hong Kong vegetarian restaurant, when he told the manager, "You're food is so good . . . why don't you become kosher."

On a Monday following the Jewish high holy days, Laura Leale asked, "How did you spend the weekend?" and Lebow answered, "In shul," implying that she should have known such an obvious point. "In temple? Fred, since when do you go to temple?" she asked in reply. "What are you talking about?" the offended Lebow shot back.

Invited as a guest of honor to the Berlin Marathon, Lebow was seated next to Kathrine Switzer at a huge prerace athlete dinner. "Fred came into the hall very late," Switzer said, and since he was wearing a yarmulke rather than his legendary running cap, she asked, "Where have you been, Fred?" to which the race director answered, "I've been to temple. It's the first night of Rosh Hashanah." Switzer, who often chided Lebow on his short attention span, continued at that point, "It's interesting, you're actually paying attention to what I'm saying," and Lebow responded, "I think it's true. . . . I've become a better person." According to Switzer, "We went on to talk about Berlin being a creepy place. He was wearing a coat. I was wearing a sweater. I said, 'It's cold here,' " and Lebow said, "Yes, it's cold . . . in more ways than one," which she interpreted as referring to the pain of his Holocaust memories that always resurfaced in Berlin.

In his new soul-searching and Jewish reconnection, Lebow extended himself not only to cancer sufferers in general, but especially to Jewish victims of the disease. Beginning in 1992, he attended luncheons of the Israel Cancer Research Fund, an organization funding Israeli scientific research. According to the group's executive director, Milton Sussman, Lebow opened up to him in discussing his Holocaust memories. "Fred was a double survivor," said Sussman. "He survived the Holocaust and he survived cancer." Sussman sensed the race director's nostalgia in references to his family. "You know, Milt," Lebow said, "I'm from a very traditional family. I'm the only one who isn't." Sussman's opinion was that Lebow "was wistful rather than resentful about the different levels of Jewish observance between himself and his family."

When his battle with cancer caused him to become unhealthily thin, Lebow saw food more realistically than he had previously. It became an instrument for adding pounds to his emaciated body. "Right now, because I have to gain weight after my bout with cancer, I eat anything, including junk food," he said. "Sometimes I don't care what I eat; I just want to gain weight." Reintroducing meat into his diet for the much needed animal protein at the time, he at first overlooked whether it was kosher, but after a short interlude, he resumed eating only kosher meat, reestablishing that connection with his family's Orthodox heritage. Twice a week he dined at Siegel's Kosher Restaurant on Second Avenue where, according to proprietor Jeffrey Speciner, Lebow came in around 8 P.M. and ate dishes such as sautéed livers, stuffed cabbage, and knockwurst and beans; read the *New York Times;* and superficially nodded to patrons who recognized him.

In his personal life, Lebow became thankful for his family and for his newest girlfriend, Heather Dominic. His four brothers and two sisters were no longer of merely minimal interest. "Family? Brothers and sisters? Who cared? I saw my brothers and sisters individually only once every year or two. But now I realized how much they cared about me. And I realized how much I cared, too." For the first time in twenty years, he started talking regularly with his siblings.

As a man, Lebow sought to help other cancer patients find strength in their suffering with the same focus he had used to develop his marathon party. Achilles Track Club's Dick Traum detected this change in Lebow. "Fred has *publicly* addressed the issue of doing good for others for the first time," he said.

As a runner, he was surprised to learn about friends and fellow runners at the Central Park reservoir who had themselves had bouts with cancer he hadn't known about. If they beat the disease, why couldn't he?

Lebow was the subject of an outpouring of support from other cancer patients after his disease became public. Cans, tubes, and jars of tablets that the race director received from well-wishers, noted the *New York Times* on July 29, 1990, made Lebow's office desktop "look like a display rack in a health-food store." "I've gotten almost 50 books, hundreds of letters, recommending all kinds of stuff." By then, his tumor had shrunk some 75 percent.

What did Lebow advise in his newly found expertise as a victorious cancer patient? Exercise, self-help, and engagement in activities were the roads to recovery. "But I say to patients, 'All I can really tell you about is my own experience. I cannot give you drugs or referrals to doctors, and I cannot give you miracles or say whether you should have [for example] a mastectomy. You have to understand that the doctors can do only so much. At some point you have to help yourself. Do some exercise to keep yourself physically fit and feel better mentally.' "

In September 1990, tests indicated that the tumor in Lebow's brain had disappeared. Dr. Lisa DeAngelis, his physician at Memorial Sloan-Kettering, declared his cancer in remission. All treatments were ended. It was a far cry from the three-to-six-month life expectancy pronounced earlier in the year! And, according to Dr. DeAngelis, Lebow's recovery was traceable to his exercise regimen and positive mental attitude; his emotional strength enabled him to deal with the disease realistically, he tapped resources of discipline and determination as an athlete, and she did not sense depression during his treatment and recovery.

By November 1990, the race director was ready for his next show, and for the first time ever, Fred Lebow was defined as the party's star. Although he had led the five-borough marathon in his pace car every year since 1976, the festival's main performers had always been its top runners, such as Bill Rodgers and, later, Grete Waitz. The disclosure of his illness through the "Fred, This Run's for You" theme—and the connection of the race with the "Stop Cancer" movement—made the 1990 running of the New York City Marathon officially Fred Lebow's race.

Before being diagnosed with cancer, Lebow had never shifted his public position about charity races—vehemently opposing the association of specific charities with specific running events. Not known as one to admit mistakes, Lebow did so now, telling *FootNotes* in winter 1990 directly: "I opposed these charity races. For 20 years, I didn't do it. In retrospect, that may have been a mistake." But, he cautioned, funding must take place "in a proper atmosphere. . . . Races that can raise money for charity, should, but the races themselves should make some money. Then some percentage [could] go to the charity . . . something like that." The notion of holding a race exclusively for charity, or turning over runners' entry fees to a charity, still did not sit as well with Lebow as did the alternative in which runners raised funds through pledged miles.

Beginning with the 1990 running, the New York City Marathon

would raise funds for New York's Memorial Sloan-Kettering Cancer Center, with a goal of contributing $1.5 million for a chair in neuro-oncology. Runners were asked to join "Fred's Team" in "26.2 miles of hope," with each participating runner finding sponsors for each mile they would complete. Among the incentives offered to encourage them to do so were a computer and a trip to London. Ever the showman, in 1990 Lebow predicted, "I wouldn't be surprised if we raised $10 million." The amount actually collected that first year was $1.2 million.

Whereas all of Lebow's prior changes of direction in his marathon vision were based on either political pressure from city hall or the rise of a new constituency in the streets, this shift reflected the race director's own soul-searching. Stricken, and more exposed to suffering, Lebow recognized the group effort involved in reaching his vision's finish line. In confronting his own mortality, he was redefining his marathon vision as he was redefining himself, and in this new context, survival no longer meant not merely being known as the promoter of the most exciting marathon party in the world. Survival, for Lebow, took on a more spiritual, humanitarian definition in the form of ensuring life for others by, for example, raising big-time funds for cancer research.

Lebow's change of mind toward using his marathon as a fund-raiser was made after a series of painful chemotherapy treatments at Mount Sinai Medical Center. "When I went there, there were two kids, a 6-year-old and a 10-year-old, both bloated, sitting there," he explained. "You know, I can accept that I have cancer, I can accept that an adult could have cancer, but I cannot accept that for these little kids. So I came back and said, 'OK you can have your fund raiser.' " Letters to marathon entrants went out from Lebow (and, after his death, from other icons of his festival, like Grete Waitz), emphasizing his indebtedness to the hospital for its medical treatment. "When he was in the hospital," wrote Waitz, "Fred's heart went out to the children he met who were so brave. That's why he started a partnership with Memorial Sloan-Kettering to raise funds for cancer research."

While still an impresario at heart, cancer had changed Lebow's outlook on life in other ways as well. In his club's *New York Running News* issue of October-November 1990, Lebow reflected:

This year, when I take my place in the pace car on the Verrazano-Narrows Bridge at the race start, I will look at the crowd of runners with a totally new perspective. Your training and tenacity, your sense of discipline and purpose, has new meaning to me. By the very act of your completing the physical and mental task of training for the marathon, and then completing 26.2 miles, [you] inspire me. You, a vision of health and wholeness, are what will keep me going in my own battle with brain cancer.

Spurred on by his new rededication to his Jewishness, Lebow quietly entered the tent at the Fort Wadsworth staging area where the annual Marathon Minyan prayer service was under way two hours before the start of the 1990 marathon. The hundred Jewish marathoners standing in shorts and warm-up outfits watched as the weakened Lebow slowly approached Rabbi Jim Michaels, the prayer leader. "Fred was so thin, that when I put my arm around him, I could feel he hardly filled out his running suit," said Rabbi Michaels, who was also planning to run that day. After Lebow prayed with the minyan for a few minutes, Rabbi Michaels interrupted the service to recite the Hebrew prayer for the ill: "May He who blessed our forefathers bless and heal Fishl . . . be filled with compassion for him to restore his health, to heal him, to strengthen him, and to revivify him." Spontaneously, the marathoners broke into Hebrew songs and danced around Lebow, asking God's blessings on the people of Israel. "There were tears in everyone's eyes," recalled Peter Berkowsky, cofounder of the Marathon Minyan.

Fittingly, the first to hail Lebow on Marathon Sunday 1990 following his prayers were the runners themselves. The cheering began as the gaunt race director, in white windbreaker and white bicycle cap, approached the pace car parked on the east roadway of the Verrazano-Narrows Bridge on Staten Island. The runners grouped along the bridge's west roadway—some wearing "This One's for You" T-shirts—applauded and shouted his name.

From the moment the pace car swung off the Verrazano-Narrows Bridge and turned right onto Fourth Avenue in Bay Ridge, Lebow clearly starred in his own street theater. "There were more people yelling for Fred than ever," said Charlie McCabe, the Chemical Bank sponsor who regularly rode in the lead car with the race director. "In other years they might yell, 'Great race,' or 'Good Run.' [But] this time they called out, 'Beat cancer,' 'Get well,' [and] things like that. Fred couldn't believe it."

In a touch of nostalgia, race organizers had ordered hot chocolate, an energy booster, and one of Lebow's favorite drinks, to be placed at all water stations along the course. "We must have stopped at 10 [stations], and none of them knew what we were talking about," said McCabe. "It's got to be a joke. We threatened to send one of the police escorts to a Dunkin' Donuts to bring some back."

McCabe witnessed Lebow's new tolerance. "He didn't yell at some of the runners who raced ahead early to be in the pictures," he reported. "In the early years, he was usually wacky about that. He was much more patient this year with people."

Lebow was surprised at his celebrity. At first it scared him. Then his self-depreciating humor took over, and he said it was so overwhelming, he felt like running for governor!

After the news conference with the winners, a weary Lebow returned to the finish line outside Tavern on the Green. As he had done in marathons past, the race director went to wave in tired runners. They drew strength from the presence of the sickly looking Lebow waiting up ahead. "The four- and five-hour finishers are very close to me," the pallid race director said. Facing the limitations of his illness with no illusions, Lebow remarked, "Today was special for me. I have cancer, and I hope to be here next year. But I'm not sure." He sensed he was not as sharp as he used to be. He was tired.

He discussed turning over his duties as race director of the New York City Marathon to his assistant Allan Steinfeld. "Allan deserved it," said Lebow. Titles no longer held meaning to the race director. As long as he and Steinfeld were involved, New York would still boast the two top marathon leaders in the world. Though Lebow's doctors declared him to be in remission, he never regained the mental agility from which sprang the initiative to hype his marathon vision. Now his salesmanship was more diffuse, his maneuverings were less original, his responses slower. The extra kick was no longer there. "There was slippage of his mental acuity," said Bill Noel, a race director at Lebow's club and formerly his third in command. "Only part of the time, he was there," said

Noel regarding Lebow's limited participation in conversations. "That wasn't Fred."

In March 1991, Lebow's recovery was marred by surgery at Memorial Sloan-Kettering to remove a cancerous tumor from his thyroid gland. His weight had dropped a dozen pounds, and he nervously read about people his own age who had died in recent months. The normally upbeat Lebow confessed that the fight was taking a toll: "I get tired, very tired, and I still have no appetite."

But even in the hospital, the marathon was never far from his thoughts. "I dreamt about the marathon in the hospital," Lebow said. "It is the event that consumes me more than any other." His morale during this hospital stay was boosted by the memory of his performance in Minneapolis a month earlier, the first race he had run in a year. He finished the five-miler in forty-seven minutes, thirty seconds.

As in his earlier hospitalizations, Lebow transformed the hallways into makeshift racecourses. "It was either 100 or 110 meters," said Lebow regarding the course he measured on his floor. "I didn't bother to have it certified!" According to his calculations, he walked around 3,000 meters. And the day after leaving the hospital, he was again walking in Central Park.

Lebow's courage inspired elite runners as well as fellow cancer patients. "Fred's illness made me realize how fortunate any of us are to have our health," said running star Joan Benoit Samuelson a few days before the 1991 marathon. "I've been injured and come back, but it's such a larger comeback for Fred." Samuelson withdrew from the 1990 marathon with a back injury, embarrassed that she canceled while the race director was summoning his limited strength to direct the festival.

Lebow's American nationalism, which had been latent in his marathon party, surfaced as the disease forced him to come to terms with life's essentials. This time, Lebow announced that he would be cheering for Joan Benoit Samuelson, as an American competitor, to capture the women's title. "I'm not embarrassed," said Lebow. "I'm a human being. It's extremely important that Joan Benoit win. I'd rather see her win in a time of 2:35 than see someone else win in 2:25. I want to see her win because we live in America and as much as I hate being chauvinistic, I want a local person to win." Previously, when Grete Waitz was his personal favorite, Lebow was not so open with his predictions. "I've changed, probably because of my damn cancer," said Lebow. "I don't pretend anymore. I used to say let the best runner win, but I don't lie anymore."

A few months earlier, Lebow had once again displayed his self-depreciating humor during a visit with President George H. W. Bush at the White House. The race director came attired in a business suit and running shoes. "I didn't have any dress shoes," said Lebow, "and I didn't want to pay $200 for a new pair." But the president, also a jogger, admired Lebow's sneakers. So when the promoter returned home, he phoned the manufacturer, who sent Bush a pair.

He also found humor in his Central Park cradle. In a run circling the reservoir, he noticed a sizable movie crew at work. Photographers, trucks, trailers, and lights were all there filming *Silver*, with Sharon Stone and Bill Baldwin. A grin crossed Lebow's face as he jogged toward the production. "Here I am," he announced, as if the cameras were awaiting his arrival!

As his strength slowly returned, Lebow began focusing on what had only been a fantasy when he lay at death's door at Mount Sinai Hospital in early 1990: running in his creation, the five-borough New York City Marathon. "I remember the day they told me I had cancer and I had six months to live," commented the race director. "I was in bed that night and I had tears in my eyes. I have never run the five borough marathon." Though he ran in sixty-eight marathons, all around the world, he never competed in his own creation because he was busy directing it from his lead car each year on Marathon Sunday.

Medically, was this recovering cancer patient in a condition to go the distance? "Yes," declared Dr. DeAngelis. She saw no medical reason to stop him from competing. But she was quick to warn that not all cancer patients should attempt such a feat. Heavy chemotherapy, she said, would weaken patients with less stamina than Lebow.

In Lebow's mind, the marathon challenge was more existential than athletic. If he could run, the disease was defeated. And the marathon run would also be the promoter's way of wishing himself "Mazel tov!" in honor of his sixtieth birthday the next June. And for fellow cancer victims, Lebow saw his running the marathon as a health-improving message.

But Lebow was still scared. What if he hit the legendary wall after fifteen or eighteen miles? What if his knees or ankles flared up in pain? He might have to walk the last ten miles. Yet complete it, he determined, he would . . . crossing the finish with raised hands. He also resolved to do his personal share to add to the $1.2 million the 1990 marathon had raised, and the $652,173 the 1991 race had raised for Memorial Sloan-Kettering for cancer research through the instrument of "Fred's Team." As a designated runner in 1992, he would be a source of contributions based on the number of miles he himself personally completed.

Through it all, even with his new persona as cancer patient in remission, he remained the resourceful impresario. Despite his talk of his newly minted spirituality and closer family ties, he hung on to the badge of promoter. Reputation in hand as a successful fighter against cancer, the race director declared in July 1990 his pride with the promoter label. It was still his defining title. "The key is, you have to be blatant," he said. "You can't just sit back. When people called me a promoter, I used to object to it. I'd say: 'I'm not a promoter. I'm a jogger and I like the sport I'm doing.' But yes, I am a promoter. We've done so many things in New York that only a promoter can do."

Convinced that the marathon movement he pioneered had developed a life of its own, he continued to throw out the prospect of revising standard athlete payments. Marathoning was secure, he argued, because of two factors: the commitment of the "ordinary" grassroots runners and the loyalty of the crowds. Cash was secondary to the race's excitement. As proof of the runners' commitment, claimed Lebow, "The marathon used to be a one-shot deal; everyone wanted to do *one*, with or without training. Now it's a lifestyle; people do one or two a year, even set their vacations around running a marathon. The emphasis is not on how fast they go but on the act of going the distance."

Urban spectators, argued Lebow, were now committed to runners sprinting through the city streets. "Any big-city marathon always gets front-page coverage and good television ratings." Since he had the crowds in tow, the savvy showman declared that "the quality of marathon fields is no longer as important as it used to be." So why shell out big bucks, he asked, if both the commonplace runner—the staple of his show—and the crowds were sold on his vision?

Persuaded that his festival no longer needed big money for elite runners to draw the public, and aggravated over bickering for appearance money by the elite athletes themselves, he proposed a financial overhaul of his party. He called for eliminating all appearance and prize money for a one-year trial period. "I think we have to experiment," he said. "I just wonder [what would happen] if you don't pay any appearance money or even prize money." He was "tortured by the idea that the elite runners don't appreciate us. . . . I don't mean to make it [strictly] a people's race [with no elite runners]," he said, "but should we spend half a million dollars if it doesn't have any effect?" He was piqued when American runner Ken Martin demanded a $20,000 appearance fee for his marathon in 1990, yet he countered with a $17,500 offer. Allan Steinfeld bristled, "Athletes and agents started calling us back and saying, 'If Ken Martin is getting $20,000, we should get at least $10,000.' "

Still, with all his talk about eliminating large purses, big money was an instrument Lebow would use when it came to hyping his show, and he now offered an unprecedented $1 million bonus for an under-two-hour marathon. Outsiders said this feat was nearly impossible to achieve, but for the promoter, it would generate publicity. "This will give the running world a little kick and that is what we need," he said. He further observed, "The sport of running has not been great in money or prizes. We're doing it to inspire the sport of running. Maybe we'll never get to the era of Dream Team basketball, [but] . . ."

Promoting the show itself was just one field of activity in which the racing icon continued to be involved. In one area, in fact, it was because he was hobbled by cancer that he became especially emboldened. It was now time to try to settle some scores with the sport's national governing bodies. He began a crusade against the TAC's 1984 decision to strip Alberto Salazar of the world record he had set at the 1981 New York City Marathon. Three years after the event, TAC had decided that Lebow's course had not been accurately measured and that Salazar therefore had not finished the distance. "[Back] in 1984, I didn't say anything," confessed Lebow.

I was quiet. I was meek. But now I speak up and it's working. Salazar never took any short cuts; he never ran the tangents. Then three years later they strip him [of the mark]. I was too weak to fight this [at the time]. If I had been stronger, I would have won easily. I should have spoken up. I didn't because I had such respect for TAC. It turns out that they are just a bunch of pencil pushers. . . . They had the fear of God in me in those days. They were the giants of our industry, so how could I object if a bunch of pencil pushers decided the course was short?

Unfortunately, in spite of the tragic irony that it was Lebow's terminal illness that had imbued him with such a fighting spirit, the race director was unable to have the decision reversed.

Though not losing his focus on his own marathon, the impresario did tinker with other projects. He held discussions with Donald Trump about a race in Atlantic City traversing two of Trump's casinos. He toyed with a race featuring Mike Tyson, the former heavyweight champion, running a twenty-second sprint. He negotiated for a Carl Lewis-Ben Johnson-Leroy Burrell one hundred-meter race on New York City's Randalls Island. And even though he was weakened by cancer and preoccupied with fine-tuning his marathon festival, he still found time in the summer of 1990 to attack a project he had launched a year earlier: a star-studded track and field meet.

Lebow's new scheme, the New York Games, was designed to move his running club beyond distance running into all facets of competitive running. It was as though he struck back from cancer with a vengeance, but improving American marathon competitors remained his main goal, even with this new endeavor. He predicted that by 2002, the year in which he planned to go for his seventieth marathon, in honor of his seventieth birthday, "The women will have broken 2 hours, 15 minutes [and] the men will run under 2 hours." He made predictions about technology, foreseeing "more high-falutin' shoes—a spring shoe [with] half a dozen springs in each shoe, and as you step on them, you'll get a little bounce." But it pained Lebow more and more, now that he was ill and didn't know how much time he had left, that leadership in the sport he pioneered had steadily slipped away from the United States, leading him to sadly prophesy, "I don't think there will be another American winner of a major marathon." Big bucks, which had lured a new international field of runners to marathoning, had led to the decline of American marathon winners, and this decline had become self-perpetuating. "We started offering prize money ten years ago to attract the best U.S. runners," Lebow observed, "but instead, it attracted the best foreign runners. These marathoners were treated like heroes at home and inspired a whole new generation of elite marathoners. Without a U.S. winner of a top marathon, American runners have no hero to inspire them."

The rise of other competitive sports was also hurting marathoning. "Our men and women are not being attracted to the distance races," he noted. "There are so many sports getting a ton of media coverage other than running and marathoning that children's interests are diverted. . . . In the 17 years that there has been a five-borough New York City Marathon, only one U.S.-born runner has won."

In support of the New York Games he was proposing, he observed:

> I think before marathoning improves, track and field has to improve; that's where the quality comes from—from the track. That's where the Shorters and Salazars come from. That's why I'm devoting so much effort to events like the New York Games. . . . The meet directors, the athletes, coaches, promoters came to me and said, "You've done a great job with the New York Marathon, you can help track and field." They told me how major colleges had dropped track and field, indoor meets had been dropping, outdoor meets have been disappearing. It seemed as if track and field had gone downhill.

But success with his marathon festival had triggered a track and field revival. "Some [pointed out that] though the Boston Marathon had been around for years, no races had made any impact until the 1976 New York City Marathon. Its instant success galvanized excitement and growth of road racing worldwide. And people said to me, do for track and field what the New York City Marathon had done for road racing."

Its name recognition would make it easier to sell this product. "What makes New York City so valuable is its name," claimed Lebow. "New York City sells around the world. If this event was called The Pittsburgh or The Albuquerque Games, it wouldn't have as much commercial value."

The problem, insisted Lebow, was one of poor promotion, not the sport of track and field itself. Observed the showman, "There is a crowd for track, but the sport has to be promoted. . . . You have to have public relations-minded leadership in The Athletic Congress, and that's what they don't have. Ollan Cassell (executive director of TAC) is a great leader, but he is not a promoter, he's not a public-relations person."

To be sure, the race director recognized the hardships in producing a track and field meet as compared with those of producing a marathon. "The marathon is much easier to put on," he said. "Marathon people make a commitment to run a marathon. They're not going to change to run 10,000 meters or 5,000 meters. In track and field, there are so many events that people will change, like the 100 to the 200 to the 400. There are alternatives. They can do different events." Lebow—the showman himself—was mostly enthralled by the sprints and hurdles. "They are incredible human performances," he remarked. "A town-house like the one owned by the New York Road Runners Club is 20 feet wide, but in the long jump, the athletes regularly jump 8 feet further. Or, they can jump 2 feet higher than my height—5 feet, 10 inches—or pole vault over a two-story building. It's hard to understand how they can surpass performances beyond normal capacity, yet it's realized in front of your eyes."

Press accounts about the race director's refusal to be overwhelmed by cancer—about his determination in "training" in hospital hallways, his plans to run in his own marathon, and the projects he was working on—appeared both during and after his hospitalization. These stories, touching something much deeper than a longing for the racetrack, seemed to fortify others fighting the disease in much the same way as Lebow's running seemed to fortify him. But "just" running was no longer enough. The showman Lebow still relished performing, admitting, "I want to come off the Queensboro Bridge and be greeted by thousands of people."

13

The Race Within

THE 2:30 A.M. WAKE-UP CALL from Steve Mendelsohn, the New York City Marathon's chief ham operator, did not reach Fred Lebow on Sunday, November 1, 1992, as it had for the previous sixteen years. That night, the sixty-year-old race director had bedded down for a few hours before the marathon, not in Manhattan's Sheraton Hotel with the Expo staff and the elite runners, but at the site of the starting line itself, Staten Island's Fort Wadsworth.

For the first time since founding the five-borough race in 1976, Lebow would be running with the pack instead of leading it with his megaphone in hand astride the Mercedes pace car. This impresario, always on the lookout for shtick to promote his spectacle, was about to act out the irresistible fantasy he had had two years earlier. He had promised himself that should his strength return, he would finally run his marathon creation. He would go with his ultimate promotional vehicle—his own weakened body—as a lesson of personal triumph.

True, the scene of this aging runner not hobbled by disease was sure to inspire. But for Lebow, the crowd counter, the feat of his gaunt body going the distance that Sunday drew a return he never expected. This showman's proud impulse to showcase his victory over cancer spurred the largest audience ever for the New York City Marathon, the event to which he had dedicated his life.

By this time, the marathon had become a celebration of New York, with some twenty-seven thousand runners threading their way through 26.2 miles of the city's otherwise discordant neighborhoods. More than any other event, it brought the Big Apple together. Marathon Sunday was the city's main fun day of the year, producing the largest single live sports audience in the world. Some two million spectators watched as runners of all shapes, sizes, abilities, and nationalities tested themselves against their dreams. Many in the crowd were on hand to cheer family, friends, and coworkers.

A lark in Central Park in its formative years, by 1992 the race drew athletes from every state in the United States and from one hundred nations, along with a television audience in the millions. Lebow's populist vision of marathoning had truly changed the nature of the sport, attracting the ordinary runner and plodder to this previously fearsome enterprise. If the marathon, as *New York* magazine reported on April 19, 1993, had emerged into a "pageant that exalts not only those who participate, but those who observe," Lebow stood as its star performer.

Attired on Marathon Sunday in his perennial running cap and running outfit, exhorting the crowds, arguing with police, hyping the media, inspecting the water stations along the course, firing up the runners, and personally waving them in at the finish line, this slight, bearded, heavily accented Romanian Jewish émigré was the trademark of the city's open-air fall festival he directed.

Every runner harbored his or her own secret reason for this seemingly bizarre challenge. In Lebow's case, four stood out on that cool autumn Sunday in 1992: his desperate desire to prove to himself that he had beaten the disease and that his remaining years would not be broken by cancer; his hope of inspiring others stricken by the disease to embrace the fitness lifestyle; it was a way to mark his sixtieth birthday, which had fallen five months earlier; and finally, simply, as a marathoner, to compete in the greatest marathon in the world . . . the show he had created. Though superficially different, these four goals fused into one for Lebow, the wily survivor. His ability to complete the marathon that Sunday became a metaphor for the struggles within his own self.

When first stricken with brain cancer and given six months to live, rather than retreat into hopelessness, Lebow had summoned his survival instincts, giving him an edge in fighting the disease. He had dragged himself out of his hospital room to the rooftop, and when snow started falling, he had switched the circuit to the hallways. In this medical setting, motion represented life; for this cancer victim, these rounds were the stubborn signposts of survival. "Other patients were looking at me running. They'd ask me. 'Why are you doing this? Why are you putting yourself through this kind of torture?' And I'd say to them. 'The question should be, Why aren't you doing this to yourself.' "

Even before the onset of his illness, a sense of loss kept eating away at Lebow all through the 1980s—never had he run his own marathon. "The New York City Marathon has consumed me more than anything in my life," he said. "I had run sixty-eight marathons in all the major capitals of the world, yet I had never run the five-borough New York City Marathon." Reaching the finish line in those years in his Mercedes rather than in his running shorts made the promoter feel "jealous and guilty." His pleasure with the marathon extravaganza was diminished by the emptiness of being a spectator at his own party. To calm those emotions, Lebow said, "I would run a marathon the week before New York so my legs would feel tired and I wouldn't feel so guilty."

On New Year's Eve 1992, his cancer having been declared by doctors to be in remission, Lebow felt that the time had come to run his own marathon. Completing the jocular New Year's Eve Midnight Run in Central Park where many runners came costumed confirmed his decision. "I hadn't worked real hard and didn't feel like I had run that fast in the race," said Lebow. "But when I finished, I realized that there were still about 1,000 people running behind me. That got me thinking about the marathon and how maybe it was possible. So I told everybody, my friends and my family, no birthday presents, no celebrations in June for my birthday. I was giving myself a gift with the marathon."

In the spring of 1992, Lebow, recognized as marathoning's main icon, was invited to the grueling Comrades Marathon in South Africa, where he saw fifteen thousand runners cover fifty-four miles along the country's scenic coast. The experience confirmed the New Year's Eve decision: "I saw some of them crawl to the finish and I thought 'I can do it.' "

Never one given to illusions, Lebow knew that if he made it to the Central Park finish, it would rank as his slowest marathon. The last marathon he had run was in Los Angeles in 1988, with a time of 3:49. His personal best had been in Syracuse in the early 1970s, with a time of 3:30. Finishing in about five hours became his stated goal. "It doesn't matter how fast I go. I'm not doing it to prove I'm a fast runner. I never was."

Central Park—Lebow's "backyard"—was his training site. "I probably know every nook and cranny of the six mile course," he noted. He entered the park near the Eighty-ninth Street town house headquarters of his running club, ran north around the reservoir into Harlem, headed back on West Drive, passed the marathon finish line at Tavern on the Green, and turned north once again to his Fifth Avenue office. Allan Steinfeld, the marathon's technical director and Lebow's eventual successor, accompanied the race director on some runs, varying these outings for both speed and endurance. Heather Dominic, Lebow's doe-eyed twenty-two-year-old girlfriend, also ran with him occasionally.

In previous years, Lebow had viewed his Central Park running as more than a sports endeavor. To the promotion-minded Lebow, appearing in the park meant a chance to see and be seen by the city's running crowd. Now he talked less, concentrating mainly on his training. But old friends had a hard time staying away. "I ran up from behind sometimes," said Laura Leale, Lebow's PR coordinator, "and kicked him in the butt to get him going."

The training regimen was erratic—some days he was too weak to run two or three miles, but at other times his distance accelerated to twenty miles. For longer runs, he joined Road Runners Club athletes who psyched themselves up by singing military songs.

In these training runs, Lebow's time translated into about ten minutes a mile, or some five hours for a marathon's distance, substantially slower than he had ever run. But cancer had changed his perspective. Speed was no longer important. "I get more pleasure out of running now, even though I'm slower. Running is a gift, a treat I give to myself. . . . I get more pleasure as a sick man running a 10-minute mile than I did as a healthy one running a seven-minute mile."

In press interviews during the months before the marathon, Lebow attributed the motives for his running the five-borough race either to demonstrating how he had vanquished cancer or to commemorating his sixtieth birthday. Sometimes, though, his understated humor surfaced: "I always hear people say the New York marathon is a good race. I want to find out if it's true."

In the spring and summer of 1992, Lebow, who enjoyed a global backdrop for his runs, competed in races in Lisbon, Oslo, and Siberia. In June, the opportunity arose to help out a marathon sponsor, always a priority for Lebow. Jack Maguire, a friend for fifteen years, invited the race director to Randolph, Vermont. As president of Vermont Pure Natural Spring Water, Maguire wanted Lebow on the scene to add stature to his company's 10K (6.1-mile) race through the green Vermont hills. Joking at the race's start as to how his illness had slowed him down, Lebow said his goal was to finish "not last, but second to last." Actually, he finished 14th from last, placing 158th out of 171 finishers.

When Lebow first conceived of running in his creation, he expected it to be a solo performance. But as though the Fates willed that the old promoter's finale would also be recorded as his biggest draw, Grete Waitz, the legendary nine-time winner of the New York City Marathon, volunteered to run with him. One of Lebow's main discoveries, Waitz had gone on to become one of the world's leading marathoners, as well as an engaging spokeswoman for the sport. When Lebow paid for the Norwegian schoolteacher's plane ticket to New York in 1978, she had never run more than twelve miles. In so much pain as a result of running her first marathon, when Waitz reached the Tavern on the Green finish, she threw her running shoes at her husband, only to learn that she had set a women's world record of 2:32:30.

When Lebow stopped at the Oslo airport in the summer of 1992, Waitz and her husband, Jack, came by to greet him. "Would you like Grete to run with you?" asked Jack.

"Would I like it?" replied Lebow. "How could she possibly run my time?"

"Don't worry," said Jack reassuringly.

Not merely a sentimental journey, the decision by Lebow and Waitz to run together stemmed from a friendship based on respect for what each had contributed to running. "All major cities in the world have a marathon and Fred started it all," said Waitz. "He's the inspiration to every race organizer." For Lebow's part, "I always said that if a computer could put together an ideal runner it would be Grete. I always say she's the Queen of the Road, but she doesn't behave like a monarch. She's a very nice person."

Running together also provided side benefits to each of them. As Lebow, still the showman who relished performing, had said, he wanted "to come off the Queensboro Bridge and be greeted by thousands of people." The thicker the crowd, the harder he was prepared to run, and with one climactic starring scene left in his show, it wouldn't hurt if he could play it as a social event. So, instead of casting his transcendent journey as a solo undertaking, Lebow accepted the moving offer from the Waitzs that the Norwegian nine-time winner of his race cover the course with him. The former schoolteacher was so beloved by race crowds that Mayor Koch called her "a New Yorker by adoption," and millions on the sidelines simply referred to her as "Grete." What better way to trigger the thunder of spectators than the sympathetic picture of the aging race director and the blonde heroine covering the formidable route together? As a couple, they would take the edge off the raw physical challenge ahead. Even for this, the extended agony of the toughest test of his life, Lebow was still thinking theater.

And for Grete Waitz, the journey would serve not only as an act of compassion; running with Lebow was a chance for the Norwegian star to experience her friend's people's marathon from the perspective of the ordinary runner—the type of runner the promoter had drawn to the sport. Not being on the front line this time, there would be no pressure to run her best, so she could reduce her stride, and, relaxed, she could learn why so many runners traveled to New York for Lebow's spectacle.

Back in 1990, Waitz, worried about Lebow's cancer, had not been able to say no when he had asked that, as a favor, she run in that year's New York City Marathon since it was dedicated to him. She finished fourth, one of the two marathons she ever ran where she failed to take top prize, and when she left New York she believed Lebow's days were numbered. "I said to my husband that year after we got home to Norway, I wonder what the Marathon is going to be like without Fred, because I was sure he would not be back."

In 1992, retired from competitive marathoning, Waitz saw herself fitting into Lebow's needs as a result of her new coaching career. "I knew it meant a lot to Fred to run his own marathon," she recalled. "My first thought, was that I worried for him. Knowing Fred, I knew that if a person doesn't give him the answer he wants to hear, he will ask another person. I had been working with people not in great shape and started them on training programs. I felt I knew how Fred could finish." Earlier that year, in response to a letter, she had run a half marathon with a retarded girl.

Though she phoned Lebow that summer once or twice weekly, Waitz, in her job as a PR consultant, came to New York, where she watched him run, regularly. She was unhappy with his overambitious goals. "In my opinion, he was doing too much," she said. "He ran five or six times a week. I was not happy when he would run a half-marathon and then another five miles."

Speed, she insisted, should not be a priority. Rather than having him push himself, she considered any finishing time less than five hours an achievement. Her strategy called for his running three miles, then walking for two minutes. "If you put in those little walk breaks, you don't get tired," she said. "It's better to be conservative. I always said, 'Take the first 18 miles as transportation. Without wasting too much energy.' Then you can run. If we can get to First Avenue . . ."

As hard as Lebow trained for the race, he could not dispel the impression that he had indeed changed into a weakened old man. He traveled in October, for example, to a racing awards luncheon in St. Paul, Minnesota, site of the Twin Cities Marathon, one of his favorites. The announcement of Lebow's upcoming marathon run received the largest ovation at the affair. He was hailed not only for all he contributed to road running but for his determination in overcoming cancer as well. But what stood out in the memory of Hugh Thompson, one of the guests, was how "frail" Lebow seemed.

Elizabeth Phillips, a member of the board of Lebow's running club, saw the race director walking in apparent pain at the Amateur Athletic Games in Central Park only a few weeks before the marathon was to take place. Concerned as to where Lebow would get the strength to go the distance, Phillips asked whether he was up to it. "I'll do it slowly," replied Lebow.

As the marathon approached, Allan Steinfeld had no doubt that Lebow would make it. "I'm not concerned healthwise about him finishing," remarked Steinfeld. "Maybe a knee blown up or something might trouble Lebow along the course." But injury would not stop the race director from crossing the finish. Lebow assured him that in desperation he would "either walk or crawl" to the end.

Persuaded that Lebow both physically and emotionally had the wherewithal to finish, Steinfeld and other Road Runners Club staff turned to the celebrity status of this recovering marathoner. How to cope with admiring crowds jamming the course? Taken with the drama of Lebow's race, spectators would want to touch, congratulate, run with, or photograph him along the route. "I was afraid he would be run down by the mob," said Steinfeld.

In order to shield Lebow and Waitz from overenthusiastic crowds along the course, a seven-member escort group or entourage was put together before the race. This type of protective escort, never before used in the Big Apple's marathon, represented a conceptual departure from Lebow's notion of a people's race. His strategy was one of crowd involvement rather than isolating viewers from the marathoners.

Waitz was in charge of the entourage, each of whose members were known to Lebow. Bill Conway, who headed a force of nineteen hundred volunteer marshals, directed the protective group's technical details. A three-time marathon finisher, Conway's experience in policing the course was considered critical in protecting Lebow from tumultuous crowds. Having worked the Central Park finishing chutes, Conway was also prepared for the pandemonium when Lebow and Waitz would complete the marathon's last few hundred yards.

In private life, the burly, soft-spoken Conway served as CEO of New York's multimillion-dollar Gotham Construction Company. Conway admired "Uncle Fred," as he called him, for his talents as a "doer." Conway compared the race director's abilities in getting results with his frustrations with the slow bureaucratic pace of Buildings Department approvals in New York's construction industry. "Being in the construction industry in New York," noted Conway, "I knew how hard it was to get something to move. Directing the marathon was even worse."

For the construction executive, protecting Lebow represented a way of winning the race director's not so readily given approval. "Uncle Fred had an intimidating air about him," said Conway. "People would work for him and accept it as a challenge to get a pat on the hand, for him to say, 'good.' "

Marathon hype for Lebow meant the obvious presence of television reporters in his entourage. The two newsmen accompanying him were Storm Field and Irv Gurofsky ("Mr. G"), both broadcast meteorologists and veteran marathoners. Field understood how Lebow categorized people. "To Fred, I wasn't a newsman," said Field. "I was a runner. In his eyes, you were either a runner or a nonrunner."

Running in Central Park one afternoon, Field heard a heavily accented voice say, "You're getting fat. You're never going to be able to run." The race director's warning failed to amuse Field until Lebow also stated his intention of running in the upcoming marathon and then said, "I want to have some of my friends around me. Do you want to do it?"

"I knew that this would be Fred's last chance to experience his creation," said Field, agreeing to join him.

The scene of Lebow on Marathon Sunday screaming from the pace car trying to clear a path for his thousands of sweaty runners always reminded Mr. G., the other meteorologist in the entourage, of General Patton leading the troops. Despite medical assurance that Lebow was in remission, Mr. G suspected that the doctors were concealing bad news. "I never knew anyone live that long with a brain tumor," he said.

Steve Loscher, the only runner in the entourage connected with a marathon sponsor, originally planned to pass up the 1992 race because of a toe injury. The regional sales manager of Vermont Pure Natural Spring Water, Loscher had finished the past five New York City Marathons. He first met Lebow when the race director traveled to Vermont to compete in the water sponsor's 10K race.

Regardless of what grandiose schemes he devised for his marathon party, Lebow knew he needed the help of the city's uniformed police and fire departments in such unglamorous work as crowd control, staffing intersections, and escorting elite runners. So the politically savvy race director included a cop and a firefighter in his escort group. Running with a cop and a fireman, reasoned Lebow, also contributed to the hometown New York City flavor of the race.

In previous marathons, Lebow had organized police and fire officers to run as a group. This move resulted in increased commitment from the three thousand cops assigned to race duty. Firehouses along the route were plastered with signs greeting runners.

"Fred always called me 'The Fireman' " said Jim Ellson, a lieutenant at Manhattan's Forty-third Street Rescue Company no. 1. Beginning as a volunteer picking up elite athletes at the airport, Ellson came to associate with the inner circle of Lebow's running club.

The first time that police officer Mike Fandal met Lebow was in the early 1980s at the Road Runners Club-sponsored Prisoner Olympics staged at the Rikers Island jail. Performing before hundreds of prisoners as a police department clown, Fandal drew a compliment from the race director. "I like your style," he commented. In earlier marathons, Fandal volunteered as a clown, entertaining runners as they cascaded over the flat surface of Brooklyn's Fourth Avenue.

Worried about possible health problems during the race, Storm Field independently invited his friend Dr. Jeff Kerner, a Long Beach, New York, ear, nose, and throat specialist, to join the escort. Though Kerner had never met Lebow, he was surprised at his decision to run the marathon given his medical history. Before the race, Kerner, a member of the board of the Long Island Hearing and Speech Society, raised nine thousand dollars in sponsorship money.

News reports in the spring of 1992 that Lebow, a cancer patient in recovery, would run his marathon for the first time enhanced his status as a running celebrity. Bill Conway saw this adulation firsthand when he accompanied the race director to view a Fourth of July race in Bloomfield, New Jersey. Always looking for ways to hype his marathon, Lebow brought some 1992 marathon posters with him to the race. Some five thousand to six thousand runners were on hand. "They were lined up fifty deep to get a poster," Conway recalled. "It became a matter of crowd control. People were bringing out anything they had to get his autograph."

As the marathon drew closer, Waitz's personal preparation included training focused on running slower speeds. She felt pain in her thighs as a result of the unaccustomed stress from these shorter strides, her nine-minute miles half the speed of her regular marathon running time. "I'm trying to get used to being on my feet for five hours or so. . . . I'm not usually on the course that long." Waitz helped Lebow show his gratitude to the Memorial Sloan-Kettering Cancer Center for the strength to run his marathon by sending out a letter soliciting money, in which she wrote, "What can I say about a man who has done more for the sport than anyone I can think of. . . . Fred has done so much for us all—now, let's do something for him."

Lebow, the week before the race, despite the need to conserve energy, engaged in the same pattern of last-minute micromanaging as in marathons past. He traveled out to the starting line at Staten Island's Fort Wadsworth the week prior to the race, checking on arrangements such as tents for the runners and the yearly reconstruction of what was hyped as the world's largest urinal. Sometimes he stopped by the home of staging-area coordinator fireman Vic Navarra for lunch, a nap, or to inquire about daughters April and Kristy.

Back in town, Lebow was busy welcoming elite runners and their coaches, schmoozing with the press during interviews, soothing sponsors at promotional meetings, and attending receptions. In the week preceding the race, he spent two nights with a city Department of Transportation crew, accompanied by girlfriend Heather Dominic, painting the legendary blue line along the marathon route.

During marathon week, Lebow made sure that the Expo held at New York's Sheraton and Hilton Hotels conformed to his wishes. He peeked in on volunteers stuffing freebie packets for the marathoners and roamed the ballroom floors inspecting the booths of Expo advertisers. The layout of advertiser booths displaying products as diverse as power sports bars and athletic jogging bras, the decoration of the halls, and the distribution of packets to runners all came under his scrutiny. He even took responsibility for tightening the lines of runners waiting in the street for entry to the Expo hotels. Some sixty thousand guests passed through the Expo, many crushing in on him, seeking to pose with him for a photo, get an autograph, or simply wish him a successful run.

Arriving in New York a few days before the race, Waitz was distressed to see how much energy Lebow was spending promoting the marathon. "Running-wise he's prepared, but I worry that he's trying to do too much organizing the race and isn't relaxing enough before the race. But that's Fred."

In addition to all the pressurized race preparations, a sudden political crisis threatened to sabotage the entire marathon. Earlier that week, a New York court acquitted Lemric Nelson, an African American accused of murdering Hasidic scholar Yankel Rosenbaum in Brooklyn in race rioting a year earlier. Fearful of rioting from Hasidim along the marathon's Bedford Avenue stretch protesting the acquittal, Lebow and Steinfeld weighed redrawing the course. Following assurances by community rabbis that the Hasidim would not interfere, the location remained intact.

Lebow's family was assembled by the end of the week to wait for him at the finish line. A brother and sister arrived from Israel, joining siblings from Cleveland, Chicago, Brooklyn, and Monsey, New York. Despite Lebow's celebrity, some siblings had never seen him race. It was the first time some of this Orthodox Jewish family, wearing traditional head coverings and dark clothing, had gathered as a group to watch their brother run.

On Saturday, Lebow was present at the International Breakfast Run where marathoners from one hundred nations jogged, flags in hand, singing home-country tunes, from the United Nations's East River headquarters to the Tavern on the Green. At the restaurant, Lebow directed the distribution of T-shirts and the buffet breakfast menu. Some ten thousand runners and their families ran the course, and for Lebow the showman, this event held special significance. Although other marathons, both in the United States and internationally, that had copied his theme of catering to the ordinary runner were closing in on the Big Apple in terms of numbers of entrants, one of the distinctions of the New York City Marathon remained its international flavor, as shown by this run from the world organization, as well as by the cacophony of languages in signs and public speaker announcements relating to the marathon.

Lebow received a grand send-off from fellow marathoners at the prerace carbo-loading party held later that evening back at Tavern on the Green. As the main attraction, Lebow circulated among the sixteen thousand diners. Busily consuming six thousand pounds of sponsor-provided pasta, three thousand gallons of sauce, and beverages designed to fuel a decent finishing time, their nutrients failing to obscure the fact that Lebow, rather than the menu, served as the main event, the runners shouted their best wishes—"All the way, Fred" and "We're with you, Fred"—as he prepared to leave for the Fort Wadsworth staging area. Skirting the aisles, the thin impresario was engulfed by emotion-filled well-wishers. Some runners so taken with the image of the old showman battling his way at tomorrow's climactic event asked him to autograph their naked skin.

Exiting the restaurant at 10 P.M., Lebow made his way in the chilly dark to the Central Park finish, accompanied by Steinfeld; Vic Navarra; David Katz, the finish line coordinator; and chief ham operator Steve Mendelsohn. Having had almost no sleep the past few days, the group welcomed the respite provided by this stopover in the cool autumn night. There, Lebow acted out his annual prerace Olympic-style flag ritual. As the flags of some twenty of the competing nations flapped in the darkness, he hoisted the American flag on a pole higher than the others. On the immediate left he raised the flag of his projected male winner, and on the right the female victor.

In an upbeat mood, Navarra drove Lebow to the Staten Island starting area. "We didn't want him to stay up all night worrying," said Navarra. "We hoped to relax him by getting away from the city." He said goodnight to the race director at 1 A.M. outside the officer's quarters.

As the old promoter lay in bed, his finale only a few hours away, his memory must have turned to a skinny boy in Arad, racing down an alley to escape a gang shouting anti-Semitic curses . . . to trips he took with his father in a horse-drawn wagon through the countryside to buy fruit from local farmers . . . to an obscure race he began in Central Park, twenty-two years earlier, where there were no banners, no television coverage, no hi-tech sneakers, and the cost of the cheap wristwatch prizes came from his own pocket . . . to the presidents and pope to whom he had presented marathon T-shirts . . . to the unathletic types who heroically went the distance in his urban theater . . . to the gorgeous "vimmen" he brought along to marathons as far away as Cairo and Caracas . . . and to the sweet-voiced kids at Memorial Sloan-Kettering who later that day would press their bald heads to window-panes, awaiting him on First Avenue.

Whatever he was thinking about, it was not an easy night for Lebow, and then, at 5:30 A.M., Navarra brought him to the Command Center. In the chill of the November dawn, Lebow went about his in-spections seemingly oblivious to the fact that in a few hours he would be running for his life. He examined the seven tents where marathoners would be limbering up and dousing themselves with gels, making sure the floors weren't damp. He sampled the hot chocolate being brewed for the runners for its warmth level. At "the world's largest urinal," he posed for photos. He made last-minute calls to a meteorologist about the expected temperature on the route. Ham operators filled him in on road conditions and the placement of barricades. He checked out the height of the balloons marking the red, blue, and green starting lines and put up last-minute decorations and frills, though fewer than in past marathons. Walking through the staging area, he bantered with the press, picked up used cups lying on the ground, and signed autographs as if it were any other year.

Marathoners started arriving, some by car, others in the fleet of 135 buses that had departed from their usual pick-up point at the New York Public Library at Fifth Avenue and Forty-second Street. Reporters interviewed Lebow one last time, announcements came through the loudspeaker in a multiplicity of languages, a crew of exercise specialists outfitted in sponsor-provided gear warmed up the athletes, and New York City politicians congratulated them for their fortitude. Despite a forty-degree chill, the marathoners exchanged running stories while doing their stretches and applying ointments. Away from the masses, the elite athletes were warming up in an indoor gym facetiously called "Ben Gay City."

Lebow, seated with Steinfeld and Mendelsohn, ate a quick breakfast of bagels and eggs, skipping the lox that one of Mendelsohn's operatives had brought into the fort. As though he recognized the role of Providence in the test ahead, Lebow slipped away from the reporters trailing him and quietly and unobtrusively entered the Marathon Minyan, planning, for just the second time since its inception, to join the hundred or so Jewish men and women—fellow marathoners dressed in their shorts and sweats—to pray with them instead of simply dropping by while making his rounds to wish them good luck and urge them to stay hydrated as he done in previous years. The only time he had actually joined the prayers was the time in 1990, the year he was diagnosed with a brain tumor, on which occasion runner and rabbi Jim Michaels had recited the Hebrew prayer for the sick, and the hundred marathoners had danced around the weary race director, singing Hebrew songs, hardly a dry eye in the crowd. "I didn't expect to see Fred that morning," said Peter Berkowsky of Lebow's 1992 appearance. "For weeks beforehand, the sports pages were reporting that Fred was finally going to run his marathon. I knew how busy he must have been. . . . He looked very weak."

After quietly reciting the Shema—a Jewish proclamation of belief in God, said three times daily, as commanded in Deut. 6:4, "Hear O Israel, the Lord Is Our God, the Lord is One"—Lebow went up to Berkowsky and quietly made a special request. For the first time since the Marathon Minyan began, he wanted to pray with tefillin, the accessory that Jewish males start to wear beginning at their bar mitzvah, at age thirteen. "I always bring my father's tefillin along in case anyone needs it," said Berkowsky, and the race director-marathoner asked for assistance in putting them on.

With help remembering how to perform the mitzvah, as such a deed commanded by the Torah is called, Lebow wrapped the black straps around his left arm seven times, positioned the black box housing various Hebrew Scriptures above his elbow, and rested a second black tefillin box on his forehead. "Loving hands helped him wrap [them]," Berkowsky recalled. After reciting prayers he remembered from his childhood in pre-Holocaust Europe, Lebow left. Clearly, he had been praying for strength to go the distance in what was to be a spiritual journey no less than a physical one.

By 10 A.M., Lebow and Waitz were positioned on the platform overlooking the blue starting line. Mayor David Dinkins, parks commissioner Gordon Davis, and other Big Apple politicos were stationed there as well. Standing below, watching thousands of runners slowly drawing closer to the start, was Lebow's escort group. In addition to those already designated to guard the race director-turned-runner, Lebow's girlfriend, Heather Dominic; *New York Daily News* race reporter Eddie Coyle; and a cadre of Mr. G's friends joined the entourage.

Lebow was dressed in a red warm-up suit under which he wore a 1992 marathon T-shirt and blue shorts and tights; his bib number displayed his age, sixty; he ran in sponsor-provided Asics sneakers; and to top it all, on his head was a light orange-colored 1992 John Hancock running cap. Waitz, dressed in black, sported bib number 39 for her age and had her sandy hair wrapped in a ponytail.

Each member of the entourage wore a blue baseball cap printed with the word *Marshal* monogrammed in large white letters. Entourage leader Conway, ready for surprises along the way, reminded the group of the motto of the marathon marshals: Expect the Unexpected.

Despite the seriousness of their task, some in the entourage came dressed hoping to lighten the pressure. Mr. G and his friends sported sweatshirts with the words *Fred and Mr. G* in large letters. Steve Loscher, in pink-and-purple running shorts, displayed a T-shirt with a picture of a Vermont Pure Natural Spring Water bottle. Firefighter Jim

Ellson wore a departmental T-shirt, and the cop-clown Mike Fandal was attired in a "March 4th (Forth) Against Crime" T-shirt on top of a blue-and-yellow New York Police Department running shirt. Entourage director Conway and Mr. G both carried cell phones to stay in touch with race officials tracking Lebow's progress.

Lebow, his characteristic chutzpah sharply diminished as the start drew closer, sought guidance from Waitz. "She'll be a guard for me," he said. "She'll protect me." Waitz, in turn, stressed how much Lebow had riding on his reaching the finish. "People have to understand, this is not a social event for Fred. This is serious business. It's my job to tell them to leave him alone."

To be sure, Lebow needed all the support he could get. To those who remembered this cunning impresario on previous Marathon Sundays, he had been transformed into a weary old man. Despite the symbolism of his running, it was the stricken quality of the cancer victim that observers noted most about Lebow in this comeback race. No longer was he the charming hustler who changed a marathon into a party; his heroics now stemmed from his refusal to complain in response to his dreadful disease. As the New York Times's George Vecsey, moved by Lebow's decline, wrote in an October 10, 1994, article: "I could see the changes in Fred. He was thinner, older, more gaunt, more preoccupied. He used to have an extra awareness of other people's personalities, even if just to flatter or criticize them for his own purposes. But now he was more introverted. He had become a case."

Two minutes before the 10:48 start, the twenty-seven thousand chilled marathoners crowding together on the entrance to the Verrazano-Narrows Bridge jostled for positions close to the starting line. Helicopters flew overhead, balloons braced against the wind, and tugboats sprayed red, white, and blue water in the harbor. For the nimble and the overweight, the boomers and the grandparents, all gathered at the starting line, these were the trappings that shaped Lebow's marathon more as a party than an ordeal.

The view that Lebow observed across the river was magnificent, but he was troubled that the runners were packed so tightly together, practically on top of one another. Suddenly, his shrewd eyes caught the worst nightmare possible for this meticulous race director: the dreaded false start he'd always sought to prevent by policing the lineup at the front edge of the marathoners like a drill sergeant. A few dozen of some of the two hundred male semielite athletes surged forward, fifty-five seconds before the official starting time, passing thirty elite male runners. The race was now under way, the starting cannon never having been fired for safety reasons. "I couldn't say 'stop' in seven languages," lamented Steinfeld. "Stay together, stay together," shouted entourage leader Conway. Curses from Lebow's escort filled the air.

"I don't want to run. I don't want to run," screamed the race director. "I shouldn't have run this race," he continued, blaming the havoc on his personally not having been stationed at the start, lining up the athletes. In this moment of truth, Lebow revealed what was most important to him: his running the marathon or the integrity of the marathon. Clearly, his dream was secondary to keeping the race's reputation intact. "I never saw Fred that upset in his life," said Mr. G. "At that moment, he needed more tender loving care than [he had during his 1990 hospitalization] at Mount Sinai."

Gently coaxing the still bewildered Lebow, Waitz climbed down from the VIP stand and, speaking reassuringly, told him, "Fred, everything will be OK. You have to take off your jacket. You have to run the marathon." She helped him slip out of his warm-up suit, and they joined the pack of runners expected to cross the finish in the 4:15–4:30 range.

Starting-line coordinator Navarra, convinced that the false start had ruined Lebow's moment of glory, drifted quietly to a corner of the bridge, starting to cry.

Tracking Lebow was a motorcycle police escort and a television camera truck. Feeling flush with excitement, some of the international athletes overtook Lebow, singing songs of their homelands as they traveled in packs over the bridge. Even accounting for his late start, the bridge was so densely packed with runners that it took Lebow sixteen minutes to complete his first mile.

A visibly tense Lebow shuffled along, hands held high, gazing straight ahead, distancing himself from the crowds. Comments from the entourage were directed to Waitz, rather than to Lebow, so as not to interfere with his pace.

Lebow passed the two-mile mark as he descended into Brooklyn from the bridge, turning onto Bay Ridge Parkway and Fourth Avenue.

He was running a twelve-minute mile, considerably slower than his standard speed, but he hoped to make up for time lost on the bridge as he traversed the level six-mile stretch that lay ahead.

The emotion of Lebow and Grete heroically threading their way through the course carried all the earmarks of a Hollywood production. The race itself was one of those magical moments in New York City history, the powerful scene of the aging marathon maven refusing to be hobbled by disease, running for his life, drawing the race's largest crowd ever. As though Lebow's prospects of crossing the Central Park finish depended on the roar of the crowds, two million spectators lined the streets, the most ever present for a single sports event in the history of the Big Apple.

Deafening cheers arose as Lebow and his blonde Norwegian guardian passed by. Early on, the intensity of the crowd's determination that he complete the course registered on the old showman. In those gritty ethnic streets, Lebow got his first inkling of the enthusiasm for his journey. The vociferous cheering for the gaunt race director was full of life. From the Irish and Italian neighborhoods of Bay Ridge and the Hispanic and Asian American streets in Sunset Park, the crowds thundered: "Thataway, Fred!" "Fred and Grete, you can do it!" and "Lookin' good, Fred!"

Among the twenty-five bands Lebow had positioned along the route was the Bishop Kearney High School Marching Band at Fourth Avenue and Fifty-ninth Street, consisting of some forty young women in green Aussie cowboy hats and green, white, and gold outfits. "The runners need us," said Sister Barbara Walsh, band moderator. "This year, we're doing it for Fred Lebow. Our freshmen are carrying signs for Fred."

Running up Fourth Avenue, Conway phoned David Katz, the Central Park finish coordinator, regarding damage control in the wake of the false start. Katz assured Conway that all the exact times had been recorded, so there was no need to worry. Conway told Waitz that everything was under control, and Waitz in turn reported to Lebow and asked him if he personally wanted to talk to Katz about the mishap. After pausing to take the phone and being briefed by Katz, Lebow inquired as to which athletes were in the lead. "Once he was told who was winning," noted Waitz, Lebow relaxed, "turning to run his own race."

Meanwhile, Fandal, the cop-clown, in an interview with a CBS reporter about his student days at Brooklyn's Lincoln High School, was adding local color to this borough's phase of the race. "Fred says to lower voices," scolded a protective Waitz.

Vermont Pure's Loscher amused Lebow and the crowd as he ran backward for a mile down Fourth Avenue. At the same time, the muscular athlete was warding off interlopers from coming close to the race director.

An overarching Lebow refused to rest at the three-mile mark on Fourth Avenue, as he and Waitz had previously agreed. "Fred," threatened Waitz, "if you don't stop now, you'll have to walk the last six miles."

In those early miles, Lebow tried establishing some sort of rhythm. The race promoter who, in past marathons, was always using his megaphone to stir the crowds from his front seat in the Mercedes pace car, now tried avoiding contact to focus, instead, on his own running, each stride drawing him closer to the finish. Waving at spectators could wait for another festival. In this marathon, he was starring as the survivor . . . the cancer patient in recovery . . . the runner bent on a life-saving mission. He had to conserve his limited energy for running this race, not hyping it. In order to conserve energy, he even kept his comments to the entourage to almost zero—conversation, as a rule, not being part of his marathon routine anyway. "I don't like to talk much while running," he explained. Waitz agreed with this tight-lipped strategy. "It wasn't necessary to talk because we had other people around to protect him."

Still, his strides were strongest where the fans were the noisiest. Not only did their cheers help push Lebow forward, but this outpouring triggered a sense of unity uncommon in the Big Apple. His escort group also felt connected with the crowd. Fandal commented how the spectators hailing Lebow found a "tremendous healing quality" in his voyage. "You saw a sense of togetherness all along the route. . . . It felt like one party, one family, one city united."

Despite the entourage's watchfulness, some spectators dashing into the streets succeeded in shaking the race director's hand as he passed by. When Lebow entered Bedford-Stuyvesant, the largest African American community in the Big Apple, he responded to the cheers with a hearty thumbs-up.

The first instance when Lebow seemed to be genuinely at ease was when he approached the Hasidic quarter of Williamsburg on Bedford Avenue. Here at the ten-mile mark stood the shtetl re-creation of the Jewish world of his childhood, and the yeshiva where he had studied the Talmud as a nineteen-year-old immigrant to the United States was not far from the racecourse. The conservatively dressed Hasidim, remembering how in past marathons Lebow had exhorted them from his pace car, "Lommen heren" ("Let's hear it"), as the runners followed from behind, shouted, "Shalom, Shalom," to Lebow, their respectful applause in sharp contrast with the raucous reception elsewhere along the course. "They definitely knew who he was and were proud of him," observed Conway. And cop-clown Fandal, attempting on his own to establish rapport with the Hasidim, called out in Hebrew, "Ma Nishma?" (loosely translated, "How are you?"), as he scooted by. Though Lebow was no longer a Sabbath observer, the Hasidim knew where Lebow's roots lay, and that he had survived the Holocaust. Tears fell down the cheeks of some of the older Hasidim witnessing their brother now running the race for his life.

For comic relief, spectators enjoyed a variety of costumed characters preceding the Lebow entourage: a runner dressed as a rhinoceros publicizing the plight of that disappearing species, a man sprouting angel wings and a halo over his head, and a Fort Lauderdale, Florida, stunt expert in a lined winter coat and wing-tipped dress shoes. Other marathoners simply sported their "traditional" marathon garb: T-shirts sending out romantic, political, religious, and inspirational messages.

At the ten-mile mark, *Newsday* sports reporter John Hanc, writing pad in hand, joined Lebow's escort. Instead of being welcomed, he was jabbed in the side by Storm Field's protective elbow. "We were blocking, trying to clear the path," explained Field. "Give him room! Give him room!" shouted Loscher as he chased fans away, but spectators were darting out to shake Lebow's hand, to snap a quick picture, or to try to run a few laps with the entourage.

The race director's guards shifted stations along the route, moving from right to left or from front to rear of Lebow and Waitz. At each water stop, escort members dashed to the tables, bringing back drinks for the race director and his companion.

Police and volunteer marshals were stationed at half-block intervals along the marathon course. Ham radio operators reported to the race's Central Park Command Center on Lebow's jaunt. When loudspeakers on Manhattan's First Avenue and at the Central Park finish interrupted their strains of "Rocky" and "Chariots of Fire," announcing Lebow's whereabouts, the crowds broke into screams.

Completing the Brooklyn leg of the marathon, Lebow passed the substantial brownstones of the Polish enclave of Greenpoint. Signs touting Lebow and Waitz hanging from restaurant windows and artists' studios served as a contemporary contrast to this Old World landscape.

Lebow crossed the Pulaski Bridge linking Brooklyn to Queens at 1 P.M., fulfilling his wish of mastering half the marathon's distance at around the same time as winners Willie Mtolo and Lisa Ondieki broke the tape at the Central Park finish.

Shuffling through the warehouse section of Long Island City, a steadily weakening Lebow prepared for one of the most formidable hurdles of the race looming ahead: the sharp inclines of the 1.5-mile-long Queensboro (Fifty-ninth Street) Bridge bringing the marathon into Manhattan. Reaching the bridge, marathoners had to make a quick decision—to run on either the pavement area or a specially carpeted walkway. Designed exclusively for this race, the carpeting was hyped to the media as the world's longest carpet.

Lebow told Conway he preferred the carpeted path. The marshal sprinted ahead, expecting to order other marathoners to move over to the pavement to make room for Lebow, but to his shock, bridge officials had already opened the paved driveway to regular auto traffic, thus shunting all of the remaining runners to the walkway. With no time to reroute traffic and Lebow drawing closer, the marshal had to make room for the race director along the narrow walkway. Conway himself was now groaning in pain, somehow having reaggravated an old knee injury during the tense traffic negotiations.

Loscher grabbed a cell phone, dialing his mother, asking that she watch on television the scene of his mounting the upward-swooping bridge.

With the Manhattan skyline beckoning ahead in the midday au-

tumn sun, helicopters on the left photographing the aging race director, and the finish still another ten miles away, Lebow was seriously
hurting—his breathing heavy, his pace sluggish, his face drawn. His escort group noticed how hard he was struggling, some predicting he
would not make it to the end of the bridge. Halfway across, Lebow
came to a complete halt and stretched. Waitz feared that the old promoter had had enough. "I realized after sixteen miles," she said, "he
was getting tired."

Drawing closer to Manhattan, Lebow was energized by the loudspeakers reporting his progress, warming up the crowds in the distance.
From his years in the pace car, he knew that runners, making the hairpin
turn off the bridge into Manhattan, are transfused by a surge from the
crowds, but never in the history of the marathon was the cheering as
heavy as it was when their beloved race director triumphantly penetrated this new borough. Crowds fifteen to twenty deep were applaud-
ing and thundering: "Go for it, Fred!" "Fred and Grete!" and "Grete
and Fred!"

Easing up First Avenue, Lebow was hailed by the overwhelmingly
yuppie spectators, many of whose lives he had changed by his mission-
izing that had brought home to them the message of fitness—the message that a footrace, or at least a two-mile run in Central Park, was
within their grasp. Now, as fellow athletes hanging out in front of cafes
and restaurants, they applauded the brave old man.

For Lebow, the seventeenth mile, passing the Memorial Sloan-
Kettering Cancer Center where he had undergone treatment, marked
the emotional highlight of the journey. In this hospital, unable to run,
he had stayed in motion as a floor walker, recruiting other patients to
plod the halls with him. Doctors and patients, too many of them children, waited on the sidewalk holding up handwritten signs: "We love
you, Fred" and "All the way, Fred." Several of the white-coated doctors
jumped onto the street, shaking his hands and hugging him. Tears in
his eyes, Lebow waved at this makeshift cancer rooting squad.

A few streets later, Fandal, who had earlier given one of the young-
sters the pair of white clown gloves and squealers he had started the race
with, choked up. "Are you OK, Mike?" asked Mr. G. "We're passing
near my house," answered Fandal. "Imagine doing this with Fred, and
it's my first marathon."

Pushing farther up First Avenue, Lebow became so confused, said Field, that there were stretches when "he wasn't even quite sure where he was going. He couldn't even run in a straight line. He would tilt toward the right, and I would bring my shoulder against his so he could get back to the center again."

At Ninety-second Street, Lebow screeched to a complete halt, bending over, clutching his stomach. The entourage whispered to one another that it was all over. Loscher jumped out, tying Lebow's shoelaces. Waitz, the only figure in the retinue allowed to talk with the race director, softly reassured him, hiding her panic. "Fooled you, fooled you," teased Lebow, bolting ahead! Even in distress, his proclivity for practical jokes remained fresh.

Though Lebow avoided shaking hands with fans who slipped through the barricades, he was still savvy enough, despite his weakened state, to accept the greetings of an NYPD inspector who rushed up on First Avenue.

During the uphill climb to the Bronx, Fandal, Loscher, and Field were still busy blocking, shouting to one another, "Pick up the guy there," to protect Lebow from enthusiastic fans dashing toward him. Over the din of blaring radios and fervid spectators, Waitz was reassuringly boosting the resolve of this tiring sixty year old. "If she weren't there with him," said Mr. G, "it would have been difficult for Fred to find the spiritual note to finish the race."

Given how much he had been struggling up to that point, the legendary runner's "wall" at the Willis Avenue Bridge—the race's twenty-mile mark, where an athlete's strength normally plummets—posed no new threat to Lebow. As he trundled through this less-than-one-mile piece of the Bronx, boisterous crowds shouted encouragement in both English and Spanish, and a lively rock band propelled the weary race director back into Manhattan.

Crossing the Madison Avenue Bridge into Harlem, the pain in Lebow's knee became so sharp that he came to a sudden halt at 135th Street. A fan produced a chair, enabling Lebow to strap on a knee brace he had been carrying. Loscher quickly changed the race director's sweated-up socks. Waitz handed Lebow a piece of the sports bar she had brought along. All the while, crowds screamed their cheers.

Passing Marcus Garvey Park, one of the Big Apple's main oases, with four miles to go, the insidious hills of Central Park loomed ahead. A Latin band celebrated Lebow's arrival.

At Fifth Avenue and 102nd Street, Lebow entered Central Park for the final drive. Across the street signs were being waved by the staff of Mount Sinai Medical Center, where Lebow had been told more than two years earlier that he had no more than six months to live.

Lebow was now back where it had all begun . . . to where, while working as a knockoff designer in New York's garment district in 1970, he had put together a marathon with 127 runners winding their way through the park. From that unheralded start, he had crafted his vision of a people's race in the guise of a party. In the arena of Central Park, Lebow had personally logged thousands of miles and had orchestrated races sending hundreds of thousands through its hills.

With three miles remaining, the deafening chorus of cheers softened Lebow's final agony. "It was beyond description," remembered Dr. Jeff Kerner. "It was sort of a surreal experience, like the crowd had a direct stake in his finishing. I've been to Knick playoff games in double overtime. This was even more. It was like life didn't exist outside the arena. The event was life itself."

A cadre of police cars and camera support vehicles surrounded the entourage in the park. Dixieland and jazz bands played. Lebow had nothing left in reserve. "It was clear," said Field, "that he was working only on sheer guts." Lebow had trouble keeping to a straight line. Runners whom Lebow had known for decades jumped out to wave him on, but he seemed unaware of their presence. His stride deteriorating, he ran for a few minutes, walked briefly, then resumed his beleaguered pace. Despite his pain, this inveterate crowd pleaser drew sustenance from his production's standing-room-only audience. Still, he had problems accepting the argument that tens of thousands of spectators were indeed waiting for hours in the November chill for him to pass. "He was all beaten up," said Mr. G. "But at that stage, his humanity and shyness came through. 'Oh my goodness,' he said. 'All those people waiting for me? Waiting for such a long time. For such a miserable runner.' I don't think Fred actually knew what he had accomplished until the end of his life."

As Lebow passed the Eighty-ninth Street town house of his New York Road Runners Club, eighty-year-old Joe Kleinerman, the club's elder statesman and confidant of the race director for more than twenty years, dashed out, tears in his eyes, kissing him. "Way to go, Fred," cried Kleinerman in the traditional runners' salutation. Moved by the poignancy of the scene of the old man and the even older man embracing, the lifestyle of running their common denominator, Waitz could no longer restrain herself. "When we ran past the club, all the people there had been waiting for us," she said. "He knew he was on home ground. I suddenly got very emotional from the support of the crowd. I knew he would make it. I got goose bumps and started to cry. Fred looked at me. He asked, 'Are you hurt?' He started to cry." Now, they were both crying, concluding that at least for the present he had beaten the disease. As depleted as Lebow was, they *both* knew that somehow he would drag his body to the finish. Hardly a dry eye remained among the tumultuous crowd as he staggered by. "We ran the last two and a half miles [holding hands] with tears in our eyes."

As Lebow hobbled through elegant Central Park South, heading toward Columbus Circle, loudspeakers that were playing sports music now concentrated on his every step. Conway alerted his marshals at the finish line that Lebow would momentarily arrive.

The Jewish Romanian impresario and the Norwegian star took a right into the park, the final hill leading to the Tavern on the Green finish up ahead. The music "New York, New York" played victoriously on the sound system.

Each minute, scores of marathoners were still crossing the finish. In order to prevent them from interfering with the race director, forty of Conway's marshals rushed out to close off finish-line chute three, which had earlier been designated for the women's winner, so that Lebow and Waitz could break the tape. Focusing the spotlight on the couple, Conway's marshals cut off Lebow and Waitz from their entourage. Some of the guards were hurt that they would not be crossing the finish as a group. "We were shunted to the side like a wrapper on a candy bar," said Field. "We did all the work," Kerner intoned. "All we wanted was a feeling of completion."

Swept ahead by the crush of marshals, Waitz ran up to the tape being held by Mayor Dinkins and male winner Mtolo. She mimicked Lebow's circular turning of his arm—his "windmill"—with which he had waved hundreds of thousands of past marathoners to their glorious finale. She then held out her hand as he shuffled to the tape, and they crossed the finish together and embraced, continuing to cry.

Most of the other runners finished hours ahead of him, but with help from friends and loved ones, Lebow managed to finish the full 26.2-mile course! The journey had taken five hours, thirty-two minutes, and thirty-four seconds. After embracing his tearful family and other race personnel, Lebow fell to the ground of his beloved Central Park, his personal Jerusalem, and kissed the finish line. *Victory was his!* In finishing the marathon that Sunday, Lebow had not only delivered a message to the crowds. For himself, he had won the race within.

The Last Mile

LEBOW, THE HAPPIEST FINISHER of the 1992 New York City Marathon, joked, "I never realized how long 26 miles and 385 yards could be! . . . Grete was hurting from running so slow, while I was hurting just from running."

In marathons past, he was too busy to connect with his brothers and sisters. Old friends merited no more than a perfunctory hello in the frenzied days leading up to the race. This time, Lebow embraced family and friends on hand to watch him finish. His self-depreciating charm still showed: "My brother, Shlomo, came all the way from Israel to see the slowest marathon ever."

Looking drawn and exhausted, the old promoter knew he would never be strong enough to run another marathon. "My last marathon," he said. "But not my last race. I'll keep running. It's what I do."

His finishing time was not what he would have preferred in his prime, yet it was another sign of his adaptability to life's new circumstances. "As you get older, your perspective changes and you adjust to adversity. But that doesn't mean you have to settle."

To prove to himself that he could at least still handle shorter distances, he made his way on foot the thirty-five blocks from his home to the next day's awards breakfast at the Park Avenue headquarters of sponsor Chemical Bank. "I could hardly walk," said Grete Waitz, who came by taxi from her hotel before 8:00 A.M. to the bank. "I asked Fred, 'How do you feel?' " "I've been walking and jogging to get here," replied the race director.

Beyond the world of runners, Lebow was startled by the inspirational message of his crossing the finish line only two years after being diagnosed with terminal brain cancer. "The emotional aftermath took me by surprise. It was two months before I could answer all the letters and phone calls from cancer patients and their families. I'm not a doctor, yet they wanted to talk with me. . . . I cannot prove it medically, but after being given six months to live in 1990, running was the best medicine for me to kill cancer."

Steve Mendelsohn, who headed some four hundred volunteer ham radio operators at the marathon, saw the humanizing change in Lebow. "Before 1992, Fred never asked me a personal question," said Mendelsohn. "When he heard I was about to become a grandfather, he called to wish Mazel Tov. Next to my mother-in-law, the happiest person about the news was Fred."

Despite the euphoria in completing his own race for the first time, Lebow was hospitalized one month after the marathon triumph, undergoing double surgery at Memorial Sloan-Kettering Cancer Center for a hernia and testicular condition. "It's just a minor thing, nothing to be worried about," commented Lebow at the hospital. "I've had the hernia for quite some time, and it bothered me during the marathon, so I felt it was necessary to do something about it. When you've had cancer, you have to be careful." Underscoring his sound health, Lebow believed, was his having run six miles only a few days prior to the hospitalization. "I hope to be out in a day or two," said the race director. Yet he was afraid: "I can't believe I'm back in the hospital again."

What made Lebow more relaxed about the surgery was that one of his doctors in the three-hour procedure was himself a veteran marathoner. "My doctor, Allan Turnball has run sixteen marathons," said Lebow with touch of *nachas* (a special sort of Jewish pride). "In fact, I recall seeing him at Boston and Berlin."

Committed to staying in motion even if the arena was a hospital hallway, Lebow walked some one hundred yards on his floor at Memorial Sloan-Kettering the day following his operation. The next day, he increased the distance to a quarter mile, calling the effort "painful."

In early 1993, there was no stopping Lebow in his comeback from brain cancer. He completed the Road Runners Club 3.1-mile Midnight Run on New Year's Eve in twenty-nine minutes, fourteen seconds. In February, he competed the same week in two Central Park races, a 3.1-mile event, and a 4-mile event held in falling snow. In the last race he clocked twelve-minute miles (forty-eight minutes, seven seconds). This sense of the heroics of his own running became more poignant for Lebow as he confronted his cancer in his last years. "I used to be enthused when I broke ten minutes for the mile, then nine minutes, then eight, then seven, then six. That was very exciting. Now I'm excited if I can break twelve minutes. You switch your excitement level, not by design but by the way you feel. This kind of illness lowers you to a level you didn't realize ever existed. You feel down, but at the same time, you get to such a low level the only place to go is up."

The new year also brought President Bill Clinton to Washington, a move Lebow welcomed for adding a renewed chic to running. Before Clinton, the jaded image of presidential jogging was provided by Jimmy Carter's collapse in a 1979 fun run. By contrast, Clinton's well-publicized morning runs spurred a national jogging boom. "Ten million people a day see Clinton out running on TV, and that's had a big effect," said Lebow. "He draws would-be runners who think they're too fat. It's a psychological boost to them that Clinton is not the slimmest man."

As the year 1993 continued, Lebow was invited for stand-up appearances due to his reputation as a running icon. In June, he made a grand entrance into the United Nations Plaza, torch in hand, followed by Police Athletic League youth, to promote the upcoming World University Games. He hosted a minimarathon (a 5K race) for Russians and Americans at Gorky Park in Moscow on July 4.

Later in the summer, Lebow served as honorary head of the track and field group to the Maccabiah, Israel's international sports event, with some 5,300 Jewish athletes scheduled to compete in various athletic contests. The last visit of his trips to Israel—he had been to Israel eight times previously, visiting his siblings Esther and Shlomo, and advising on marathons—it would turn out to be a bittersweet occasion. Early on the day of the meet, he participated in a press conference with New York City mayor David Dinkins, and the Big Apple official embraced him, praising him for his contributions to New York. When Lebow marched in, leading the 650 athletes in the American delegation, the spectators at Ramat Gan National Stadium cheered wildly, knowing that this Holocaust survivor had revolutionized the running movement. But his poor personal performance in the Maccabiah's masters half marathon—he finished last, not reaching the stadium finish line until nightfall—underscored for Lebow the reality of his waning strength. The half marathon in Israel was the last major run of his life. To add sweet to the bitter, when he was presented with an honorary medal after his race, thousands cheered.

During his trip to Israel, Lebow visited his sister Sarah's son Eli, a student at the Jerusalem yeshiva Aish HaTorah. Wearing a New York City Marathon International Breakfast Run T-shirt, Lebow was given a tour by the yeshiva's project coordinator, Seth Clyman. The aging race director had a hard time holding his balance as he was shown the sites of the old city, but ever the running-movement missionary, Lebow didn't forget to urge Clyman, and other Israelis he met, to take up marathoning. "He wanted to promote marathoning not as a sport," according to Clyman, "but for its health value." And when, in a meeting with the yeshiva dean, Rabbi Noah Weinberg, Lebow argued that Orthodox Jews should do more running, the black-frocked rabbi chuckled, "He must have meant me too."

Among the other organizations honoring Lebow in his more "Jewishly involved" stage of life was the Emanuel Foundation, named after actor Tony Curtis's Hungarian-born father. Dedicated to revitalizing the Jewish community of Budapest, the organization named Lebow its guest of honor in 1993. In accepting the award at New York's Grand Hyatt Hotel, Lebow in tuxedo, sneakers, and running cap told the audience he was raised Orthodox, "but I forgot a lot—I was too busy running." In Budapest shortly beforehand to observe a marathon, he had visited the Doheny synagogue: "It took me back forty years. I saw the memorial for our lost Jews. I was very moved." Presenting the award to Lebow, sportscaster Dick Schaap said he always thought Lebow was a Romanian. "And now he is being honored by Hungarians. What a social climber!"

In addition to his status as a running celebrity, Lebow took on a new role as a celebrity in the battle against cancer. Attired in signature running cap, tuxedo, and sneakers, Lebow was honored by the Israel Cancer Research Fund at its 1993 fund-raising dinner. "We knew he turned down other requests, and we felt honored that he considered us worthy," remarked Milton Sussman. Seated at Lebow's table were girlfriend Heather Dominic; his sister Sarah, her husband, Manny, and their son Moshe; Road Runners Club volunteer Muriel Frohman with her husband, Paul; and George Spitz, the race director's bachelor friend for more than two decades. Lebow told Sussman that, despite having endorsed Memorial Sloan-Kettering Cancer Center fund-raising drives at two past marathons, he would have directed money to the Israel Cancer Research Fund as well had he been aware of its role earlier.

In addition to his marathon's fund-raising for Memorial Sloan-Kettering and his support of the Israel Cancer Research Fund, toward the end of his life Lebow began sponsoring the women's cancer run, "The Race for the Cure." But reaching out to people fighting his disease, he found, required different talents than simply hyping them to go the distance and raising funds for research to find a cure. The common denominator in both struggles—to run the miles and to fight the disease—said Lebow, was belief in one's self. He became a regular at his Road Runners Club Cancer Support Group for Athletes. Before the disease struck him, the notion of casually schmoozing was totally foreign to this driven, time-conscious promoter. "I'd never gone to a support group, and I've had cancer since 1990," he noted. "People need this. Has it helped me? Yes, definitely. It helps just to share experiences, and hopes and fears." Instead of just succumbing to a dismal prognosis, he dealt with the disease pragmatically: "But . . . life has to go on," he said. "You cannot live a life worrying about a disease when you have nothing . . . [T]here's nothing you can do about it."

Lebow reached out in particular to other runners struck by cancer. Sonja Stollman already shared two life definitions with Lebow. She was a Holocaust survivor and suffered from brain cancer. Displaying a Lebow-like positive attitude, Stollman dedicated the last year of her life to sharing a third dimension with the racing impresario by training to complete the 1995 New York City Marathon. "She arranged her radiation and chemotherapy treatments around her marathon training," said Dick Traum, president of the Achilles Track Club for disabled athletes. "She felt that exercise reduced its side effects." According to Stollman's marathon escort, Arlene Eneman, "It was Fred's encouragement and [later] his memory that kept her going. He told her how wonderful it was that she was going to have surgery, and offered other encouraging words."

Summing up his contribution in an interview with the *Jewish Week* newspaper, Lebow observed, "Looking at my wall, I am moved by all the Jewish and non-Jewish organizations that have chosen to honor me for my cancer work and other causes." His raspy voice breaking with emotion, Lebow continued, "I realized I created something without even knowing or planning for it."

As is common with people coming to terms with their lives as a result of a terminal sickness, Lebow's Jewishness continued to become more and more prominent, especially in his relationship with Heather Dominic in the early 1990s. Contrasting with his earlier romances, Lebow made the defining aspect of his Jewishness clear to Heather. "He enjoyed teaching me what he knew," said Heather regarding their conversations about religion. "He loved the high holy days and loved Passover." Together they lit Chanukah candles, facing the street window of the race director's apartment.

In the final stage of his life, the race director had clearly softened. He was more dependent on Heather than he had ever been on a woman. Maneuvering and hustling, so characteristic of the past, were no longer dominant themes. He was mellowed by his illness. References to the future, not only the immediate present, were obliquely inserted into his conversation. Most strikingly, the aging race director relented in opposing direct professions of love. Finally, he could be true to his emotions, unfettered by manipulative designs. On a card to Heather in December 1993, Lebow wrote: "Heather, you have given me the best years of my life. Thank you. Thank you. I love you very much."

Though officially in remission from cancer, Lebow gave signs to friends in the running community that he was weakening. Running competitively became more of an ordeal. "Fred's short attention span was reduced to no attention span," said Bill Noel, his former third in command at the Road Runners Club. At a Central Park workout of the Achilles Track Club, Dick Traum asked him a question, "and Fred jabbered, but not in any single language I could understand."

Although in past years Lebow ignored critics on the board of his New York Road Runners Club, now they insisted on hemming him in. Previously, there were never any showdowns with Lebow, because the board respected his savvy style in getting results. Now that the board saw that the old promoter was slipping, action had to be taken to protect the club's treasury. "People were taking advantage of his not being all there," admitted Dick Traum. To guard the club's finances from Lebow's impaired judgment, the board passed a resolution requiring a countersignature to Lebow's authorizations. Lebow was also stripped of the presidency of the New York Road Runners Club, the job he had held since 1972. Replaced by his alter ego, Allan Steinfeld, Lebow was named chairman of the club instead. To be sure, the change in Lebow's title had little impact on club affairs, since his day-to-day responsibilities had diminished as his illness progressed. But for the event closest to his heart, the New York City Marathon, no attempt was made to remove him as director.

Preparation for the marathon must continue regardless of how strained he felt. Never one to take himself too seriously, a weakened Lebow directed traffic at that summer's New York City Marathon Tune-Up outside the Port-O-Sans. "Keep moving, keep moving," he ordered, opening up doors, peaking in, barking commands in his thick accent, waving to the next runner in line. "This one . . . open. In here." With the marathon approaching in November, a *Washington Post* article concluded, "Lebow cannot be described as the picture of health. His frame has always been spare, but the illness has rendered him gaunt. His voice is faint."

The inaugural press conference for marathon countdown week at Tavern on the Green featured the usual shtick, such as an oversized athletic shoe behind the podium. The deputy mayor of Caen, France, was on hand to present Lebow the official medal of the city. Paul Dubourget, the deputy mayor, announced that a fourteen-kilometer race held along the beaches of Normandy would be renamed the Fred Lebow Challenge. The Lebow race was to take place the following year in conjunction with the Marathon de la Liberté, commemorating the fiftieth anniversary of the Allied D-Day invasion at Normandy. The race had until then been known as the Pegasus, after the bridge at its starting point that was the first French territory to be liberated on D-Day. In awarding Lebow his city's gold medal, Dubourget called the race director "a symbol of man's will and courage." Everyone in the audience knew that the French official was referring to the heroic stories brought home by French competitors about Lebow's fight for life. The connection between France and the New York City Marathon was strong, Dubourget declared. "For many years, the people in Caen and Normandy have come to New York to run the marathon. All these marathoners told me of Fred Lebow when they came back. Fred is the symbol of marathon running. He is known by all marathon runners as someone who incarnates effort and human will."

Moved by the award, Lebow said, "I've been in more than 1,000 races and received hundreds of awards, but I've never had a race named after me." As a way of reciprocating, Lebow promised to join the runners on June 12, 1994. "I would like to run 1:25," he said irreverently. "But I will take 1:30."

As flattering as this French gesture was, it did not erase the *tzores* (pain) plaguing the race director for a year. In November 1992, during marathon week, David Downs, vice president for sports marketing at ABC-TV phoned Lebow with bad news. ABC was going to drop the marathon broadcast. "I knew this would be an unbelievably tough call," said Downs. Professionally, he was proud that his network broadcast the marathon, an event whose technical achievements "set us apart" from other networks. He also respected Lebow, "enough of a showman and promoter who understood certain things he must do for TV." But ABC, after televising the marathon for ten years, had seen its ratings steadily drop. Despite new shtick from Lebow, the television audience showed less and less interest in a race dominated by non-American champions. Besides, other football contests in the fall needed the skills of ABC's top technicians. The decision was made not to renew its contract to televise the marginally profitable New York City Marathon.

In Lebow's utopia, canceling television coverage spelled devastation, because his vision pitched the marathon to the masses. So important was TV that in his marathon's early days it had not mattered to Lebow whether he paid the network or the network paid him for this exposure.

"I got some bad news for you, Fred," stated Downs on the phone. In recounting the story, Downs said, "Rather than acknowledging that I said these words, or asking if there was anything he could do to change my mind, he blithely continued to talk like I had just offered an extension of the contract." So Downs continued: "Fred, you didn't understand me." And after the second go-round, Lebow got the message.

"What do you want to do it for," asked Lebow, trying to negotiate a good price. "You'll be making more money." To which Downs responded, "Price isn't an issue." "I remember thinking to myself, 'here is a person who can't take no for an answer.' I knew how painful this news was for him, especially because he was sick. I also knew that his event wouldn't be able to get network TV." But Lebow's agent, Barry Frank, came to the rescue, convincing Downs to delay for one year the cancellation of ABC's broadcast. "We would have lost sponsors [without another television agreement in hand]," argued Frank.

During Frank's search for new TV sponsorship throughout 1993, Lebow continued to weaken. Frank noticed the difference while exploring alternatives to the bad news from ABC with Lebow and sponsor Jack Rudin at Manhattan's Brasserie Restaurant. "Fred was philosophical, waiting for divine intervention," Frank observed. "Jack was much more forceful."

The explorations of the trio were successful, and a new television broadcaster, New York's WPIX, Channel 11, picked up the coverage, and ESPN featured a national highlight package. This switch, which would begin with the 1994 marathon, would have the positive feature of adding more of a New York City focus. "ABC's mission was different. Because it had a national audience, they had to treat it like an elite marathon," said Jim Bukata, senior vice president of Trans World International, which coproduced the race with WPIX. "That's the way we presented it to Fred," added Paul Bissonette, WPIX's station manager. "He was happy with ABC, but I think he liked our ideas. We thought we could foster the feeling of a New York event, by promoting it on the air, by coming up [every] ninety minutes to get the scene, by intensively following the race itself, and not only the top runners." Conveying the local color of the marathon show, WPIX prepared eight forty-five- to sixty-second features on neighborhoods like Bedford-Stuyvesant and deployed mini news units along the route, such as outside the Brooklyn Academy of Music and the Memorial Sloan-Kettering Cancer Center where Lebow was treated for his tumor.

During 1993's premarathon events, Lebow's intimates noticed increasing deterioration. Steve Loscher—who just a year earlier had served as part of Lebow's entourage for the race director's heroic running of his own marathon—recalled that when he approached Lebow in the elite-athlete suite at the Hotel Sheraton, "Fred had no idea who I was."

Premonitions that this might be his last New York City Marathon came through in an interview. He expected to stand at the finish line, as in years past, greeting his ordinary runners in their moment of triumph. "The leftovers, I call 'em,' " said Lebow. "They'll have been out there a long time. They'll need to see a friendly face. Me, I'll run my seventieth marathon in my seventieth year in 2002 . . . if I live that long. Otherwise, I've had plenty."

When he reached the finish line in the Mercedes pace car, Lebow was far too weak to wave in his runners. With hardly any energy left, the race director needed to be helped out of the car. Holding onto supporters as he was led to the marathon's trailer, he told chief ham operator Steve Mendelsohn, in a faint voice, "You know what has to be done. Do it." An alarmed Mendelsohn said later, "Heaven to God, I thought he was going to go then and there."

Regaining some strength, six weeks later Lebow could be seen slogging through his club's Midnight Run in Central Park. Jerry Henkin, whose wife, Marsha, competed, busied himself during the race roasting chestnuts in a microwave oven in the club's trailer. An officer of the Northeast Nutgrowers Association, Henkin had brought twenty pounds of chestnuts to the pageant. "Fred was very tired when he came into the trailer after the race," said Henkin. "He couldn't move his legs well. I helped him get on stretch pants." Instead of good-naturedly urging Henkin to follow his wife's example and take up running, as he usually did whenever they met, this time Lebow simply enjoyed the nut grower's chestnuts. "Fred ate so much," recalled Henkin. "He was enamored of the chestnuts. He didn't want to give them up." Henkin attributed Lebow's enthusiasm for this food to his European roots, where chestnuts were not considered as exotic as they were in America.

Next on Lebow's running agenda for 1994 was a race he had been advocating for years. What more flattering climax for his vision of the fun marathon than for one of his "people's races" to be staged at Disney's Magic Kingdom in Orlando, Florida? This maven of popular culture had for years urged New York City Marathon runners from Gainesville, Florida, to launch a marathon at Disney World. "Wait till it gets to the masses," Lebow had confidently told John Hughes, one of the Florida marathoners, regarding his vision. Disney was the perfect setting for a marathon festival, agreed Hughes. "Disney was where the masses go to have fun."

But first, Disney executives needed to be convinced to hold a "serious" run in the "fun" park. Georgia Keith, Disney's manager of special events, turned to Lebow for behind-the-scenes coaching to help her sell the marathon idea to Disney higher-ups. Lebow explained to her, "Disney owned the property in which to hold a marathon. If I could persuade New York City politicians to stage a five-borough marathon, then you could persuade Disney."

In 1993, Disney decided to inaugurate a marathon the following year and asked Lebow to serve as honorary chairman. Flown to Orlando in spring 1993 to advise on this magical marathon, he was readily recognized by vacationers, and many New Yorkers came up and took pictures with him.

Since he had pioneered the concept of marathoning as entertainment, Lebow was not worried about the Magic Kingdom, with all its indigenous props, competing with his Big Apple spectacle. Deep down, Lebow must have felt that running through the arches of Cinderella's Castle, past the breathtaking Spaceship Earth, and down Hollywood Boulevard would still hold less excitement than the magic of New York. "He was willing to share for the good of the sport," remarked Keith.

In addition to giving advice about the course layout, Lebow stressed the need for the presence of crowds to energize the marathoners. "Runners draw energy from the spectators," he told Keith. Since spectators were not likely to be out in full force for the race's 6 A.M. start, Lebow told the marathon's planners to arrange for bands and entertainers along the course.

But Disney race director Hughes detected that despite Lebow's enthusiasm, illness had dulled his judgment. "At times he was not all together," noted Hughes. He cited the small area recommended by Lebow for the marathon's start as an example of his declining acuteness. Lebow's heavily accented comments reminded Hughes of his grandparents. "I grew up with Italian grandparents who spoke a broken English," he said.

Lebow's attendance at the Disney Marathon's January 1994 debut "gave us prestige," declared Hughes. "He was like a magnet. People had to see him at the Expo. He was our best marketing tool." In prerace festivities, running greats from Lebow's past, such as Frank Shorter and Alberto Salazar, were nostalgic and sad at the sight of the frail impresario.

In thirty-eight-degree temperature in January 1994, some eighty-two hundred starters began the trek through the magical miles of Disney. Aping Lebow's fun theme, finishers' medallions were designed in the form of Mickey Mouse's ears. The runner's T-shirt was also distinctive—a long-sleeve garment celebrating the marathon.

Despite his weakened state, Lebow, accompanied by girlfriend Heather Dominic, joined the starters. Disney officials were amazed that he was running. As a precaution, an undercover paramedic ran alongside the promoter. Although he dropped out after six miles, "a lot of runners were thrilled to run alongside him," reported Keith.

Hughes did not forget Lebow's prediction after he was named founding director of the Disney Marathon. "Fred knew that good runners eventually aspired to run a marathon [but] now the office secretary or the delivery person also had that goal. They would see people just like them run a marathon, and would tell themselves, 'I could do it.' " Florida's citizens now had a local marathon party they could aspire to attend, and Lebow could return to New York to continue work on the next rendition of *his* popular show.

But a marathon without Mercedes-Benz sponsorship. . . ? Standing triumphantly in the white Mercedes, the charging pack behind him—this was Lebow's classic pose as he led his people's party. Now, however, the automaker was convinced that track and field had lost popularity in America and decided to withdraw from sponsoring the New York City Marathon. "The dollar value wasn't there anymore," explained Rolf Waldeis, Mercedes' manager of events and auto shows, himself a runner. But given the close personal ties between the race director and Mercedes' American executives, the decision was reached painfully. "Would Mercedes have stayed these eleven years," asked Mercedes' media consultant, Bob Thompson, "if [Fred] hadn't been there? Fred and the event became one and the same." Thompson respected Lebow as a class act different from other race directors. The latter, he felt, were intent on pursuing personal exposure. "Most race people are primarily interested in getting on TV," he said. "Fred was in it for the love of running."

Ignoring his illness, a proud Lebow nevertheless phoned Waldeis, inquiring about "the rumor I heard" regarding Mercedes' plans to leave his marathon. "I was surprised he called, because he was very sick," said Waldeis. "The marathon was close to my heart, and still is." But Mercedes did not reverse its decision to withdraw.

More bad news followed. Lebow's secret fear ever since he had been declared to be in remission suddenly turned to reality in February. An MRI taken at Memorial Sloan-Kettering Cancer Center revealed a return of lymphoma of the brain. He had been urged to seek medical evaluation after exhibiting forgetfulness and unusually severe absent-minded behavior. At the hospital, Lebow received the first of five scheduled chemotherapy treatments. He was to be readmitted every two weeks for the remaining treatments.

Despite the nightmare's recurrence, Lebow still orbited his future on the single great force in his life. In a statement released by his running club, Lebow said, "I'm looking forward to celebrating the 25th anniversary of the New York City Marathon this November. We're planning all kinds of special events and activities to honor the occasion." But would he make it that long?

As someone who always got by in life by grit and knowing all the angles, it was quite a change for Lebow when this recurrence of his disease plunged him into an uncharted period of dependency. Often staying overnight at his apartment, Heather made sure he took his daily quota of some fifteen pills, brought him to doctors, prepared meals, and kept him clean. Struggling to stay ahead of the disease, the persona he built as king of the road changed. Instead of running to meetings in a sweat suit, he took taxis. His appetite disappeared, "because everything tastes like straw." And the ordeal brought out more of the human side that had not been very apparent while he was building his show as the hard-bargaining hustler.

Where Lebow used to run the stairs to his tenth-floor apartment—thirty-nine seconds up, fifty-eight seconds coming down—now weakened, he was again taking elevators. "You know the nice things about elevators?" he asked. "I'm meeting my neighbors for the first time."

Spiritually, Lebow sought haven in simple Jewish beliefs, despite the flamboyant schemes that he promoted as a race impresario. In the spring of 1994, as he sensed his impending death, he dramatically showed just how far his transformation had gone. When the angel of death would appear, this world-class celebrity wanted to be known by his childhood name, Fishl Lebowitz, not as Fred Lebow. When he was originally diagnosed with cancer, Lebow had confessed in the hospital to Steinfeld, "It's that time again. I don't have four years, maybe just a few months. I was born Fishl. I will die Fishl." But since he was in remission, he never pursued going back to his Jewish shtetl name. In April 1994, his club put out a stunning and somewhat surprising release: the race director wanted to be known by the Jewish name he bore in Arad, Transylvania, Fishl Lebowitz. Jewish customs and observances, noted the release, always held meaning for the race director. On April 28, the *New York Daily News* reported that Lebow had "started the process of reverting to his original name." Explaining his move, Lebow said, "I've always observed the Jewish holidays and always been proud of my heritage and its time I return to my original name."

That same month, "Fishl" attended the Passover Seder at his sister's home. Whereas during each of the four preceding years—the years since Lebow had been stricken with cancer—Allan Steinfeld had been able to mention in his traditional annual review of the "Orphans' Seder" how good it was to have Lebow at the table, the mood at the 1994 Orphans' Seder, as Phil Greenwald recalled, was "more somber" than usual, in Lebow's absence.

For Mr. G, the weatherman and runner with whom Lebow bantered about their Jewishness, the assertion of the race director's roots as shown by his changing his name indicated the end was near: "When people are preparing to die they go back to the time where they will find the most comfort and peace."

Three weeks before he died, Kathrine Switzer visited Lebow for what both must have known would be the final farewell. When Switzer, who had called him Fishl throughout their twenty-five-year friendship, asked, "Why do you want to change your name after all these years?" he replied, softly, "I see it's now near the end. I want to be known by my real name, my real self."

Praying Saturday mornings at the Park Avenue Synagogue, a block away from his club's town house, became a ritual for Lebow. Accompanied by synagogue member Robert Towers, a tennis publicist, Lebow unobtrusively took his seat at the left-hand rear of the congregation.

"He felt comfortable here," said Barrie Modlin, the synagogue's executive director, referring to Lebow's joining the four hundred-member congregation at collations following services. However, Lebow poignantly clung to his identity as race director and never removed his marathon running cap at the synagogue, not even when honored with an aliyah (being called in front of the congregation) during the Torah reading.

When he was strong enough, Lebow attended social events. When the Church of the Heavenly Rest sponsored a Saturday-night fund-raising dinner dance in May to repair damages from a serious fire a year earlier, Lebow appeared, feeling loyal to the facility because it was a site where his runners used to change for Central Park races before the club acquired its town house one block away. The Sunday May 29, 1994, *New York Times* "Society Page" carried a head shot of a smiling Lebow attired in tuxedo and a John Hancock marathon running cap.

Visits from friends continued to trigger Lebow's ironic sense of humor. He had always enjoyed tweaking L.A.'s race director, Dr. Bill Burke. Each of the impresarios continually worked on making the other laugh. "I never bonded with another guy in the way I did with Fred," Burke noted. But bonding or not, business had always remained uppermost for the two entrepreneurs. Neither lost sight of their main focus, how best to hype their marathon shows, so, joking aside, they each denied the other the list of runners in their marathons in order to retain their own party's edge.

In late spring 1994, Burke phoned Lebow at his Road Runners Club office to inquire about his health. Burke described the conversation: "Fred got on the phone, not with his regular voice, but with kind of a child's voice. He said, 'I miss you.' " Unaccustomed to such sentimentality, Burke explained: "I'm a black guy from the streets. I don't remember anyone else saying in his life that he missed me." Still, he answered, "I miss you too. . . . I'm anxious to come see you." "Come soon," advised Lebow faintly, so Burke cancelled all his engagements and boarded the red-eye flight from L.A. that night to rush to see his ailing friend.

"We would meet in the morning at a deli" was, according to Burke, their plan. "Fred had a deli for everything." Arriving at 6 A.M. in New York City, Burke rode in a cab to the deli. "I ordered a hot chocolate, and about twenty minutes later Fred came through the door. It was unbelievable for me that he was using a walker. He was really in bad shape. He told me he was going for a treatment later that day." Then Lebow unexpectedly threw out a proposition to his fellow race director: "Let's do a marathon together in Las Vegas. We'll kill 'em." The New York director asserted that an American must win, reflecting the worries of both race directors over the decline of American triumphs in the sport.

When would this extravaganza be held? Burke wanted to know. "The first Monday in March," insisted Lebow. By this point in the conversation, Lebow no longer spoke faintly. "The adrenaline started flowing," said Burke. And then he caught on. The date Lebow proposed was the day after the first Sunday in March, and that first Sunday in March was the date of the L.A. marathon. "He was giving me the needle," Burke realized. "He had one of the major events in the world, but deliberately chose a date to compete with me."

Lebow made it to France for the ceremonies inaugurating the race name in his honor, but he was too sick to derive much pleasure. "He didn't know what was going on," reported Alice Schneider who, together with her husband, Allan Steinfeld, had accompanied Lebow. Somehow, as sick as he was, the perennial race promoter still managed to be on the lookout for shtick for his own marathon, and watched as over the Normandy beach, planes shot out plumes of colored smoke to hype the new Lebow race. What an exciting piece of glitz for his own show, thought Lebow, and according to Steinfeld, "He called me from his hotel room in the middle of the night [and] said, 'We must do this.'"

Later in June, in response to Lebow's failing health, USA Track and Field, in a special election, named Fred Lebow the 151st member of the National Track and Field Hall of Fame. Rather than wait for the September balloting, the group in Indianapolis suspended its normal procedures since time was of the essence. A waiver made it possible for Lebow to be inducted right away, instead of waiting for the December ceremonies. In nominating Lebow, Ollan Cassell, the group's executive director and sometime rival for the post of the most powerful figure in American running, said, "He is one of the sports world's all-time greatest showmen." Years back, Cassell had invited Lebow for lunch at the New York Athletic Club whose rules required a tie and jacket for ad mission. Dutifully, Lebow appeared properly attired, but since he was wearing his running shoes, the club's doorman blocked his entry. Cassell took the race director around the corner and bought him a pair of dress shoes so they could dine at the club.

In a fitting tribute, Lebow's August induction into the Hall of Fame took place at the site where it all began, at Tavern on the Green, across from the Central Park finish line. In his honor, New York City declared the occasion "Fred Lebow Day," and according to Larry T. Ellis, president of USA Track and Field, "We thought the timing was good in light of Fred's health, and we thought it was in his best interest to have it all this time. We [didn't] know whether he could travel well in the future, and who knew what his treatment schedule might be."

"He brought the race to the people," said Allan Steinfeld in his tribute at the fete. Steinfeld had in mind the hundreds of thousands of marathoners who had crossed the nearby finish, many of them originally everyday runners, stirred by Lebow's challenge.

Supported by a metal cane, wearing his signature running cap and jogging suit, an emotional Lebow accepted the award in a barely audible whisper: "I'm flattered and honored and I don't deserve it. I'm just a peon. I'm awed and embarrassed. . . . [F]irst they told me I had six months to live, and I'm here today, but I'm stronger now, and I'm looking forward to running again. . . . I want to run."

Though stripped of his ability to run, promoting the marathon remained Lebow's main focus. The race director's Orthodox sister Sarah arranged for Rabbi David Kleinerman of Aish HaTorah yeshiva to stop by Lebow's town house office for Torah lessons, but Lebow, in spite of being ravaged by cancer, was still dwelling on marathon details. Rabbi Kleinerman found Lebow "not with it, jumpy," so he was completely unprepared when the race director queried him about leads for marathon sponsorship. "He knew he was a dying man," said Rabbi Kleinerman, "but he asked me questions about sponsoring or advertising the marathon." Lebow also bounced off Rabbi Kleinerman his scheme for color coordinating the marathon start that he picked up in his French trip. "I felt very sad," recalled Rabbi Kleinerman. "He made his world through the marathon, and wanted to keep it still."

Six weeks before his death, Lebow walked through the chambers of the New York City Council, handing out to the hardened politicos "In

Training for the 1994 New York City Marathon" T-shirts. Lebow always tried to keep on the good side of these politicians in order to ensure the city services they furnished his party. "They grabbed his hands and patted him on the back," wrote *Runner's World* publisher George A. Hirsch, "to thank him for creating New York's finest day."

Holding firm to feelings of intimacy with God, Lebow insisted to Heather that she bring him to synagogue services on Yom Kippur eve, the Day of Atonement. "He proudly explained to me that he was going to synagogue that night," said Heather. "It's the time that Jews confess their sins," Lebow told her. "When a Jew puts a tallis [prayer shawl] over his head, he becomes a king again." At the service, a weakened Lebow managed to stand during a few prayers, but his pain worsened so dramatically at the synagogue, confessed Heather, "I was positive he was going to die."

By September, Lebow was transported mainly in a wheelchair, his voice hardly audible. He drifted in and out of coherence. The race director, as well as old friends, sensed that the journey was nearly over and that it was time for good-byes. Central Park, his Road Runners Club office, and the Gracie Mansion residence of the mayor were the sites for these farewells.

"Any babies?" he asked Françoise Levinsohn in Central Park following her run. Levinsohn, who in addition to warming up marathoners at the Fort Wadsworth start, had modeled running outfits for Lebow's shows in past years. "He knew I wasn't running much because I was busy modeling," said Levinsohn. "The way he asked about babies wasn't to tease," she continued. "I sensed by the way he said it that he wanted the best for me."

Laura Leale, his public relations associate, saw him last in his office. When she told him, "I love you. What could I do for you?" he assured her, "You've done whatever you could."

The late-afternoon reception at Gracie Mansion hosted by Mayor Giuliani was the city's annual premarathon send-off. Giuliani's predecessors Ed Koch and David Dinkins had held similar gatherings to boost one of the city's most exciting events. "This time instead of Fred thanking the city for its support," reported Steve Mendelsohn, the marathon's chief ham radio operator, "the city was thanking him." Without being billed as such, the cast of three hundred composed a

"This Is Your (Marathon) Life, Fred Lebow" production. With the exception of a few relatives on hand, the guests had all helped orchestrate Lebow's marathon theater—running club officers and staff, volunteers, athletes, sponsors, journalists, police brass, and more.

Giuliani paid tribute to the marathon's wondrous contributions to the city and to Lebow's pivotal role in the race. Allan Steinfeld thanked guests for attending, recounting the marathon's history in connection with its upcoming twenty-fifth anniversary. Speaking at the mayor's reception was a new role for Steinfeld who had always been the behind-the-scenes technician for the relentless Lebow. "Fred was constantly pushing me to be in the limelight," said Steinfeld. "Not that I was reticent. In my mind, there should be only one person representing the club." But that night, with Lebow frail and disoriented, Steinfeld assumed a more up-front posture. "I spoke more aggressively than I ever had, trying to let people know someone was in charge, and that someone was me. It was something I didn't want to do but when I saw Fred, I realized I needed to."

Steinfeld's remarks completed, Heather wheeled in Lebow through the hushed crowd. Though near death, he wore his signature running outfit. Heather carefully "guarded" Lebow, reported Achilles Track Club for disabled athletes founder Dick Traum. "His cheeks had an ashen color," said Vermont Pure Natural Spring Water owner Jack Maguire regarding Lebow's appearance.

George Spitz and Ted Corbitt, conceivers of the five-borough marathon, approached the race director together. "Fred grabbed our hands," according to Spitz, "but we knew it was hopeless, based on what Norb Sander said." Sander, a medical doctor, won the marathon in 1974.

Tiffany's Jim Quinn wished Lebow luck, shaking his hand. "It was the first time I ever saw Fred sitting down at a function," said Quinn. "I hope to see you at the marathon" were his parting words to the race director. "People there knew it may be the last time they would see Fred."

"You've won," confessed Lebow to Vince Chiapetta, his cofounder of the first 1970 Central Park New York City Marathon. Over the years, Chiapetta had challenged Lebow for keeping the running club officers in the dark as to his wheeling and dealing. Now, the rivalry having come to end, the definition of winning for Lebow meant longevity on life's calendar.

Dick Traum thought that in his prime the pragmatic promoter would have felt uncomfortable at such a sentimental affair. Lessons he learned from Lebow crossed his mind. "I learned from him how to develop an event," asserted Traum, whose Achilles Track Club by then numbered thirty-five hundred handicapped athletes. As for organizational politics, another lesson Traum picked up from Lebow was "When you use power, use it sparingly." According to Traum, this meant to avoid saying no in such a definitive way that room for maneuver, or future relationships, would not be impaired.

Seiko's David Strauss's good-bye consisted of "stepping in front of his wheelchair, grabbing his hand and telling Fred, 'I love you.' I'm not even sure Fred knew what was happening. Not too many people understood what he said." Jack Maguire disagreed: "Fred knew exactly who he was. I said, 'I'll see you at the finish line,' " and Lebow replied, "Jack, it's good to have you here." Leaving the reception, Maguire and a few guests stopped off at a nearby restaurant. "We speculated whether he would live long enough to be at the marathon," Maguire relayed.

A life-size sculpture memorializing the imagery of Lebow's autumn dream was unveiled at the end of the month in San Diego, California. For four years, Daniel Mitrovich headed a New York City Marathon Tribute Committee focusing on the Lebow statue, to be placed at the Central Park finish. Mitrovich launched his campaign for the statue after running the New York City Marathon in 1990. "Fred was fighting cancer then, as he is now," stated Mitrovich. "He is a friend of mine and what he has done to touch the lives of people in 91 nations is simply amazing. He is totally one of the most unselfish persons one would every meet."

The sculpture, by Professor Jesus Dominguez of San Diego State University, depicts Lebow in his trademark running outfit and cap checking the watch on his left wrist, as marathoners cross the finish. Though the statue was not to be installed until the Friday two days before the marathon, a replica was displayed at a Tavern on the Green press conference. Bill Rodgers was seated next to Lebow at the gathering. No runner had more of a role than Rodgers, winner of the first five-borough run in 1976 and three subsequent marathons, in showcasing Lebow's urban theater in the early years than he. "He was in a great mood," said Rodgers. "He was so pleased. He kept showing me the ring he received when he was inducted into the US Track and Field Hall of Fame. That's how I'll remember him. He's the guy who developed New York into the world's biggest marathon, and everybody copied it. Isn't imitation the greatest form of flattery?"

In these last weeks, Lebow's sister Sarah Katz, the closest of his siblings, moved into his apartment to take care of him. His body grew increasingly bloated as it was ravaged by the advancing disease. Drifting in and out of consciousness, and in another terminal move to find truth in his life, the little conversation he shared with Sarah was mainly in the languages of their childhood, Yiddish and Hungarian. Not giving up his running persona completely, however, Lebow insisted on wearing his warm-up suits and running cap.

Sarah brought Lebow to his last race a week before he died—the Discover Card Mile that he had inaugurated in 1981, capturing the glamour of Fifth Avenue as a backdrop. From his wheelchair at the finish line, he watched the runners and cheered as his sister Sarah, who had walked the distance in the race, crossed the line.

Athletes who performed at his party came by for a last visit. Eamonn Coghlan, the indoor-mile record holder and one of the great runners of the century, took Lebow for a walk in his wheelchair. "Although the poor man was suffering, he still talked about coming back. . . . I remember two Freds: the vibrant, electrifying Fred and the courageous Fred—battling his illness."

Finally, Grete Waitz, perhaps the runner with whom he was closest and his accompanist in the triumphant running of his own marathon, the first time in his life, as a cancer patient in remission in 1992, visited on Thursday, October 6. "He recognized me," remembered Waitz, "and waved his finger to let me know he knew me." She reappeared Saturday evening, "I came there with nine roses for each of my victories and one for what I hoped would be his victory over cancer. I bent over and told him. He woke up and squeezed my hand. I like to think he knew I was there."

On the following morning, "Marathon Tune-Up Sunday," October 9, 1994, Fred (Fishl) Lebow died. Preparing him for burial,

Lebow's bearded, black-hatted Orthodox family followed the teaching equating a human body with an impaired Torah scroll no longer suitable for religious services. Revered for the function it once filled, the deceased (similar to the damaged Torah scrolls) was tenderly and respectfully prepared for burial by the Chevra Kadisha (the burial society literally meaning "Holy Fellowship"). Though Lebow had facetiously told sportscaster Dick Schaap he wanted to be buried in a running suit, when the end came, he was dressed in traditional Jewish white shrouds. The burial was scheduled as quickly as possible, and his body was accompanied at every moment until the service was held.

After the traditional religious service at the West Side's Plaza Memorial Chapel, Lebow's Orthodox relatives were treated to one final bells-and-whistles flourish befitting the deceased showman race director. Rather than a quiet ride to Mount Hebron Cemetery in Queens, banker Charles McCabe arranged for eight police motorcycles, their sirens blaring, to lead the funeral motorcade to the Central Park finish line. There, a lone Scottish bagpiper played dirges, a funeral rite Lebow's Orthodox family had never previously witnessed. The procession stopped briefly outside the town house headquarters of the Road Runners Club, allowing Lebow's comrades to honor him.

At the cemetery Steinfeld spoke about Lebow, the caring man. He remembered that Lebow, despite his own failing health, took him to an eye doctor for his damaged retina, and how he comforted him following the death of his mother. Family members insisted on digging Lebow's grave themselves, rather than having paid cemetery workers do the work. Heather, unaware of the starkness of Orthodox burials, innocently placed a solitary rose on his grave.

As though Providence was displeased with "Fishl Lebowitz's" attempt to erase "Fred Lebow's" record of going the distance in the marathon of life, his remains lie at the cemetery's block 26 line.

Even in death, Lebow's tombstone evidences the dichotomy of his identity. Was he the running world impresario or the Jew from prewar Transylvania? In capital letters, the tombstone's slope states, FRED LEBOW, and the inscription, "He was humble in his greatness." Chiseled between his dates of birth and death is the symbol of the New York Road Runners Club—the Big Apple with a runner in its middle.

But from the Hebrew lettering on the tombstone's face, it seems that a different man was buried below: Ephraim Fishl Lebowitz. Beneath the Hebrew name are four Hebrew lines, each line beginning with a letter from the name Fishl. Translated, the inscription reads:

> (F) His mouth abounded in truth
> (I) He was beloved by all
> (SH) His name was universally known
> (L) His heart, as his name, so he was.

His heart . . . Lebow, in Hebrew, literally means "his heart."

Since the *levaya* (funeral) was held in relative private, two days later, on October 12, the site of the Central Park finish was the location of a huge noontime tribute to Lebow. The autumn day, crisp and clear, was waffled by a slight breeze. It would have been ideal marathon weather.

Drawing between three and four thousand people, the gathering was the largest memorial held there since John Lennon died in 1980, and attending were well-known runners, city political leaders, a rabbi from Lebow's childhood in Arad, sponsors, and more. The gathering itself, much like his populist marathon, drew all types, including people in suits, people in running shorts, and even some people emulating Lebow's signature bicycle cap. Some came in wheelchairs, others with baby strollers. Deborah Carabet, a runner, showed up with her boyfriend, Jeff Berman, a leukemia patient and founder of the runners' cancer support group. Since she was training for her first marathon, Deborah wore running shorts and a knee brace so she could run later. For her, Lebow was "an inspiration who taught that you could do whatever you want to."

Some mourners remembered Lebow for his runs in the park, others were connected by no more than a glimpse of him in the marathon pace car, and still others paid tribute for his gutsy battle with cancer. Those who were marathoners mourned not only a fallen race director, but also someone in the entertainment business who gave them each a chance, regardless of skill, to perform across the great urban landscape. They sparkled on those Sundays because their charged footwork was so out

of step with their otherwise benign lives. The crowd's unpretentiousness registered on the *New York Times*'s George Vecsey:

> On this gorgeous afternoon, everybody held hands as we walked
> past the finish line, and I wound up holding hands with a good
> friend of mine on my left and a stranger on my right, and that was
> the point.
>
> We liked each other. . . . I liked the people who surged forward,
> talking of the races they had run and the races they had watched.
>
> And I realized I liked this crowd a whole lot more than the
> crowds I observe at the great arenas we have built with our own tax
> money for the millionaire owners and the millionaire players. I feel
> good every year at the New York City Marathon, an event that en-
> courages and celebrates the average plodder. I don't feel the wariness
> I feel when I walk toward a stadium, waiting to encounter boisterous
> louts, to say nothing of the fans.

The single floral display lying in front of the speaker's platform was
a gift from a running club in Japan. One woman left a solitary rose behind a barrier just past the finish line. Attached was a note thanking
Lebow for the rose he had presented to her when she finished her first
marathon in 1982.

"Where the speeches were made was within fifty yards of the starting line when we had the race entirely in the park," said Paul Fetscher,
recalling the early obscure Central Park marathons Lebow produced.
"We had more people standing at the starting line today than we used
to have running or jogging in the entire park on a weekend."

"Fred Lebow was a New Yorker" were the opening words of Mayor
Giuliani in his brief eulogy. "The marathon is a living legacy that few
people can claim. It advertises the city in a positive light all over the
world. It is a legacy to the city." When the twenty-fifth anniversary of
the marathon is held, added Giuliani, "everyone who crosses the finish
line will dedicate the race to him."

Grete Waitz, his good friend who had accompanied his valiant
1992 marathon in spite of her original plans to retire from running in
1978, rose to speak. It had been in succumbing to Lebow's chutzpah

that she had originally competed in New York, on a whim, emerging as one of history's most celebrated women distance runners. "He touched a lot of lives, mine included," said Waitz, her voice breaking. "He always wanted me to win 10 New York marathons, but crossing the finish line with him in 1992 meant more to me than a possible 10th victory."

Allan Steinfeld, the last speaker, had worked with Lebow for more than sixteen years. He was choked with emotion as he said, "Today is a beautiful day, the type of day that Fred would have loved to be in the park and running. . . . I know that when Mayor Giuliani fires the gun to start the marathon, until the last runner finishes . . . Fred will be there." Adding a humorous, yet touching thought, he captured the magic that T-shirts had held for the impresario race director, saying, "[I am] overwhelmed by those who came to honor Fred, even without the promise of a T-shirt!"

At the end, people held hands, shuffling silently across the finish line. Some, crossing the finish line, pretending they had gone the 26.2-mile distance, triumphantly threw up their hands. Others tossed bouquets of flowers at the finish line, reminiscent of the roses Lebow handed women finishers. A red carnation and a white carnation rested undisturbed on the New York City Marathon apple logo painted on the road.

Grief mixed with the humor of "Fred stories" marked a memorial service held a week later, on October 18, at the United Nations. The Sri Chinmoy Peace Meditation and the international organization's Athletic Club sponsored the program. Sri Chinmoy and his students, who admired Lebow, had composed two songs in his honor previously and had volunteered at his marathons in large numbers. At their service, Lebow's successor, Allan Steinfeld, tweaked the impresario for his media savvy in orchestrating his departure from this world on a date so close to the upcoming marathon. "Fred was a great PR man, and he timed his death perfectly. What better promotion for the New York City Marathon than what occurred?"

Peter Roth, treasurer of Lebow's club, tried figuring out the race director's salesmanship skills:

> He would go to meetings with all kinds of officials all over the city, the country, the world, and get them to do things that they wouldn't or-

dinarily do. How could he do that? My feeling is that it was because Fred appeared to be different. He would never dress like anyone else. He always dressed the way he wanted to dress, and it was different. He acted differently and he controlled his emotions differently. He upset the way we see things so that we couldn't read him the way we understand most people. So there was nothing left to bank our decisions on. We couldn't put him into any of our typical categories.

His club's public relations director, Raleigh Mayer, cited Lebow's shameless hyping of his marathon: "I'd like to tell you that individuals from 99 countries are entered in this year's New York City Marathon. If Fred were editing as I talk, he would say, 'No, no, say "Over ninety-nine"!' Then I would say, 'But Fred, there aren't one hundred yet.' And he would say, 'You don't know that; some of these people may not know where they come from.' "

Just a month following Lebow's death—on Marathon Sunday, November 6, 1994—Fishl's Hasidic brother and sister-in-law from Cleveland, Mr. and Mrs. Morris Lebowitz, along with one of his nephews, were in attendance at the Marathon Minyan early in the morning. The marathon that year was being dedicated to their loved one. After the service, Lebow's relatives asked minyan cofounder Peter Berkowsky to help them find the Command Center in order to be taken by car to the Central Park finish line. Berkowsky described this "incongruous-looking group" walking through the Fort Wadsworth staging area:

> Announcements were coming across the loudspeakers in all languages. Thousands of runners from Japan, Italy, and so on were walking around. I was wearing my military fatigues. I was holding the hand of Fred's black-hatted Hasidic brother who was walking behind me. He was holding the hand of his wife wearing her *sheitel* [wig or head covering]. Walking behind her was the nephew. I started to shout, "Come meet Fred's brother from Cleveland!" Hundreds of runners came up to shake his hand. He had no idea how famous Fred was. Fred wasn't the kind of person who would talk about himself. Then we met Grete [Waitz] who kissed his wife, and she said she would take care of them.

A little while later, as the last marathon festival to be orchestrated by Lebow kicked off, a squadron of five military propeller airplanes flew through the clouds over the starting line at the Verrazano-Narrows Bridge, streaming plumes of red, white, and blue smoke in the sky. Exactly the jets so admired by Lebow at the race named after him at Normandy, on the fiftieth anniversary of D-Day, these planes were not. Improvising in the spirit of his teacher, the old garment-center knockoff artist, Steinfeld pulled off the shtick using smaller planes. Skywriting sponsored by Chemical Bank spelled out the message, "For you Fred." Hanging ten thousand feet in the air, eight miles across, these words reminded some twenty-nine thousand marathon starters that their dream maker was gone. The tribute was repeated at the eight-, seventeen-, and twenty-mile marks, and at the finish line.

The party was decorated with twenty balloon arches, hung at various points along the route, each holding one thousand balloons. Avoiding the specter of a cookie-cutter marathon, the arch at the twenty-five-mile mark was outfitted with silver balloons.

At the twenty-five-mile water station, at Central Park and Sixty-sixth Street, silver commemorative drinking cups were given to runners. Volunteers manning the water station were dressed in tuxedos, Lebow's second-favorite attire (running clothes being his first choice, of course).

So that the excitement and energy of the party would not be mistaken for an old-fashioned sweaty race, forty bands along the course played rock, jazz, marches, and blues. This music mainstreamed Lebow's marathon into pop culture, the fun beats spiking runners to work harder.

Dusk settled on the city. Most runners, having already completed the race, trudged through the park and nearby streets in Mylar blankets. Passersby hailed their achievement. The Empire State Building was lit with blue lights, symbolizing the marathon's "long blue line."

At journey's end, each finisher was awarded a medal matching the marathon T-shirt, both *tchotchkes* of Lebow's theater. Every woman finisher carried away a red rose, Lebow's overtly sexist symbol.

To the left of the finish line stood the new bronze life-sized statue of a preoccupied Lebow in signature running outfit checking his watch as the marathoners crossed in their moment of glory.

"I hope he will always be there where he is now," wished Grete Waitz, considered by many his adoptive sister. "In that way, he can watch the finishers every year."

The Awards Ceremony—
Vignettes

AFTER HIS PASSING, Fred Lebow's sister Sarah Katz continued to attend the New York City Marathon festival events he had created— events like the Marathon Expo. What greater tribute could the late racing impresario receive? The recognition from his Orthodox siblings certainly must help him rest in peace.

Of course, there has been professional recognition aplenty, with Hall of Fame inductions, races named for him, and continuation of much of what he instituted in his life and what his life stood for.

Established by the National Distance Running Hall of Fame in 2000, the Fred Lebow Award honors the spirit and commitment of Lebow, who cofounded the New York City Marathon and worked tirelessly to build the race into a world-renowned event that unifies nations, races, and cultures. The award celebrates Lebow's dedication, passion, leadership, creativity, and foresight: "The New York City Marathon is Fred Lebow. Without his vision and devotion, the marathon would not have the impact internationally that it does," said John Petrone, codirector of the National Distance Running Hall of Fame. "We want to honor individuals like Lebow who rise to the occasion and demonstrate characteristics that set them apart, that selflessly work to show us all that is possible." *Upstate N.Y. Runner* reported that the "National Distance Running Hall of Fame: Class of 2001" included "the late Fred Lebow, founder of the New York City Marathon and popularizer of long-distance running around the world." Lebow's listing on the official Web site of the National Distance Running Hall of Fame (http://www.distancerunning.com) states:

> Many in the running world credit Fred Lebow with helping to raise distance running to its current status as one of the world's most widely respected sports that is frequently participated in world-wide . . . not only an avid runner, but a racing pioneer. He founded many major road races, including the Fifth Avenue Mile, the Empire State Building Run-Up, and the Women's Mini Marathon. He is perhaps best known for founding and directing the world-renowned New York City Marathon . . . every year since its inception in 1970 through 1993. He transformed the marathon from a local event in Central Park with 55 finishers to the world's largest marathon with over 25,000 finishers running through all five boroughs of New York City. . . . president of [NYRR] for 20 years, growing the group from 270 members initially to 31,000—making NYRR the world's largest organization of its kind. He was promoted to chairman of the group in 1993, and heralded as the trailblazer for running groups nationally.

In an update from *NYRR Online: Official Site of New York Road Runners:*

> At the end of his life, Fred encouraged marathon runners to get friends and relatives to sponsor their runs to raise money for cancer research. One of those runners who responded was a woman named Aubrey Barr. Then came The Aubrey Fund for Pediatric Cancer Research. Aubrey, who developed leukemia at the age of four, was treated at Lebow's hospital, the Memorial Sloan Kettering Cancer Center [MSKCC], and was cured. Aubrey has been raising funds for MSKCC through participating in marathons for ten years. In 1997, she courageously gave her name and her story to be used to inspire other runners by helping to establish *The Aubrey Fund for Pediatric Cancer Research.* The Aubrey Fund is the beneficiary of the funds raised through Fred's Team.

"Look at what we've done," the article continues. "Since 1995, *Fred's Team members have raised more than $13 million for cancer research.* Over $11.5 million of that total has benefited *The Aubrey Fund for Pe-*

diatric Cancer Research, and more than $1.5 million dollars has gone directly toward other types of cancer research as requested by runners and their sponsors." The NYRR Fred Lebow Classic, a five-mile (8K) race, and the NYRR Fred Lebow Cross Country 5K Youth Run in Van Cortlandt Park are held each September.

According to *Runner's World Presents the 2000 New York City Marathon* (http://www.runnersworld.com), a "Fred Lebow Room [was] dedicated at Ronald McDonald House. . . . In conjunction with the continuing efforts of 'Fred's Team' to use the New York City Marathon as a vehicle for raising funds for pediatric cancer research, the Fred Lebow Room has been dedicated at Manhattan's Ronald McDonald House."

Hundreds upon hundreds of listings come up when a search for "Fred Lebow" is done on the World Wide Web—the impact he left on the world has truly been global and lasting.

Bibliographical Essay

AS WITH ALL CELEBRITIES, the print record reveals only a small part of Fred Lebow's life. Particularly in the case of this race director, who worked so much behind the scenes to transform, in effect, American popular culture with his marathon vision, it was necessary to interview a wide variety of people involved in his struggle to succeed. Those interviewed included athletes, other race directors, sponsors, politicians, police officers, rabbis, journalists, meteorologists, restaurateurs, garment-center businessmen, girlfriends, publicists, social friends, marathon staff, club officers and personnel, and more. Together they helped flesh out Lebow's vision, Lebow the promoter, and, most important, Lebow the man. Independently, many of these individuals would never have crossed the lives of other sources. Combined, they represent a cast as unlikely as the notion of shutting down the streets of the world's most hyper city one day a year for a people's race.

Published Materials

New York City newspapers cited were the *New York Post, New York Times, New York Daily News, New York Newsday,* and *Village Voice.* Regional newspaper sources were the *Bergen (N.J.) Record* and *Chicago Tribune.* National papers included the *Wall Street Journal* and *USA Today.* In both *Reader's Digest* and *People* magazine, Lebow was the subject of feature articles. Various running publications such as *Runner's World,* his club's *New York Running News,* and the Road Runners Club of America's *FootNotes* provided ongoing data on the evolution of Lebow's marathon. *Road Race Management* discussed the administrative side of distance running. The *New Zealand Runner* contained a tribute from 1974 marathon winner Kathrine Switzer.

Lebow, together with Richard Woodley, authored *Inside the World of Big-Time Marathoning* (New York: Rawson Associates) in 1984. Since the work appeared before Lebow was stricken with brain cancer, it failed to include the

281

greatest struggle of his life. Robert Brody in *Whatever It Takes: Athletes Against Cancer* (Waco, Tex.: WRS Publishing, 1993) devoted a chapter to Lebow's response to the disease. The New York Road Runners Club's *New York City Marathon—Twenty-five Years,* a picture book with text by Peter Gambaccini (New York: Rizzoli, 1994), showed highlights of Lebow's theater. Lebow, Gloria Averbuch, and friends wrote *The Complete Book of Running* (New York: Random House, 1992) from which certain anecdotes are cited. Following Lebow's death, the Sri Chinmoy Marathon Team published a booklet, *Fred Lebow: A Celebration of His Life* (Jamaica, N.Y., 1994), containing tributes made to the race director at a memorial service.

Works by running contemporaries of Lebow were Bill Rodgers and Joe Concannon, *Marathoning* (New York: Simon and Schuster, 1980); Frank Shorter with Marc Bloom, *Olympic Gold: A Runner's Life and Times* (Boston: Houghton Mifflin, 1984); Dick Traum and Mike Celizic, *A Victory for Humanity* (Waco, Tex.: WRS Publishing, 1993); and James E. Fixx, *The Complete Book of Running* (New York: Random House, 1977).

Pamela Cooper gave Lebow's achievements historical perspective in *The American Marathon* (Syracuse: Syracuse Univ. Press, 1998). Earlier she described Lebow's promotional contribution in "The 'Visible Hand' on the Footrace: Fred Lebow and the Marketing of the Marathon," *Journal of Sports History* (winter 1992).

Internet Resources

Postscript information was culled from several Internet sites, including *Upstate N.Y. Runner;* the official Web site of the National Distance Running Hall of Fame at http://www.distancerunning.com; *Runner's World Presents the 2000 New York City Marathon* at http://www.runnersworld.com; and *NYRR Online: Official Siter of New York Road Runners.*

Individuals Interviewed

Phil Angel, assistant to the chairman of BFI Industries
Sharon Applebee, race director of the New York Road Runners Club
Peter Berkowsky, cofounder of the Marathon Minyan (Jewish Prayer Service)
Beth Bonner, women's winner of the 1971 New York City Marathon
Chris Brasher, founder of the London Marathon, Olympic gold medalist, 1956
Dr. William Burke, president of the City of Los Angeles Marathon
Dody Burkey, friend of Lebow

John Carroll, sports marketer at Capital Sports

Joe Cea, lieutenant in Operations Unit, New York Police Department

Vincent Chiapetta, cofounder of the 1970 New York City Marathon, president of the New York Road Runners Club, and president of the Road Runners Club of America

John Chodes, author and playwright

Nat Cirulnick, president of the New York Road Runners Club

Seth Clayman, director of special projects at Aish HaTorah yeshiva, Jerusalem

Bill Conway, head marshal of the New York City Marathon and president of Gotham Construction Company

Gary Corbitt, media consultant

Ted Corbitt, president of the New York Road Runners Club and champion distance runner

Eamonn Coghlan, winner of the Wanamaker Mile and champion track star

Jeff Darman, president of the Road Runners Club of America

Maurice Dickson, comptroller of Tucker Knits, garment-center employer of Lebow

Heather Dominic, friend of Lebow

David Downs, vice president of sports marketing for ABC-TV

Jim Ellson, New York City Fire Department, member of Lebow's 1992 marathon entourage

Paula Fahey, friend of Lebow

Mimi Fahnestock, librarian of the New York Road Runners Club

Michael Fandal, New York City Police Department, member of Lebow's 1992 marathon entourage

Jim Ferstle, sports journalist

Storm Field, TV meteorologist, member of Lebow's 1992 marathon entourage

Ellen Finn, elite-athlete coordinator of the New York City Marathon

Lee Flaherty, president of the America's Marathon, Chicago

Tom Fleming, winner of the New York City Marathon in 1973 and 1975

Barry Frank, senior corporate vice president of the International Management Group and Lebow's agent

Henley Gibble, executive director of the Road Runners Club of America

Jerry Goldman, Scottex Corporation, a garment-center associate of Lebow

Joy Gordon, executive director of Maccabi USA/Sports for Israel

Curt Gowdy Jr., coordinating producer of *ABC Wide World of Sports*

Phil Greenwald, race director of the New York Road Runners Club

Irv Gurofsky (Mr. G), TV meteorologist, member of Lebow's 1992 marathon entourage

Art Hall, board member of the New York Road Runners Club

Linda Harris, manager of the New York City Marathon Expo

Jerry Henkin, director of the Northern Nutgrowers Association

Dick Hochschild, member of Lebow's party at the 1982 Moscow Marathon

Susan Hoffner, staff member of the New York Road Runners Club

John Hughes, race director of the Walt Disney World Marathon

Logan Hurst, construction manager and designer of world's largest urinal (located at Staten Island start of New York City Marathon)

Craig Jenkins, manager of the Sports, Student, and Athletic Travel Department for Finnair

Carl Jonasch, commander of the Central Park precinct, New York Police Department

Don Kardong, president of the Road Runners Club of America

David Katz, finish-line coordinator of the New York City Marathon

Georgia Keith, manager of special events at Walt Disney World

Dr. Jeff Kerner, member of Lebow's 1992 marathon entourage

Rabbi David Kleinerman, faculty of Aish HaTorah yeshiva

Joe Kleinerman, registrar of the New York Road Runners Club

Edward I. Koch, mayor of New York City

Nina Kuscsik, winner of the New York City Marathon in 1972 and 1973

Jan Laster, public relations associate at Asics

Robert Laufer, attorney for the New York City Marathon

Laura Leale, public relations associate of the New York Road Runners Club

Françoise Levinsohn, friend of Lebow

Ed Levy, president of the Pioneer Track Club

Steve Loscher, regional sales director of Vermont Pure Natural Spring Water and member of Lebow's 1992 marathon entourage

Rod MacNicholl, commercial artist

Jack Maguire, president of Vermont Pure Natural Spring Water

Jules Marder, garment-center associate of Lebow

Charles McCabe, executive vice president of Chemical Bank

Steve Mendelsohn, chief ham radio operator of the New York City Marathon

Dick Metz, New York City golf coach

Bill Michaels, sports promoter and race director of the Denver Mile High Marathon

Rabbi Jim Michaels, cofounder of the Marathon Minyan (Jewish Prayer Service)

Ilkka Mitro, passenger sales manager at Finnair's New York City office

Barrie Modlin, executive director of the Park Avenue Synagogue

Tom Monetti, managing direct of Tavern on the Green

Beth Powell Morass, friend of Lebow

Joanne Navarra, friend of Lebow

Vic Navarra, coordinator of the Staten Island staging area for New York City Marathon

Michael Nishi, general manager of the LaSalle Banks Chicago Marathon

Bill Noel, race director of the New York Road Runners Club

Anna Noel-Mayberry, head of the carbo-loading party for the New York City Marathon

Angel Nunez, director of the Urban Running Program, New York Road Runners Club

Patricia Owens, elite-athlete coordinator for the New York City Marathon

Barbara Paddock, vice president of Chemical Bank

Marie Patrick, executive vice president of the City of Los Angeles Marathon

David M. Patt, executive director of the Chicago Area Runners Association

Elizabeth Phillips, board member of the New York Road Runners Club

Victoria Phillips, marketing associate for the New York Road Runners Club

Cary Pinkowski, race director of the LaSalle Banks Chicago Marathon

Al Puma, coordinator of the twentieth-anniversary celebration of the New York City Marathon and designer of T-shirts

James Quinn, corporate executive vice president of Tiffany's and Company

Walter C. Rauscher, manager of Tavern on the Green

Larry Rawson, sportscaster for ABC-TV

Dave Romansky, running coach

Peter Roth, treasurer of the New York Road Runners Club

Lewis Rudin, Rudin Management, founding sponsor of the five-borough New York City Marathon

Tom Ryan, commanding officer of the Traffic Division, New York Police Department

Martin Schloshberg, president of Berg & Berg Knitting Company and garment-center employer of Lebow

Alice Schneider, head of Information Services for the New York Road Runners Club

Lisa Sepulveda, senior vice president of Edelman Public Relations

Sandy Sislowitz, Expo coordinator for the New York City Marathon

Morris Sopher, friend of Lebow

Jeffrey Speciner, proprietor of Siegel's Kosher Restaurant, New York City

George Spitz, New York State civil servant and conceiver of five-borough marathon

Allan Steinfeld, technical director of New York City Marathon under Lebow and Lebow's successor

Henry J. Stern, parks commissioner for New York City

Chris Stewart, British marathon star athlete

Phil Stewart, publisher of *Road Race Management*

David Strauss, assistant to the president of Seiko

Steve Sultan, photographer of the New York City Marathon

Tracy Sundlun, executive director of the Metropolitan Athletic Congress

Milton Sussman, executive director of the Israel Cancer Research Fund

Percy Sutton, president of the borough of Manhattan

Ellen Kate Sweeney, manager of Marketing Communications for Hoechst Celanese

Kathrine Switzer, winner of the New York City Marathon in 1974 and sports commentator

Hugh Thompson, running official in St. Paul, Minn.

Robert Thompson, media consultant for Mercedes-Benz

Erma Tranter, Friends of the Parks, Chicago

Dick Traum, founder of the Achilles Track Club

Arlene Trebach, friend of Lebow

Grete Waitz, nine-time winner of the New York City Marathon and Lebow's accompanist in 1992 marathon

Stephen L. Wald, board member of the New York Road Runners Club

Rolf Waldeis, manager of events and auto shows for Mercedes-Benz of North America

Rabbi Noach Weinberg, dean of Aish HaTorah yeshiva, Jerusalem

Priscilla Welch, winner of the New York City Marathon in 1987

Judith Woodfin, vice president for public affairs at Hertz Corporation

Larry Wydro, New York City Marathon Center coordinator

Index

New York City Marathon (*cont.*)
181, 257; rivalry with Chicago
Marathon, 130, 136, 164, 167–70,
179; support services for, 22–23,
24, 25, 33, 57, 58, 59, 132,
144–45, 150, 184, 185–86,
188–92; women runners in, 24–25,
27–28, 31, 45, 51, 97, 162–63,
166, 167, 171, 271–72. *See also*
Central Park Marathon; marathons
New York City Marathon Tune-Up,
254, 269
New York City Police Department,
239, 242, 245, 269; escorts runners,
49; at premarathon warm-up
meetings, 144; relationship with
Lebow, 3, 21, 35, 49, 104–5, 117;
role and responsibilities during NYC
Marathon, 87, 103, 104–5, 159. *See
also* Fandal, Michael
New York Games, The, 219–20
New York Metropolitan AAU, 20
New York-New Jersey Buick Dealers
Association, 130
New York Post, 75
New York Public Library, 57, 145, 148,
182, 234
New York Road Runners Club, 20–21,
30, 73, 98–99; accused of wanting a
monopoly, 103; board of directors
of, 73, 96, 99–101, 123–24, 254;
budget of, 133; cancer support
group of, 252; as a charity, 106–7;
concerns about charity races, 106–7;
critics of Lebow in, 134; early years
and races of, 16–19; Lebow elected
president of, 27; Lebow joins, 18; as
Lebow's family, 192–96; and
Lebow's 1992 run, 237–38, 245;
office/headquarters of, 25, 30, 38,
45, 100, 132; rift with parent
organization, 109–10; safety patrol,
150; survey of, 135; symbol of on

Lebow's tombstone, 270; urban
running program of, 89, 104; and
wheelchair participant controversy,
107. *See also* Cherry Tree Marathon;
Chiapetta, Vince; Corbitt, Ted;
Roth, Peter; Steinfeld, Allan
New York Running News, 16, 150,
151–52, 170, 212
New York's City Council, 265
New York State Division of Human
Rights, 107
New York Times, The: on Central Park
Marathon, 22, 47, 53, 54; on
Lebow, 78–79, 262; on New York
City Marathon, 22, 47, 53, 54, 111,
113, 118–19, 123–24, 127,
134–35. *See also* Starr, Roger;
Vecsey, George
1964 Civil Rights Act, 152
Nissan, 130
Noel, Bill, 102, 144, 185, 214, 253
Noel-Mayberry, Anna, 68, 74, 190
Normandy beach, 263
Northern Nutgrowers Association, 257
Norwegian Christian Home & Health
Center, 175
Nunez, Angel, 89, 104
Nyad, Diana, 45
*NYRR Online: Official Site of New York
Road Runners,* 276

Oakleys, 119
The Observer (London), 91
Olympics, 111, 152. *See also*
Lillehammer Olympics; Shorter,
Frank
Olympic Airways, 28, 30, 37, 122
Olympic champions/marathoners. *See*
Corbitt, Ted; Juantorena, Alberto;
Lopez, Carlos; Moore, Ken; Ross,
H. Browning
Onassis, Aristotle, 28, 30
Onassis, Jacqueline, 28